Roc the Mic Right

D0870809

Roc the Mic Right is the first in-depth, book-length analysis of the most pervasive yet least examined aspect of Hip Hop Culture—its language. Hip Hop Culture has captured the minds of youth "all around the world, from Japan to Amsterdam" (like the homie Kurupt say), shaping youth identities, styles, attitudes, languages, fashions, and both physical and political stances. Written in both "Hip Hop Nation Language" and "academic discourse," Alim takes the reader on a journey through Hip Hop's inventive linguistic landscape, deconstructing its discourse and poetics, while highlighting relationships between language, identity, and power (from the groundbreaking exploration of the Muslim "transglobal Hip Hop *umma*" to the critical study of Black Language in White public space).

What sets this book apart from many on the subject is Alim's extensive ethnographic fieldwork and his close contact with the Hip Hop community, from multiplatinum superstars to street-level, underground heads. Drawing upon an impressively broad range of theories and methodologies, from sociolinguistics and anthropology to cultural studies and poetics, Alim places the Hip Hop artists—such as Mos Def, Pharoahe Monch, Ras Kass, JT the Bigga Figga, Eve, and Juvenile—in the center by viewing them as interpreters of their own culture. The result is a fascinating insider's view of what can arguably be referred to as the most profound cultural and musical movement to rock the late twentieth and early twenty-first centuries.

H. Samy Alim is an Assistant Professor in UCLA's Department of Anthropology and author of *You Know My Steez* (Duke, 2004) and co-author of *Street Conscious Rap* (Black History Museum, 1999). His research interests include language and race, global Hip Hop Culture, and the street language, culture, and music of the Muslim world (from Chicago to Cairo).

Para César y toda
mi familia de Nayarit
con mucho cariño . . .

Ya tu sabe!

Roc the Mic Right

The Language of Hip Hop Culture

H. Samy Alim

Routledge
Taylor & Francis Group

NEW YORK AND LONDON

First published 2006
by Routledge
270 Madison Ave, New York, NY 10016

Simultaneously published in the UK
by Routledge
2 Park Square, Milton Park, Abingdon, Oxon OX14 4RN

Routledge is an imprint of the Taylor & Francis Group, an informa business

© 2006 H. Samy Alim
Typeset in Franklin Gothic by Keystroke, 28 High Street, Tettenhall, Wolverhampton
Printed and bound in Great Britain by MPG Books Ltd, Bodmin

Library of Congress Cataloging in Publication Data
Alim, H. Samy.
  Roc the mic right : the language of hip hop culture / by H. Samy Alim.
    p. cm.
  Includes bibliographical references and index.
  1. African Americans–Languages.   2. English language–Social aspects–
United States.   3. Black English–United States.   4. Hip-hop–United States.
  5. Popular culture–United States.   I. Title.

  PE3102.N42A45 2006

  427′.97308996073–dc22   2006003029

British Library Cataloguing in Publication Data
A catalogue record for this book is available from the British Library

ISBN10: 0-415-35877-9 (hbk)
ISBN10: 0-415-35878-7 (pbk)
ISBN10: 0-203-00673-9 (ebk)

ISBN13: 978-0-415-35877-4 (hbk)
ISBN13: 978-0-415-35878-1 (pbk)
ISBN13: 978-0-203-00673-3 (ebk)

Contents

Foreword

Every rare once in a while, a scholar-activist comes along, like the balm of Gilead, giving hope to those of us laboring in the vineyards. When I first met Dr. H. Samy Alim, he was an inspired and inspiring undergraduate student at the University of Pennsylvania. Early on, it became starkly clear to me that here was someone to take stock of over the years, someone who would make a mark in the world. 'Cause this bad young boy was on a mission. And I do mean "young." Now, Stanford University Ph.D.–Fulbright Fellow–Duke University Postdoctoral Fellow–UCLA Assistant Professor–three books–numerous articles–later, he is still a few years under thirty. And his own labor in the vineyards has borne rich, delectable fruit, some of which you holdin in your hands right now.

This third book of this self-avowed "combat linguist" not only stamps his unique intellectual and scholarly imprint on the game, but also elevates the game to a whole nother level, setting forth a global, interdisciplinary agenda that Alim calls "Hip Hop Linguistics." In a sense, this book represents Alim's attempt to centralize what he believes to be the primary way of "reading," that is, understanding and making sense of, Hip Hop. As language-centered as Hip Hop is (it's all about the skillz, baby), there has been a huge void in Hip Hop Studies scholarship on the very medium of the Hip Hop message—its unique, innovative and powerful language. *Roc the Mic Right* not only fills this void in Hip Hop Studies and in cultural studies, but also problematizes the work of linguists/linguistics and poses the provocative question: Of what value is it? His answer: Linguistics can play a major role in social transformation. In Alim's relentless quest for truth about the language of our people, he boldly fuses multiple research traditions and methodologies—ethnography, linguistic anthropology, quantitative sociolinguistics, poetics, and discourse analysis. He charts new, important territory as he hooks up linguistics, anthropology, cultural studies, and other disciplines in the Academy, with the streets, Hip Hop Nation Language and Culture, Islam, and the classroom. Like Old School folk say, "People git ready, cuz a change gon come."

Alim's focus on Hip Hop Nation Language (HHNL), what he refers to as this "synergistic combination of speech, music, and literature," lends itself to a wholistic treatment of all elements of Black Language. These come into play in the Hip Hop cipha—call–response, signifyin, tonal semantics, narrative sequencing, verbal battlin, flow, and poetics. His central message is profound even as it is deceptively simple: We need to throw out the old world of "linguistic supremacy" and usher in a new world of "linguistic equanimity." Taking us on a journey through HHNL, Alim reveals possibilities for achieving this socio-cultural change. Teachers, especially, need to know about the power of HHNL and Black Popular Culture. In these days of No Child Left Behind (or as someone signified recently, "No Child Left"), HHNL can bridge the home and school cultures of Black and other marginalized youth. To make this happen, teachers must accept the fact that Hip Hop has its own "innovative and inventive poets," as powerful as Chaucer and Shakespeare—or Langston Hughes and Sonia Sanchez. It is not a question of substituting one for the other, but including *all* as we seek to set afoot a new generation in the twenty-first century.

Black Language (BL) is central to Hip Hop Nation Language (HHNL), and HHNL is central to BL. To take it even further, as Alim so astutely puts it, "While scholars have made mention of the centrality of language to Hip Hop Culture, hiphopography presents language as not only central to the notion of a Hip Hop Nation, and to reading the HHN theoretically, but as central to its study in the field and the narration of its history." Hip Hop rules. Alim locates it in subject, not object position—and rightly so. Hip Hop, its power, its nuance, tone, essence, its cultural lifeblood permeates every chapter of Alim's book. In so doing, he comes decidedly *correct*. Word.

There is much to like, learn, and praise in *Roc the Mic Right*. I like the inclusion of the voices of students, who hail from what a Wilsonian (Julius, that is) social analysis would call the "underclass." The "Sunnysidaz" and Philly Town students whom Alim worked with for several years conduct sociolinguistic autobiographies in which they righteously—and correctly—analyze their Hip Hop language use. Astoundingly, teachers are not as linguistically astute: "Not only does the teacher erroneously point out 'he was' and 'she was' as cases of BL . . . [she also implies] that BL has a random system of negation ('we ain't not' is actually not found in BL, or any language variety in the US)." I also like the presentation of Black Arts poets of the 1960s/70s in conversation with Hip Hoppas—a rich, cross-generational dialogue that has much to teach us. Then there are the voices of myriad Hip Hop artists, from East to West Coast, from Chi-town to Cairo, spittin rich, unique rhymes as they glide beneath the mainstream radar. And it's been a looooong time since I read anything with the power and eloquence of Alim's chapter on and interview with Hip Hop artist Pharoahe Monch.

Reading Alim's text, I was especially moved by "Verbal *Mujahidin* in the Transglobal Hip Hop *umma*: Islam, Discursive Struggle, and the Weapons of Mass Culture." In this chapter Alim impressively deconstructs Islam in Hip Hop. Headz up to readers: you gon be forced to reassess and revise your conceptions of both of these powerful forces in the life experiences of Black people in the

U.S. and other countries. Alim positions Islam in Hip Hop as a "verbal jihad" and "discursive struggle against oppression" here in the U.S. and globally. It is a refreshing departure from staid, old, tired stereotypes of both Islam and Hip Hop. Check out how he acknowledges and treats women in Islam and Hip Hop. Ain nobody other than this intellectual playa coulda brought this kinda heat. His in-depth knowledge of the Arabic language and Islamic Culture and his participant-observer-scholar mindset in Islam and Hip Hop is in full effect here. I also like . . . look, this whole book is bad! It is a seminal work in which Alim's own voice echoes those of the many "defiant giants"—students, Old School poets, Hip Hop artists—whose voices he shares with us. Alim's approach gives center stage to the "culture creators" of Hip Hop, thereby providing a rare, edifying *emic* perspective on one of the twentieth century's most important cultural, musical—and linguistic—movements.

A final note. In this book, Alim boldly sets forth a critical area of study, which he refers to as "Hip Hop Linguistics (HHLx)." This work is focused centrally on language and language use within Hip Hop communities around the world. The studies are not only relevant to African American, Latino/a, and other marginalized groups in the U.S., but Hip Hop Linguistics also tackles a worldwide agenda that seeks social transformation from Brooklyn to Baghdad. "Since language ain't neva neutral," and Alim ain neva scared, like that bad brotha Bone Crusher, "HHLx interrogates the development of unequal power relations between and within groups in an effort to make a contribution to our understanding of the world around us." Elucidating, illuminating, educating, causin readers to do some marinatin . . . it's "real talk" time up in *Roc the Mic Right*. As Alim does at the end of his book's introduction, I, too, send out a clarion call to young scholars of all disciplines, from all over the Hip Hop globe. A new generation of scholars is needed to help build this area of research that Alim lays out in this foundational book. Step up, yall, and enter the cipha of Hip Hop Linguistics!

Peace up,

Geneva Smitherman, Ph.D., aka Dr. G
University Distinguished Professor of English and Director,
My Brother's Keeper Program, Michigan State University
Author, *Word from the Mother: Language and African Americans*

Shout outs

Bismillah Al-Rahman Al-Rahim. In the Name of Allah, the Beneficent, the Merciful . . . Yo, first and foremost, as always, All Props and Praises due to the Most High. One Love. You still wit me after all these years, after all my ups and downs, after all my trials and tribulations. I know I'm strugglin in the process of what my brothas Common and Cee Lo call G.O.D. (Gaining One's Definition), but as the chorus say, "I just wanna be happy with being me." And through all of this, you been hittin me with blessings like it was *nobody's* business. Can I ever thank You enough? Most of all, thanks for the gift of family, and what I have often referred to as "the most valuable gift anyone could ever ask for"— that is, a mother and father who spent their whole lives livin for their children, makin sure that their baby boys were well taken care of and prepared to handle a world that, like the big homie Pac say, we were given. Minky, Tex, Wiss, Willo, Lisa, and Deanna (my beautiful, lil niece), thanks for all the family love. You all are the reason why "Nobody beats the Alims!" ☺

   Alright, y'all, time to give a madd shout out to all of the dope-ass Hip Hop artists who have helped me out over the years by openin up their doors and their hearts to me in honest and engaging conversation about their lives, loves, hopes, fears, and most of all, this beautiful thang we call Hip Hop. Y'all know, like my man Juelz Santana be sayin, this ishhh is so much more than what these people call "music." That's real talk. This is a Global Hip Hop Cultural Movement. Props to the modern day pharaoh walkin the streets of Queens, Pharoahe Monch. Thanks for sharing your thoughts and insights with me all while I was workin on this book (and before). It couldn't have been written without you, Bro. Special shout out to Brother JT the Bigga Figga for all of his support, above and beyond this book, but especially for the many meetings we done had over the last six or seven years. You continue to be an inspiration. It ain't for play, JT. Keep bangin. Also central to the clarity of the ideas in this book is the sincere and honest participation (and in-depth metalinguistic insights) of some bad-ass, street-conscious street linguists and street poets such as Afrika Bambaataa, Kurupt, Beanie Sigel, Freeway, Ghostface, Raekwon and the American Cream Team (R.I.P. to Bankie Santana), Mos Def, Ras Kass, Chuck D, Zion I, Eve, Juvenile, Big Daddy Kane, Common, Saafir, Lil Kim,

LL Cool J, Bahamadia, Boots, DJ Hi-Tek, the Delinquents, Guru, San Quinn, Jubwa of Soul Plantation aka Johnny Afro, Brother Brian Rikuda and Conduit Entertainment, and the Sugarhill Gang, among many others. And to the *mutha* of them all, a sista who ain't gotta say "wassup?" cuz she already *know* wassup—Sista Sonia Sanchez. Thanks for layin it down. One love to the Global Hip Hop Nation for representin and stayin true to what you do—it is through my engagement with you that I have become firmly convinced that culture *is* the revolution.

Several scholars have been pivotal to the writing of this book, but I gotta take y'all back to my undergraduate years at the University of Pennsylvania in Philly to arrive at the real genesis of this work. I think it was 1998, the year after the Ebonics controversy. I remember sittin on Penn's campus one day havin this all-out, intense, critical discussion with Hip Hop historian, scholar, critic, James G. Spady. And, yo, by the end of this heated battle, I remember bein so *into* what we were talkin about that I realized that it was *this*—these critical issues of Language and Culture—that I wanted to devote my intellectual life to. But how? Here I was feelin trapped in an Ivory Tower full of stuffy, boring, tight-ass scholars, very few of whom knew anything about Hip Hop Culture, or even gave a shit. How was I gon study the thing that I loved in an environment that, for the most part, didn't even know that thing existed, you know what I'm saying? For those of you who know me personally, you can imagine the angst with which I asked Spady, "How I'm supposed to do all this shit, sociolinguistics, education, anthropology and Hip Hop Culture, all at the same time, man?!" Spady's response was simply to look at me directly and say, "Of course you can do it, Alim. It's actually much more related than you think it is, even if others don't see it. In fact, it's all the same." At this stage in my career, I realize how lucky I was to have met someone like Spady at such a critical time for me. Of course, now I look back at my question with a chuckle, because it is obvious to me how all these issues are interrelated. What's more obvious is that just because there was no current space in the academy for the type of work that I wanted to do, didn't mean that it couldn't be done. While nothing was exactly what I wanted to do, there were previous models which were similar, and I could use those models to create my own space in the academy for critical Hip Hop inquiry, particularly in the areas of language and literacy. And here, you have it in your hands, *Roc the Mic Right*, the culmination of seven years of thought and effort to come up with a way to do what Spady said I could do. Thanks, Bro, you set me off on this quest by teachin me how to be critical and you've always made yourself available since. I'm sure you'll see that next, other Umum ishhh all up inside the pages of this text. As always, the Black History Museum crew, the UMUM BALLERS (Charles G. Lee, Leandre Jackson, Stefan Dupres, Samir Meghelli and others), got a lotta work to do. Let's keep bangin!

Several scholars have been key to the writing of this book. Beyond John Baugh's incredible intellectual impact on my work, he is, in an important way, responsible for this book. Yo, you might not remember this, Bro, but it was *you* who came up with the idea of writing this book some time in early 2003. We was walkin out the back of the Stanford Cubberley Education building—I don't know, prolly walkin out after your class or something—and I was proud to report to you that I had published an article. You said these words, "You've published so much on Hip Hop and Language already, Alim, that I can see you writin a book on this topic soon." Well, thanks, man, for those words, cuz I took off the minute you said that and began plannin this book. I didn't realize how much work it would be, but yo, it's here. Thanks, homie.

Major props and thanks to the one and only Docta G, Geneva Smitherman, who continues to be an intellectual guiding light and the moral consciousness of a couple of generations of scholars. Is there any way to really thank you for all of your intellectual and personal investment? Your work, your words and your wisdom have served as models for me since the Penn days. Of course, you know all this, cuz you stay in constant contact with a brotha and never let me forget my mission. Check this out, though: Could there have been a *Roc the Mic Right* without "The Power of the Rap"? And would I be sittin here testifyin if there wasn't no *Talkin and Testifyin*? Keep doin your work on Black Language, Education, and Social Change. We need a word from the mother. Like you said to me early on, long before I could ever know what you meant by it, "We need your work!" Word to the *mutha*.

Major shout out to John Rickford who was with me throughout the Stanford years and supervised my Master's thesis in linguistics on "Street Conscious Copula Variation in the Hip Hop Nation." Some of the work that you see here, particularly in Chapter 5 of this book, began back in that Rickford lab, and other work stems from an early invitation to contribute a chapter on the unique language of the Hip Hop community in the US, "Hip Hop Nation Language." Bigtime support. Good lookin out, homie. Peter Sells also made helpful comments on early drafts of this work, which have also benefited from the insights of Arthur Spears (thanks for the many great conversations), Sonja Lanehart, Elaine Richardson, Marcyliena Morgan, and Mary Zeigler (some of whom appeared on the same panel in the 2001 American Dialect Society's meetings in DC, where this research was first presented). I am also indebted to Ed Finegan for his scrupulous reading of "Hip Hop Nation Language" and for his valuable support and insights.

Shout out to my homegirl, Christina Paulston, for her critical eye and for the lively intellectual exchanges that most certainly produced better work. I also wanna thank Ray McDermott for his encouragement, insights, and readings of early drafts of this work. I'd like to thank Angela Rickford and Arnetha Ball as well, who were with me when I first presented some of this research at the annual meeting of the American Educational Research Association 2003 in Chicago. Portions of this work benefited greatly from the insights of Paul Kiparsky, who supported and supervised independent research on Hip Hop poetics and made several important suggestions upon reading the manuscript. I'd also like to give props to Mia Mitchell for the hours spent in our "lyrical analysis battles." Yo, where you at? Also, in addition to their reading of portions of the text, I'd like to acknowledge the encouragement offered by Connie Eble and Charles Meyer. Others who were helpful to the ideas in this book are the AILA 2005 cipher, Alastair Pennycook, Awad Ibrahim, Michael Newman, Mela Sarkar, and again, Elaine Richardson, who tore it up in Madison, Wisconsin. My colleagues, the Ling Anthro CLIC at UCLA, who have been very helpful, Alessandro Duranti, Marjorie Goodwin, Chuck Goodwin, Paul Kroskrity, Claudia Mitchell-Kernan, Elinor Ochs, and Doug Hollan, and the AFAMily and the Ralph Bunche Center, including Darnell Hunt, Lisbeth Grant-Britton, Alex Tucker and Scot Brown. Also, madd shout to the UCLA Graduate Hip Hop Studies Reading Group (and other grad students), especially Melanie Schmidt, Jooyoung Lee, Emilee Woods, and Lauren Mason (dippin in the Lo-Lo). Bill Labov, Ira Harkavy, Farah Griffin, Ron Butters, Walt Wolfram, James Banks, Pedro Noguera, Maisha Fisher, Derrick Alridge, Lisa Green, Penny Eckert, Robin Kelley, James Peterson (uknowhowwedo), Shirley Brice Heath, Mary Bucholtz (one of the most careful readers of this work), Jane Hill, Jennifer Roth-Gordon, Carolyn Adger, Jabari Mahiri, Austin Jackson, Ana Celia Zentella, and George Yancy have also been helpful at various points. Of course, the Spencer Foundation and the Fulbright Foundation have provided me with the necessary support, space, and *skrilla* to complete much of what you read here.

A special long-distance, trans-Atlantic shout out goes out to all of my dear friends and colleagues from the Cairo Linguics Group for the many ongoing dialogues on the language of Hip Hop Culture, particularly the language of Black America, and the links between language, discourse, and racism in institutions. Thanks, too, for your encouragement, wonderful Egyptian-style hospitality, and for all that you've done for me in Egypt. I would especially like to thank the editors of *Al-Logha*, Madiha Doss and Gerda Mansour of Cairo University, for inviting me to do a lecture series on language in the USA, and Helmi Sharawi, the Director of the Arab and African Research Center, for being such a warm and welcoming host. Helmi, your critical questions, along with the questions, suggestions, and ideas of the participating scholars from Cairo University, Helwan University, and other institutions, helped me to better understand the Egyptian linguistic context at the same time as they helped to hone my own understanding of the American context. I have hopes, Insha'Allah, that all of us will be in contact with each other in the future. *Elf shukr.*

I also wanna give a shout out to Dalia El-Shayal and Maha El-Said of Cairo University's English Department, and former Egyptian Fulbrighters to the US, for their passion, interest, and research in Black American art, literature, language and history, as well as their ability to see parallel activities within the Egyptian context. Our many conversations about everything from the main man, *Shaaban Abdel Rehim*, to the relationship between creativity and oppression, have greatly enhanced my work and will undoubtedly continue to shape my future work. Maha and Dalia were among the many scholars, artists, and religious leaders who were present at the Mubarak Public Library in Cairo for my lecture on Hip Hop Culture, Language, and Spirituality. Major shout outs to Eliza Al-Laham, Ahmed Naguib and the US Embassy in Cairo for sponsoring the lecture and for makin sure everything was perfect. I have incorporated much of the feedback from that lecture into Chapter 2 of this book. *Itsharafnah.* Thanks also to all of my Fulbright colleagues for enhancing my intellectual life in unforeseen ways, but mostly, for being there and supporting me, especially my roommate Nicholas Lanoie who saw how much of this book came together and offered critical feedback. Yo, thanks, homie. And if a shout out could be a hug, it would go out to the one and only, Sobhi, who held me down for nine months while I was in Egypt. *Inta bitiwhashni yakhooyah. 'ayzeen nishoofek tani orayyib, Insha'Allah, wa nis'el 'aleik. Ana makutish ha'dur akhalas el-kitaab deh min gheirak, ya seedi. Elf, ELF shukr.*

I'd also like to thank Manar El Shorbagy, the Academic Director of the American Studies Center at the American University in Cairo, for her work in organizing the conference on American Popular Culture and for her invitation (on the recommendation of the AUC History Department's Joseph Walwick) to give the keynote lecture on the Globalization of Hip Hop Culture. Thanks also to AUC's Alaa El-Gibali who was instrumental to my being in Cairo. I can't thank you enough for your support. Thanks also to my friends and colleagues at the Egyptian Folklore Society, Sayed Hamad and President Ahmed Morsi, for meeting with me and supporting my work. Also, major props to Hani Shukrallah and Dena Rashed for publishing my article, "Hip Hop Islam," in *Al-Ahram Weekly* and for your support of this line of research. Your interest in this topic, along with the others present at the American Popular Culture conference, has reinvigorated my drive to do this important research.

On the topic of Hip Hop, Islam, and discourse, madd people been supportin me in this work. I would like to acknowledge my colleagues miriam cooke, Bruce Lawrence, Ebrahim Moosa and the Center for the Study of Muslim Networks who were the first to invite me to present this line of research at the John Hope Franklin Center at Duke University. Their exploration of Muslim networks has opened up a much-needed space in the academy, and their support of my research has improved the quality of this work tremendously. I would also like to acknowledge Ayat El-Noory and all of her colleagues at the Muslim Artists Collective at the University of Illinois, Urbana-Champaign, for supporting earlier versions of this work and for inviting me to build with them during the month of Ramadan. As my Duke colleagues have created an academic space for Islam and popular culture, I thank you for opening up a creative space where art, culture, and Islam can be in healthy dialogue. And many, many thanks to Ramzi Salti and the Middle Eastern and African Languages and Literatures program of Stanford University and Jennifer Bloomquist of Linguistics and African American Studies at Gettysburg College for their support of research on "Islam and popular culture" and "activism in the vernacular."

Peace to James G. Spady and Samir Meghelli for helping me work through some of these ideas. The influence of the Black History Museum Committee in

Philadelphia is all up in this piece, i.e., clearly evident in this work. Keep documentin the living culture in *Tha Global Cipha: Hip Hop Culture and Consciousness*, as Grandmaster Flash said, "one page at a time, one life at a time, and one story at a time." Yo, Dee, you know wassup. I can't even count the number of conversations we've had about the issues raised in this book. And, damn, thank *God* Skype was free or we'd both be broke! Seriously, though, you don't know how much you've helped me during the years that this book was written. Thank you for *still* bein a frieeeennnnnnnd. And, yo, a MADD SHOUT OUT to all my students at Stanford, Duke and UCLA in "The Language of Hip Hop Culture" and to all the Sunnysidaz from my high school Hip Hop class who are now out there causin havoc in the world. I'm watchin and waitin. Put yo stamp on this game. Y'all know who y'all is. Thanks for pushin me. One Love.

Finally, this book goes out to all the dope MCs, street poets and street linguists that's spittin lyrical flames and knowin that it be about much more than language. To all of those who, like Mos Def, get rashes on they lips from speakin the "King's English"—who be committed to page, writin rhymes, sometimes don't finish for days. To all of those like Common who gon stay "forever puttin words together." And lastly, to allay'all who be choppin heads, man, or like brotha Afu Ra spit it, killin us with yo syllables . . . "but never softly." This is for you, the Hip Hop Cultural Movement. Keep spittin that slick-ass Black Language. Much props, thanks, and love.

P.E.A.C.E.
not war . . .

Chapter 1

'The streetz iz a mutha'

The street and the formation of a Hip Hop Linguistics (HHLx)

The Black Language is constructed of—alright let me take it all the way back to the slave days and use something that's physical. All the slavemasters gave our people straight chittlins and greens, you feel me, stuff that they wasn't eatin. But we made it into a delicacy. Same thing with the language. It's the *exact* same formula. How our people can take the *worst*, or take our bad condition, and be able to turn it into something that we can benefit off of. Just like the drums. They didn't want the slaves playin drums because we was talkin through the drums. "What the hell did my slaves do? Oh, no, cut that! Take them drums!" you feel me? So through the music, that's kinda like goin on now with the rap thang. It's *ghetto* music. People talkin about they issues and crime and, you feel me? "Don't push me cuz I'm close to the eeedge!" [Rappin Grandmaster Flash and the Furious Five's "The Message"] You feel me? He talkin about, "Man, I'm so fed up with you people in this society, man." So this is the voice of the ghetto. The rap come from the voice of the ghetto . . . Hip Hop and the streets damn near is one, you might as well say that . . . Straight from the streets.
        (Interview with rapper JT the Bigga Figga, cited partially in Alim 2000)

Finally, of what use is linguistics? Very few people have clear ideas on this point . . . But it is evident, for instance, that linguistic questions interest all who work with texts—historians, philologists, etc. Still more obvious is the importance of linguistics to general culture: in the lives of individuals and societies, speech is more important than anything else. That linguistics should continue to be the prerogative of a few specialists would be unthinkable—everyone is concerned with it one way or another.
        (Ferdinand de Saussure, *Course in General Linguistics* [1916], 1960: 7)

I begin this book with an anecdote from the "Hiphop Community Activism and Education Roundtable," at Harvard University's W. E. B. DuBois Institute for Afro-American Research. The roundtable was organized by Marcyliena Morgan, Director of the Hiphop Archive (now at Stanford), the first national archive established to preserve, document, and support the development of Hip Hop Culture around the globe.

On September 28, 2002, Harvard brought together many of the leading scholars in their respective fields with pioneering and progressive Hip Hop artists and community activists from around the US. Looking around the roundtable, one could see a wide range of participants including Black American literary critic Henry Louis Gates, Jr., "the Godfather of Hip Hop" Afrika Bambaataa and representatives from the Universal Zulu Nation, urban education scholar Pedro A. Noguera, politically conscious Oakland-based Hip Hop artist Boots of The Coup, journalist and pioneering Hip Hop scholar-historian James G. Spady, LA-based Hip Hop artist Aceyalone, Rap Coalition's Wendy Day, political scientist Michael Dawson, and many, many others.

I begin with this anecdote from the conference because it illustrates, in part, the motivation for the type of work that I do. In addition, it reflects the fact that Hip Hop Culture is an egalitarian forum and an enabler of dialogue among and between diverse communities. With such an eclectic group of participants, all of whom have dedicated their lives to the development of Hip Hop Culture and Black American youth and youth around the world, there were bound to be some *heated* moments. These moments of critical engagement seemed to be fashioned after the intense rhyme battles that occur in the Hip Hop cipha— they were carried out in a highly energetic and expressive space that is both competitive and communal. The cipha offers all participants a chance to sharpen their skills, while sharing ideas in the spirit of both teaching and learning. As James G. Spady commented during the meeting, "Upon entering the cipha, all borders disappear." That means that conventional notions of power, authority, and the hierarchical construction of knowledge melt within the flow and exchange of ideas. The idea takes center stage. Like a Hip Hop sista once told me, capturing the essence of the value of critical thinking to the Hip Hop Nation (HHN), *all we is is our ideas*.

One moment, in particular, helps to frame this discussion. Cashus D, a member of the Universal Zulu Nation, was considered by many to be the "conscience of the conference," since his presence and that of Afrika Bamba-aataa and the other artists kept the scholars honest. Throughout the day-long event, he made several passionate statements about the nature of Hip Hop Culture that, to some participants, seemed like an idealization rather than an accurate depiction of what Hip Hop truly is, that is, how it is played out in the lives of everyday people. After Cashus D finished his powerful statement about the cultural unity and nationhood found within the HHN, one Black American literary critic stood up, grabbed the mic and entered the cipha. In a two-minute flurry of some of the most animated talk at the conference, he challenged Cashus D and posited that Hip Hop Culture may actually be a drug to seduce young Black Americans from a productive lifestyle into one of criminality and nihilism. In other words, here at Harvard, we were observing two colliding constructions of "Hip Hop Culture" at battle in the cipha: (1) a Hip Hop-centered idealization and (2) a mainstream-centered, pathological perception of Hip Hop Culture. Critical Hip Hop studies (Rose 1994, Perry 2004) reveal that Hip Hop Culture is neither of these; rather, Hip Hop is constituted by popular cultural production and practices that are as contradictory as they are conscious (or like Jigga say so concise on *The Black Album*, it's like Che Guevara with bling on, complex).

The literary critic continued to lambaste the HHN and asked what seemed, to many in the room, to be a strange series of questions. Bemoaning the educational reality of most Black Americans (and it *is* something to moan about), he asked, "Where are our writers?" "Where is the wonderful, literary tradition found in centuries of African American literature?" "Where is the literacy tradition?" He continued to make several comments that clearly privileged written literacy over oral literacy, and commented on how Hip Hop artists and those interested in Hip Hop should be working towards "moving Black youth from oral forms to written forms." In his conclusion, he suggested that the most politically subversive act of the HHN—"the Blackest thing you can do," in his words—would be to take the "white man's literacy" and empower Black youth.

There are several assumptions in this critic's remarks that need to be addressed. First, the "blackest thing" we can do, as a Nation of Hip Hop Headz, is to *appreciate our own culture, history and traditions*. I say this for two reasons. First, Black people are not only the first people to produce spoken language, but they are also the first to invent writing systems. In addition to privileging written literacy over oral literacy, the critic was also quite nostalgic about older Black American literary forms while completely failing to recognize the literary, linguistic, and poetic sophistication of young Black American Hip Hop MC's. The second point, in particular, represents the pervasive attitude that young Black Americans face everyday in America's schools, an attitude that emerges due to the cultural-linguistic disconnect between Black American culture and school culture, and is ultimately rooted in racist views of Black people. It is important to note that such a well-respected scholar, one who clearly has a healthy respect, love, and admiration for Black American literary forms, did not comment on the artistry and creativity found within the Hip Hop Cultural Movement. In moments like these, I often ask myself: Will we appreciate the full complexity and creativity of our contemporary culture and literary production only after it's dead and gone? At what price will we continue to ignore the extraordinary linguistic, literary, and literacy skills of this generation of young Black Americans? One could argue that the great lesson from Harvard's Hiphop Community Activism and Education Roundtable is that the "blackest" thing we can do—that is, the most politically subversive strategy—is to learn to appreciate the totality of Black American culture, its contradictions, fluid possibilities, dynamism, and the power potential evident in the newly emerged (and constantly emerging) Hip Hop Nation Language.

The scholar and the Hip Hop-saturated street

It ain't even necessary for me say that this scholar is not alone in his misguided critique of Hip Hop Culture. He is but one of a legion of folks who are still *sleepin* on what some critics see as the most profound lyrical and musical movement to rock the twentieth century. The Hip Hop Cultural Movement has captured the minds of youth "all around the world, from Japan to Amsterdam" (like the homie Kurupt say) as it "whirlwinds through cities, from Chicago to Cairo" (like the god Afu-Ra say) shaping youth identities, styles, attitudes, languages, fashions, and both physical and political stances. Still, many scholars who comment on Hip Hop Culture do little more than reproduce the public discourse. There are a variety of reasons for that and much of the confusion is surely due to a complex array of class and racial politics. However, when we consider the research methodology informing the critiques, it becomes clear that far too many commentators are simply too socially distanced from the locus of Hip Hop cultural activity—the street. Writing in *Black Street Speech*, in a chapter entitled "The scholar and the street: Collecting the data," Baugh (1983: 36) notes the challenges of collecting speech data in Black and other marginalized communities: "It is one thing to recognize the need to gather data from representative consultants, but it is another matter altogether to get the job done." Can we imagine Baugh's (1983) classic study of "Black street speech" being carried out anywhere else but in the streets? Can we imagine the study of Hip Hop Culture beginning anywhere but in the streets?

Hip Hop Culture is sometimes defined as having four major elements: MC'ing (rappin), DJ'ing (spinnin), breakdancing (streetdancing), and graffiti art (writing). To these, KRS-One adds knowledge as a fifth element, and Afrika Bambaataa, a founder of the Hip Hop Cultural Movement, adds overstanding. Bambaataa, in an interview with noted Hip Hop journalist Davey D, provides a more comprehensive definition of "Hip Hop:"

> People have to understand what you mean when you talk about Hip Hop. Hip Hop means the whole culture of the movement. When you talk about rap you have to understand that rap is part of the Hip Hop Culture. That means the emceeing is part of the Hip Hop Culture. The Deejaying is part of the Hip Hop Culture. The dressing, the languages are all part of the Hip Hop Culture. So is the break dancing, the b-boys and b-girls. How you act, walk, look and talk is all part of Hip Hop Culture. And the music is . . . from whatever music that gives that grunt, that funk, that groove, that beat. That's all part of Hip Hop.

Rappin, one aspect of Hip Hop Culture, consists of the aesthetic placement of verbal rhymes over musical beats, and it is this element that has dominated Hip Hop cultural activity in recent years. Thus, language is perhaps the most useful means with which to read the various cultural activities of the HHN.

Sociolinguists and linguistic anthropologists have always been interested in analyzing language and language use within varying contexts. Given these scholars' healthy respect for vernacular languages, and given the richly varied and diverse speech acts and communicative practices of the HHN, it is surprising that until the late 1990s no American sociolinguist had written about Hip Hop Culture in any major academic journal. It was a Belgian student of African history and linguistics at the University of Ghent who first collected data about Hip Hop culture in the Lower East Side of New York City in 1986–87. In his quest to learn about the social and cultural context of rap performances, Remes (1991) produced one of the earliest sociolinguistic studies of rappin in a Hip Hop community. His pioneering study provided a brief account of the origin of rap, identified several "Black English" linguistic features found in rap, and highlighted the communicative practices of call-and-response and verbal battling. Only in 1997 did sociolinguist Geneva Smitherman publish her pioneering analysis of the communicative practices of the HHN (Smitherman, 1997; presented before an audience in South Africa in 1995).

Since then, language scholars have presented papers at professional conferences and published in academic journals. In 2001 at the thirtieth anniversary meeting of NWAV, the major gathering of sociolinguists, I participated in a panel called "The Sociolinguistics of Hip Hop: New Ways of Analyzing Hip Hop Nation Language." Every year since then, scholars of language at various professional conferences in anthropology, sociolinguistics, cultural studies, education, and others have presented academic papers on language and Hip Hop Culture. Most recently, in July 2005, I participated in a symposium about Hip Hop Culture, ethnicity, and the politics of language education at the Fourteenth World Congress of Applied Linguistics. To paraphrase the poet-dramatist Amiri Baraka, a leading figure of the Black Arts Movement of the 1960s and 1970s, scholars of language are now celebrating Hip Hop Culture and beginning to see that the "Hip Hop Nation is Like Ourselves."

To be fair, at least since 1964, there has been considerable scholarship on language use within what are now called Hip Hop communities. It started with investigations "deep down in the jungle" in the streets of South Philly (it's like a jungle sometimes it makes me wonder how I keep from goin under) that recorded "black talkin in the streets" of America (Abrahams 1964, 1970, 1976), the analysis of "language behavior" of Blacks in Oakland (Mitchell-Kernan 1971), the narrative syntax and ritual insults of Harlem teenagers "in the inner city" (Labov 1972a), the critical examination of "the power of the rap" in the "Black Idiom" of the Black Arts Movement rappers and poets (Smitherman 1973, 1977), and an elucidation of the "language and culture of black teenagers" who skillfully "ran down some lines" in South Central Los Angeles (Folb 1980). In myriad ways, then, scholars had prepared the field for the extraordinary linguistic phenomenon that was about to leave an indelible mark on many languages of the world. This linguistic phenomenon is, of course, Hip Hop Culture. Most of the works cited above (with the exception of Folb) were published before the advent of the first Hip Hop recording in 1979, the Sugar Hill Gang's "Rapper's Delight." By describing the linguistic patterns and practices of Black Americans in the "inner cities," these scholars were studying the linguistic forebears of the HHN.

The work of these pioneering scholars, and others, demonstrated the creativity, ingenuity, and verbal virtuosity of Blacks in America by examining language use at the very loci of linguistic-cultural activity. One scholar puts it succinctly: "The street is hardcore and it is the rhythmic locus of the Hip Hop world" (Spady in Spady and Eure 1991: 406, 407). Foregrounding the streets as the site, sound, and soul of hiphopological activity allows one to gain a more thorough understanding of the origins and sociocultural context of Hip Hop Culture, which is critical to understanding language use within this Nation.

My own research on HHNL and Hip Hop Culture in general has led to the streets, homes, cars, jeeps, clubs, stadiums, backstage, performances, hotels, religious centers, conferences, and ciphers (highly competitive lyrical circles of rhymers) where Hip Hop lives—up inside the "actual lived experiences in the corrugated spaces that one finds reflected in the lyrical content of rap songs" (Spady *et al.* 1995). What I have attempted to do in this book is to demonstrate the creativity and complexity of language use in contemporary Black American expressive culture, particularly HHNL, language use in the Hip Hop Nation Speech Community, and the Hip Hop cultural modes of discourse. By excavating the broad range of linguistic-cultural activity of the HHN, I hope to have deepened our understanding of this highly complex discursive zone. However, each of the aspects of HHNL covered in this book deserves more critical attention. I have used various sources in the writing of this book, but it is important to note that my research is informed by members of the HHN—from underground street-level heads to multiplatinum, international playas. The main point is that this research utilizes Hip Hop's culture creators as a primary point of departure. As we shall see, the Hip Hop artists represented in this book, from Mos Def and Pharoahe Monch, to Ras Kass and Kurupt, to Eve, Juvenile and JT the Bigga Figga, are all quite capable of being the interpreters of their own culture.

Language scholars of the Hip Hop generations (we are now more than one) are needed to uncover the linguistic inventiveness and innovativeness of HHNL speakers. In order to *represent*—to reflect any semblance of Hip Hop cultural reality—these scholars will need to be in direct conversation with the Hip Hop communities under study. More fieldwork in the Hip Hop-saturated streets of America, and the world, is required to elucidate the dynamics of this black-culture-turned-global-culture. It's time for a Hip Hop Linguistics.

The formation of a Hip Hop Linguistics (HHLx)

What I have attempted to do in this book is to provide a modest example of a new area of inquiry, Hip Hop Linguistics (HHLx), and present a diversity of approaches to the study of the language of Hip Hop Culture, from sociolinguistic variation and applied linguistics, to poetics and the critical approach of cultural studies, to the ethnographic fieldwork required in anthropological studies. Through this work, I seek to contribute to all of these areas, as well as the broader field of Hip Hop Studies. There is a cross-disciplinary legion of scholars who are now producing more and more work in Hip Hop Studies as Hip Hop scholarship enters a new phase of maturation and expansion (see Forman and Neal's *That's the Joint: The Hip-Hop Studies Reader*, 2004). As Michael Eric Dyson writes in the foreword to that reader,

> Hip-Hop is being studied all over the globe, and the methodologies of its examination are rightfully all over the map. They are multidisciplinary in edifying, exemplary fashion, borrowing from sociology, politics, religion, economics, urban studies, journalism, communications theory, American studies, transatlantic studies, black studies, history, musicology, comparative literature, English, linguistics, and many more disciplines besides.

While the reader is described as an "intellectual mixtape," I offer this book as a full-length album in HHLx. I present this study in the hopes that it will launch a series of in-depth analyses of the many varieties of HHNL—analyses that will collectively represent the creativity and complexity, the dynamism and diversity, and the power, politics, pleasure, and the potential of youth language.

HHLx gives props and pays homage to the studies of Black Language (BL) mentioned above, cuz them the ones that really laid down the foundation for what we do. Without them, without that intense field-based inquiry into Black street culture, HHLx would have no academic legs to stand on. Much respect due. HHLx is informed by the recently codified "Black Linguistics" (Makoni *et al.* 2003) and shares with it the mission of "decolonizing Black language and thought," as Ngugi wa Thiongo wrote in the foreword. More generally, we are interested in exploring the relationships between language, literacy, life, and liberation.

Some two decades before the publication of *Black Linguistics*, one of the pioneering researchers of BL stated: "Black scholars now define the role that their white allies can play in advancing the study of Black English . . . Members of an oppressed people have entered an academic field, taken up the tools of linguistic research, and used them for the advancement of their nation" (Labov 1982: 24, cited in Baugh and Smitherman in press). Many Black linguists approach the study of BL as more than merely an academic pursuit. In fact, linguistics is often seen as a direct means to quantify and reverse the myriad social injustices facing Blacks in America, including educational, economic, and political subordination.

Since language permeates all aspects of our lives, for Black scholars, the scientific study of language provides one way to make a way outta no way in the wilderness of North America. Black scholars have been at the forefront of educational, cultural, historical, and legal debates involving language, culture, race, and racism. Recent sociolinguistic scholarship (Baugh 2003) has

examined the relationship between racial profiling and "linguistic profiling"—
the racial identification and discrimination of an individual or group of people
based on their speech and/or writing. This research seeks to address the very
real problem of housing discrimination (among other forms of discrimination)
against linguistic minorities on the basis of their speech. Recognizing a Black
or Latino/a voice on the opposite end of the phone, for example, they falsely
claim that there are no apartments for rent. Such research is a quintessential
example of how the scientific study of language can be utilized to create social
change.

Black linguists have long been concerned with issues of social justice and
social change. Long before the "Ebonics controversy" caught the media's
attention, Black linguists (Bailey 1969, Smitherman 1981, Taylor 1985, Rickford
and Rickford 1995, Baugh 1999) have been committed to the educational
welfare of Black American students. They have joined forces with many Black
American educational researchers who view BL as a resource to be utilized
rather than a problem to be eradicated (Lee 1993, Ball 1995, Perry and Delpit
1998, LeMoine 1999). These researchers support policy and pedagogy that
acknowledge the linguistic resources of Black American students and further
the development of "standard" English proficiency. (See DeBose 2005.)

Black linguists have also provided numerous insights into the dynamic nature
of BL structure and use. From detailed descriptions and analyses of language
use within the Black American community (Mitchell-Kernan 1971, Smitherman
1977, Morgan 1991) to the identification and quantification of several "new"
linguistic features (Baugh 1979, Spears 1982), Black linguists continue to
enhance our understanding of how Black American speech breathes. Struggling
for linguistic liberation, Black linguists have been instrumental in shattering the
myth of the *linguistic tabula rasa*, i.e., the myth that the African Holocaust
completely eradicated any trace of African linguistic heritage in Black Americans.
Many Black linguists and scholars (Turner 1949, Bailey 1965, Williams 1975,
Rickford 1977, Alleyne 1980, Baugh 1983, Asante 1990, DeBose and Faraclas
1993, Smith 1998) have demonstrated the linguistic connection between BL
and creole languages (as well as African languages) in an effort to provide a
more accurate historical account of BL. Early researchers were responding to
the White supremacist view that Black Americans were intellectually inferior
and, therefore, could not produce "the white man's English." Later, many
became involved in producing a historical reconstruction of BL that recognized
the linguistic contributions of both Anglican *and* African sources.

The central focus of HHLx is language and language use within Hip Hop
communities. Since language ain't neva neutral, HHLx interrogates the development of unequal power relations between and within groups in an effort to
make a contribution to our understanding of the world around us. As cultural
theorist Raymond Williams wrote about language in his classic *Keywords*: "A
definition of language is always, implicitly or explicitly, a definition of human
beings in the world" (Williams 1976: 21). There is a reason why Hip Hop

communities resist others' attempts to control their language varieties (you can slap on all the "explicit lyrics" stickers you want). Heads know that policing language is a form of social control that amounts to nothing less than policing people. And we already got too many pigs up in this piece, you know what I'm saying?

As much as HHLx views the poetics of puns, wordplay, and playin with words as a source of pleasure, HHLx situates Hip Hop expression within what we know are highly politicized contexts. Like JT the Bigga Figga can be heard sayin, "This shit ain't for play, cuz it's not a game no mo." As editor of a special issue of the *Black Arts Quarterly*, which focused on "emergency art," I contextualized Hip Hop voices within larger discursive and political struggles against oppression:

> We are talking/ writing/ painting/ photographing/ analyzing/ poeting/ collaging/ languaging/ creating in a critical time. Attempts to censor Black liberatory voices and perspectives continue. From the Anti-Defamation League and New Jersey Governor James McGreevey's grievous call to remove Amiri Baraka from his post as poet laureate of New Jersey . . . to MTV's (Viacom's) censoring of Public Enemy's latest video, "Give the Peeps What They Need" (they requested that Public Enemy delete images of Mumia Abu Jamal and remove the word "Free" from the phrase "Free Mumia"—you can peep the uncut video on www.rapstation.com), to the political ousting of progressive Black politicians Cynthia McKinoy (D–GA) and Earl Hilliard (D–AL) (both of their opponents reportedly received outside financial support from AIPAC—The American Israeli Public Affairs Committee), to the death threats used to intimidate Congresswoman Barbara Lee (D–CA) for her opposition of Bush's "war on terrorism," to the British and Israeli government's ban on Minister Louis Farrakhan from speaking to their constituents (out of fear that his speech will further divide an already racially divided nation, on the British side, and fears of "anti-Semitic" comments on the Israeli side), to the censoring of the cover art of dead prez's Hip Hop album (the cover art for *Let's Get Free!* which contained an image of South African schoolchildren raising rifles in solidarity during the 1976 Soweto Uprising; they were fighting for the right to be educated under an oppressive apartheid regime), among other high profile incidents in recent times.

Writing about the psychic and symbolic violence enacted upon colonized Africans and their relationship with the French language, Frantz Fanon (1967) stated plainly, but heavily, "To speak means to be in a position to use a certain syntax, to grasp the morphology of this or that language, but it means above all to assume a culture, to support the weight of a civilization." HHLx takes as its point of departure the linguistic culture of the HHN. That is, language is far more than linguistic variables, polysyllabic utterances, and turn-taking in conversation, though all of those are important aspects of language. HHLx takes a broad, multidisciplinary approach to the study of language. As Ferdinand de Saussure, who some refer to as the "founding father" of modern linguistics, wrote in 1916 (see this chapter's opening quotation), HHLx is not the domain of a few specialists known as "linguists." As an interdisciplinary area of inquiry, HHLx includes studies of language and language use from various methodological and theoretical perspectives. While studies are grounded in the streets, contributions come from cultural studies, communications studies, ethnic studies, literacy studies, philosophy, sociology, anthropology, sociolinguistics, poetics, literary analysis, and discourse analysis, among other approaches to the study of language.

We begin with language as power, that is, the view that language *is* the revolution, a powerful discourse in and of itself. We know that the most powerful people in society tend to control speech and its circulation through mass media. We know, cuz the Wu-Tang Clan's Rza told us, that "words kill as fast as bullets." Words are far more than parts of speech; they're weapons of mass culture to be deployed in the cultural combat that we, invariably, as humans, find ourselves in. Unfortunately, with teachers of young Hip Hop Heads still sayin that the language of their students is the very thing that they "*combat the most*," we learn this lesson very early on. In this sense of cultural warfare—the micro and macro forms of social control through culture—Hip Hop Linguists are "combat linguists." Yeah, we know it's a war goin on, but don't get it twisted. We are never the aggressors. The task of the Hip Hop Linguist is to both analyze and mediate the struggle. We operate like the Arab-American combat linguist who recently saved an Iraqi family's house, and possibly their lives, from being destroyed. What US soldiers thought were terrorist plots scribbled on pieces of paper throughout the living room turned out to be sewing instructions. The combat linguist's Arabic language skills helped him explain that fact to the other US soldiers. In an analogous situation, Hip Hop Linguists are cultural translators who mediate between Hip Hop Culture (and its languages) and the dominant classes and societies (and their languages) within which they exist.

While this book is mostly about the Black American Hip Hop community, the HHLx agenda focuses on Hip Hop language practices in global context, with particular attention to the global social and linguistic processes that both gave rise to HHNL in the US and reformed and reconfigured HHNL varieties as they are spoken in other contexts (such as Brazil, France, and Japan, for example). HHNL, as a variety of BL in the US, was formed by the sociolinguistic and sociopolitical processes of creolization, as language structure and use were reconfigured in the involuntary transatlantic movement of the African slave trade. As Hip Hop Culture continues to be adopted/adapted by heads all over the world, the syncretization of local street languages and Black American language practices has produced multiple HHNL varieties. HHLx seeks to explore these "global linguistic flows" (Alim and Pennycook in press) of a world-wide movement that has impacted youth language from Tanzania to Turkey. How have Algerian youth, rapping in Arabic, French, and an English influenced by the HHNL model (Meghelli 2005) adapted Hip Hop Culture and HHNL to suit their needs and tastes? How do we begin analyzing Palestinians and their trilingual "lyrical *intifada* (uprising)" (Arabic, Hebrew, and a HHNL-inspired English)? What do we make of South African rappers who spit heat in five languages (Xhosa, Zulu, Tsotsi-Taal, Sotho, and a HHNL-inspired English), or the codeswitching and codemixing that take place in Canada when Haitian, Dominican, and African immigrants practice Hip Hop as a critical site of identification with Black Americans and the development of hybrid identities (Ibrahim in press, Sarkar and Allen in press)? HHLx is clearly an international enterprise and heads are needed from every corner of the Hip Hop globe to study the HHN's expressive richness and diversity.

Hiphopography: Contents under pressure

My particular approach to HHLx has been strongly influenced by five related, and in my mind, overlapping perspectives, each with diverse theoretical traditions and a multi-methods approach—those of "hiphopography" and Hip Hop Studies, language and cultural theory, sociolinguistics and anthropology, education and literacy studies, and English and literary analysis. Hiphopography, coined by Hip Hop scholar-critic-historian James G. Spady, of the Black History Museum Committee in Philadelphia (see the Umum Hip Hop Trilogy beginning with *Nation Conscious Rap: The Hip Hop Vision*, 1991; *Twisted Tales in the Hip Hop Streets of Philly*, 1995; and *Street Conscious Rap*, 1999), has had a critical and central impact on the way that I conduct my research. Hiphopography is to my research what the streets are to Hip Hop Culture—as Method Man say, "it's where I got my stripes at."

Importantly, the hiphopography paradigm integrates the varied approaches of ethnography, biography, and social, cultural, and oral history to arrive at an *emic* view of Hip Hop Culture. It is hiphopography that obligates HHLx to directly engage with the cultural agents of the Hip Hop Culture-World, revealing rappers as critical interpreters of their own culture. We view "rappers" as "cultural critics" and "cultural theorists" whose thoughts and ideas help us to make sense of one of the most important cultural movements of the late twentieth and early twenty-first centuries. Hiphopogaphy's insistence on direct engagement with the "culture creators" also demands the inclusion of theories of linguistic practice into the study of Hip Hop Culture. While scholars have made mention of the centrality of language to Hip Hop Culture, hiphopography presents language as not only central to the notion of a Hip Hop Nation, and to reading the HHN theoretically, but as central to its study in the field and the narration of its history.

Hiphopography began as the study of Hip Hop cultural practice, a Hip Hop Cultural Studies, if you will—not as a subparadigm within cultural studies, but as a movement lying somewhere between cultural studies and cultural anthropology. My own studies seek to reinvigorate cultural studies' commitment to the people and put into practice what cultural anthropology espouses, that is, a nonhierarchical, anticolonial approach that humanizes its subject. What captured my mind as an undergraduate at the University of Pennsylvania in Philly was that deceptively simple point. Hiphopography humanizes Hip Hop. Check it. While most folks was busy talkin about Hip Hop's impact on today's youth, or on this or that culture industry, or on the far corners of the globe (all important areas of inquiry)—what it meant to *be* Hip Hop, to exist in a Hip Hop Culture-World, to possess a Hip Hop mode of being and way of viewing the world was lost in obscure analyses, shit that ain't even feel like Hip Hop to me. To paraphrase Mos Def (peep his already classic album, *Black on Both Sides*, 1999), as he holds up a mirror to Hip Hop critics, Hip Hop ain't no big ole giant livin on the hillside comin down to visit the townspeople. He adds emphatically, in an effort to put a face on Hip Hop, "We *are* Hip Hop! Me, you, everybody, we are Hip Hop. So Hip Hop is goin where we goin." Mos, frustrated by the construction of Hip Hop artists as somehow supernatural, grotesque or non-human, asks critics to take a look at themselves the next time they find themselves asking where Hip Hop is going. Hip Hop is cultural practice embedded in the lived experiences of Hip Hop-conscious beings existing in a home, street, hood, city, state, country, continent, hemisphere near you. Too often in scholarship on Hip Hop Culture, Hip Hop artists and practitioners are talked about, but very seldom are they themselves talking. It may seem extreme, but this can be seen as both tragedy and tyranny. How have we as scholars reproduced the hierarchies that we are trying to dismantle? How has our methodology silenced and disempowered the very folks we claim to be giving voice to and empowering? These are questions that I have grappled with in the writing of this book and will undoubtedly continue to grapple with in my future work.

In Chapter 2 of this book, "Verbal *Mujahidin* in the Transglobal Hip Hop *Umma*: Islam, discursive struggle, and the weapons of mass culture," I view BL and HHNL not as checklists of linguistic features, but as discourse, that is, as potentially powerful weapons of mass culture (WMC). I discuss the complex relationship between Hip Hop Culture and Islam, which have both been separately constructed by dominating discourses as "threats to American civilization." As Foucault (1984: 110), and history, have constantly taught us, "discourse is not simply that which translates struggles or systems of domination, but it is the thing for which and by which there is struggle; discourse is the power which is to be seized." Hip Hop Culture represents a counter-discourse that is not only mass-based, but also mass-mediated, circulated, and communicated to millions of youth.

Like the Islamic *umma*, the Global Hip Hop Nation functions as a worldwide network of "believers" around the world who have created "nationhood" through imaginary, ideological, and discursive means. In this chapter, I view Hip Hop artists—particularly those engaged in what I have called the "trans-global Hip Hop *umma*" (Alim 2005)—as "verbal *mujahidin*," with their speech activities serving as alternative media sources narrating the beliefs and experiences of a "nation." Their very experiences, when verbalized, represent a discursive struggle against oppression. I also show how Hip Hop artists are engaged in a battle over the manipulation and control of discourse on both Hip Hop Culture and Islam. This battle is not fought in the language of classical religious texts—it's fought in that sacred, steetified, slick-ass BL.

It is that same sacred, streetified, slick-ass BL that is dissected in Chapter 3, "Talkin Black in this White Man's World: Linguistic supremacy, linguistic equanimity and the politics of language," where I analyze the language and linguistic practices of Hip Hop youth. In the chapter, I discuss issues of language, racism, and power in American institutions, particularly schools. I show how even well-intentioned teachers are enacting whiteness in their pedagogical praxis and subscribing to a hidden ideology of linguistic supremacy within a system of daily cultural combat. One of the major goals of my research in this area has been to make the invisible visible" by examining the ways by which well-meaning educators attempt to silence BL in White public space by inculcating speakers of heterogeneous language varieties into what are, at their core, White ways of speaking and seeing the word/world, that is, the norms of White, middle-class, heterosexist males. As Fairclough (1989: 7–8) argues, the job of sociolinguists should be to do more than ask, "What language varieties are stigmatized?" Rather, we should be asking, "How—in terms of the development of social relationships to power—was the existing sociolinguistic order brought into being? How is it sustained? And how might it be changed to the advantage of those who are dominated by it?"

This chapter explores the politics of language in order to call for the eradication of the ideology of *linguistic supremacy*—the unsubstantiated notion that certain linguistic norms are inherently superior to the linguistic norms of other communities, and in this case, the practice of mapping White norms onto "the language of school," "the language of economic mobility," and "the language of success." In its place, I argue for *linguistic equanimity*, which, simply put (but difficult to achieve), is the structural and social equality of languages.

In Chapter 4, "'Bring it to the cypher': Hip Hop Nation Language," I move from issues of discourse and power (though never leaving them behind) and begin to explore the anatomy of language and language use within the HHN, providing a thorough description of HHNL. My research on the language and linguistic practices of the Hip Hop Nation Speech Community examine how HHNL both builds upon and expands the Black American Oral Tradition. The chapter outlines several Hip Hop discursive practices and cultural modes of discourse—*call and response, multilayered totalizing expression, signifyin* and *bustin (bussin), tonal semantics* and *poetics, narrative sequencing* and *flow, battling* and *entering the cipher.* While some scholars (like the one mentioned at the beginning of this introduction) and educators (like those in Chapter 3) are quick to point to Hip Hop Culture's "illiteracy," Hip Hop Headz are even quicker to point to Hip Hop's ill literacy. ("Yo, that's *ill*, yo!") From the perspective of the HHN's linguistic culture, one must come prepared to speak "Advanced Street Language (the study and application of Street Communication)," which is:

> commonly referred to as "Black English," "Urban Slang," and "Ebonics," it is Hiphop's street language and linguistic codes; the verbal communication of the "streets." Advanced Street Language includes the correct pronunciation of one's national language as it pertains to life in the inner-city. Its practitioners are known as "Hiphoppas." Popularized by Rappers, Comedians, and Hiphoppas.
>
> (KRS-One, "Refinitions," www.krs-one.com)

Hip Hop artists *been* knowin that they language is "advanced." KRS is reversing "standard" notions of correctness and appropriateness, realizing that the HHN has distinct values and aesthetics that differ from the majority culture (although simultaneously and implicitly reproducing values of "correctness"). Jubwa of Soul Plantation builds on this Hip Hop-centered perspective and refers to "standard English" as *limited* and "Black Language" as *limitless*. This move takes the burden of the communicative work off of the speakers of marginalized languages and puts it squarely onto those of dominating languages. Sounding a lot like Toni Morrison, who wrote about the Black child who suffers the "cruel fallout of racism" in school because he possesses more present tenses than the school's language (see Chapter 3), Jubwa describes the language education process for Black Americans as one of learning a "limited version" of language:

> You have to teach them that in everything there's limits. You have to teach their mind limits. To grammar. To everything. Because it's structure. They want the words to come in this order. If the words don't come in this order, these people [speakers of "limited English"] that live by this language and thrive by this language, won't understand what you're talking about. So, you have to get the word order in the way *they* want it to be in cuz they're limited.
>
> (Unpublished interview with author, 2000)

Maaan, talk about flippin the term "Limited English Proficient" right on its head!
      "Standard English," in Jubwa's words, is limited by its own prescriptivism: "You're only right when you do it the way that the rules prescribe." While recognizing that BL is a rule-governed system of speech ("It's the speech pattern and stuff like that"), he states:

> But it's not defined at any state in time, and it's not in a permanent state. It's sorta like—and this is just my opinion—it seems to be limitless . . . So, I feel that there's no limit and there's no real rules of structure, because

they can be broken and changed at any time. And then a new consensus comes in, and then a *new* one will come in. And it will always change, and it will always be ever free-forming and flowing and it'll be reflected in the artform.

Chapter 4 exemplifies the power of the hiphopographic approach. There is no way to arrive at the meaning of some of these linguistic practices without direct engagement with the culture creators. One example of this is in the rich, linguistic description of *flow*. When rappers like Lil Kim say they "ridin a beat," they are talking about what is known as *flow* in HHNL. Flow can be defined generally as the temporal relationship between the beats and the rhymes. In discussing the concept of flow with rapper Raekwon, I asked him directly what he meant by flow, in order to develop an understanding from the artist's perspective. His definition provides useful insight:

> Flow is like, *how* you say it. Flow is like poetry going to the beat, but you making it connect like a bridge, you know what I mean? It's like building a bridge with your rhymes. You want to be able to let everybody know that, "Yo, I could rhyme like this, but off of this type a beat. But when it comes to another beat, I could switch it up," you know what I mean? And make it still flow, but just a different way of using it, you know what I mean?
>
> (Alim 2000, unpublished interview)

In discussing the relationship between rap and poetry, Pharoahe Monch provides additional insight with his definition:

> P: I mean, poetry is a awesome art form in itself. I dabble in it before I write some of the songs that I do. I try to be poetic with some of the songs. Hip Hop is based upon a mixture of that, but more writing musically. Points and timing, you know. So is poetry. But on a level where it's based upon the music, you have to be more rhythmatically connected with your listener and crowd, in terms of rhythm, you know. And *how* are you riding that beat. You know, you could do the same thing with poetry without any music at all, you know what I'm saying? Get a response rhythmatically. So, I'm not disrespecting that. I'm just saying, Hip Hop, it's about where you are on that fourth bar, where you are on that first bar . . . You got to have flow, and I think that's something that just comes natural.
>
> A: What exactly do you mean by that, by flow?
>
> P: I mean, how the person rides the beat, you know. Some MC's ride the beat soulfully 100 percent like Slum Village, and they're funky with it. Some MC's go against the grain of the beat, but they're so on point and you understand what they're doing, you know.
>
> (Alim 2000, unpublished interview)

One of the most remarkable aspects of Hip Hop poetics is that the artists manage to convey a message of great import to the Hip Hop community while flexin these off tha hook rhyme skillz. For instance, peep the perfectly put paragraph by my potna Saigon, who know he ain't no P.I.M.P. even though he rap about "I do got a pistol in my pocket." Here, he levies an internal critique of Hip Hop Culture (what's externally referred to as the "conscious" vs. "commercial" Hip Hop debate), all while *P'in* on those pretenders who purposely perpetrate. "Personally, I preach prophecy/ these punks puttin out poems about pimpin, pushin, and property, *pleeeaase* . . ." Then without missin a beat he changes up the *flow* real quick to match the staccato beat, "people ain't prepared to be persuaded by political paraphrases." Gettin real street widdit, Saigon boasts about his rhyming abilities by using humor to work a clever metaphor—he ain't gotta shit on other MC's, he just be P'in on 'em with his skillz!

In Chapter 5, "Spittin the Code of the Streets: The strategic construction of a street-conscious identity," we realize once again that the streetz iz a mutha. That is, the streets gave birth to, nourished, and raised Hip Hop Culture, and continue to advise it well into its adult years (the mother of creation). At the same time, like my man Kurupt say, "the streetz iz a *mutha*" . . . *shhhh, hush yo mouf*, and he stops short like Sista Sonia did on stage in the 1970s (see Chapter 6). In this chapter, I present an analysis of the conscious stylistic variation in the language of Black American Hip Hop artists. Specifically, I focus on an analysis of two artists' (Eve and Juvenile) lyrics *and* conversational speech. Recognizing the high degree of linguistic creativity and verbal virtuosity present in the HHN, this research demonstrates how Black American youth, like the Hip Hop youth in them Sunnyside streets in Chapter 3, possess extraordinary, chameleon-like linguistic capabilities. Further, this chapter focuses on Hip Hop artists' strategic construction of a street-conscious identity through language. By consciously varying their language use, these rappers are forging a linguistic-cultural connection with the streets (meaning both members of the Black Street Culture and the sets of values, morals, and cultural aesthetics that govern life in the streets—peep the Geto Boys' "G-Code," *The Foundation*).

While drawing upon variationist methodology, I explore variation in BL with the additional perspective of linguistic anthropology, which views language as social practice and as a tool for constructing one's identity. This chapter challenges sociolinguists (particularly scholars of BL) to go beyond the mere quantifying of linguistic variables and to problematize the perceived passivity of linguistic variation and change. Speaker agency, the conscious and strategic use of language, must be considered when discussing these processes. At the same time, linguistic anthropologists are urged to embrace quantitative analysis, which would add tremendously to their already rich descriptions.

Chapter 6, "'Every syllable of mine is an umbilical cord through time': Toward an analytical schema of Hip Hop poetics," takes a close look at the literary ingenuity of Hip Hop lyricists. Importantly, this chapter does not simply state that "Hip Hop is poetry," in an attempt to legitimize Hip Hop lyrical production. While many scholars emphatically claim that Hip Hop *is* poetry—and it is—Hip Hop Headz are sayin, "Don't just limit us by sayin what we do is just poetry." What Pharoahe Monche's comments earlier and other Rappers' comments reveal is that Hip Hop is similar, but different, to most poetry in that multiple layers of complexity are required in order to "get a response rhythmatically."

The chapter begins with an exploration of the relationship between the Black Arts Movement of the 1960s and 1970s and the Hip Hop Cultural Movement. I take the reader straight into a conversational cipher between Hip Hop artists and Black Arts Movement poets. We hear from baaaddDDD poets like Sista Sonia Sanchez and Brotha Amiri Baraka and dope Hip Hop artists as diverse as Chuck D, Zion I, and the self-proclaimed "baddest bitch," Trina. From there, we move into an in-depth, or deeply deep, poetic analysis of Hip Hop lyrical production. My analysis of Hip Hop poetics reveals that Hip Hop artists not only use the conventional poetic constructions (feminine rhyme, masculine rhyme, end rhyme, etc.), but they travel far beyond that, using innovative rhyming techniques such as *chain rhymes, back-to-back chain rhymes, compound Internal rhymes, primary and secondary internal rhymes*, polysyllabic rhyme strings of *octuple rhymes*, and creating a *multirhyme matrix* that is unparalleled in American poetics. There is an educational point to be made here: Rather than using Hip Hop Culture in urban classrooms only as a means to cultivate an appreciation for poets such as Chaucer and Shakespeare (those that use the so-called "white man's literacy"), or even Amiri Baraka and Sonia Sanchez, and their use of poetic devices, why not turn our attention to the study of some of contemporary Black America's most innovative and inventive poets (like Pharoahe Monch, Eve, E-40, Busta Rhymes, the Rza, Redman, Method Man, Ludacris, Talib Kweli, Mos Def, Common, Lauryn Hill, Beanie Sigel, Black Thought, Nas, Bahamadia, Raekwon, Kanye West, Jay-Z, and Scarface, to name a few off the top of the dome)? After all, it is these rhymers who are continually influencing contemporary musical and literary production around the globe, like the poetics of Japanese Hip Hop artists (Tsujimura *et al.* forthcoming), for example, or the rhymes of Hip Hop youth from China, Germany, Brazil, Tanzania, Australia, and Singapore, to name a few sites examined in recent literature on the Global Hip Hop Nation (Ibrahim *et al.* forthcoming).

In Chapter 7, "'I'm Pharoahe when I'm on stage; I'm Troy when I'm home in Queens': An interview with Pharoahe Monch," the final word is left for the Pharoahe. It is one thing to analyze an artists' lyrical production, and quite another to speak with the artist himself. I caught up with Pharoahe Monch in San Francisco's Maritime Hall after one of the livest Hip Hop tours to sweep the country in 2000, "The Spitkicker Tour," which featured artists like De La Soul, Biz Markie, Common, Talib Kweli, DJ Hi-Tek, Pharoahe Monch and others. After viewing and photographing his performance, I was invited backstage where I conducted interviews with many of the artists on the tour. I connected with

Pharoahe as we rode in the jeep to his hotel where we conducted an exclusive one-on-one interview. This interview, combined with the poetic analysis in Chapter 6, allows us to go far beyond an analysis of lyrical production alone. Not only was Pharoahe instrumental in the interpretation of his lyrical skills (we sent this manuscript back and forth several times before it actually went to print—thanks homie), but his interpretation of Hip Hop Culture contextualizes cultural production in ways that greatly enhance our understanding of this literary and linguistic phenomenon.

Enter the cipha of HHLx

Hip Hop cultural modes of discourse are at their peak in the *cipha*, the hyper-activated, communal, and competitive Hip Hop lyrical testing and stomping grounds of verbal mastery. If HHNL itself is both a communal and competitive discourse, and it is, then the cipha is the height of community and competition within the HHN. In the opening anecdote to this introduction, I likened the heated verbal exchanges between those present at Harvard's "Hiphop Community Activism and Education Roundtable" to an intellectual cipha. Conventional notions of authority, power, and the hierarchical construction of knowledge disappear in the cipha, and the flow and exchange of ideas take center stage. The cipha offers all participants a chance to sharpen their skills, while sharing ideas in the spirit of both teaching and learning—but you gotta have *heart*. Let's take our lead from Pharoahe Monch and his cohort of word warriors. Listen in as he describes the value of having a competitive community of lyricists to help sharpen his skillz:

> I'm just so inspired, you know, just watching how the people are reacting to Talib and Common and De La. And it's what's inspiring me to go back and record my new album, which is what I feel this is all about. *360 Degreez of Inspiration*. You hear my album, you're like, "Okay." Friendly competition, you know. "When I put my shit out, I'ma let the people know!" And that's healthy for Hip Hop because it keeps it elevating on a lyrical level and a music level. I mean, you got to come with some *shit* now to come better than the Common album. You got to come with some *shit* now to come better than the De La album. Talib's letting me hear his new album, I'm like, [Eyes buggin] "Yo, man!" . . . I got to go *back*! . . . It's dope. And, I mean, we did a song for Lyricist Lounge where me and Common and Black Thought were just, you know, freestyling on it, rapping, some written, some off the top. And we were just saying how—Black Thought was saying how straight up and down he picked up the Pharoahe Monch album, enjoys it, listens to it. But then he's like, "Fuck *that*!" You know?! "When my album come, I'm comin better than that!" You know what I'm saying? And I expect him to elevate. And I expect him to inspire me when he drops his shit. That's what art is about, you know.

Let's bring all of our varying methodological approaches and theoretical perspectives to the HHLx cipha. In the spirit of Pharaohe's *360 Degreez of Inspiration*, let's build a community of scholars that's real enough to offer critical advice, comments, and suggestions in a communal flow of information so that we can arrive at a more thorough description of HHNL—from the streets on up. Let's take the tools of our varying fields, as elitist and hierarchical as they may be in their current condition, and revise them. Let's bring that Hip Hop flava up into the academic study of language. Let's take, like my man JT the Bigga Figga said in the opening quotation of this introduction, straight chittlins and greens and turn them into a delicacy.

Chapter 2

Verbal *Mujahidin* in the Transglobal Hip Hop *Umma*

Islam, discursive struggle, and the weapons of mass culture

Hip Hop is a light. It's like the light of the sun which strikes the Earth and causes the Earth to rotate. Just as the sun is burning at a temperature of 14,072 degrees, it sends out light at 1,086 miles per second, striking the Earth at its very center, causing it to revolve and rotate at 1,037 miles per hour . . . The best of Hip Hop is like the sun, because it's hot. When it's a dope beat it pumps you up, it heats you up, it causes you to sweat. And when you have light giving, revolutionary, spiritual lyrics, that light travels and it strikes you in your mind, and it causes your mind to rotate like the Earth, causing you to think differently, causing you to act differently, causing you to bring down the world of white supremacy in your mind. Hip Hop is a great light, and it is also God's music today . . . Let us not forget the root of our light. When you hear the Poor Righteous Teachers, when you hear X-Clan, Public Enemy, Paris, the Defiant Giants, Brand Nubian, Kool Moe Dee; when you hear them rap of black consciousness, they rap from our father, all of our fathers, the lessons of the Honorable Elijah Muhammad. That's where we rap from.

(Defiant Giants in Spady 2004: 486)

I took my *shahada* [Muslim testimony of faith] four years ago . . . Well, I had been advised that when you do works that go out to the public—written works or spoken works—that you should bless them like that, you know [by opening with *Bismillah Al-Rahman, Al-Rahim* ["In the name of Allah, the Beneficent, the Merciful"]. It makes sense to me. The spiritual level just puts the seal on it. Like I'm making a effort to reach *Allah* ["The God" in Arabic] with this, and *Insha'Allah* ["If it be the will of God"], my efforts will be accepted.

(Mos Def in unpublished interview with the author 2001)

I just took a trip to Saudi Arabia . . . It was beautiful. Everything, the people, just you know—I've been Muslim all my life and that's like—in Islam there's something called the Five Pillars of Islam and that's one of the pillars. If you get the means to go to Saudi Arabia then you're supposed to do it because that's where everything started at. It was beautiful ya know? The people were real hospitable. It was nice.

(Freeway interviewed by Allhiphop.com 2005)

What happens when Beanie Sigel, one of the hardest Rappers in the United Streets of America, clenches his jaws and spits in that South Philly Black street speech, "I fear *nu'in* [nothing] but Allah"? What has attracted such a large number of Rappers to seek Islam as a means of establishing their faith claims? More generally, how much do we know about the relationship between "Hip Hop" and "Islam"? In what ways are the two compatible? This chapter explores aspects of the complex relationship between two entities—Hip Hop Culture and the Islamic Faith—which have both been separately constructed by dominating discourses as "threats to American civilization." To some practitioners, Hip Hop Culture represents a counterdiscourse that is not only mass-based, but also mass-mediated, circulated, and communicated to millions of youth. Like the Muslim *umma*, the Global Hip Hop Nation functions as a worldwide network of "believers" around the world who have created "nationhood" through cultural, ideological, and imaginary means. In this chapter, I view Hip Hop artists—particularly those engaged in what I have called the "transglobal Hip Hop *umma*" (Alim 2005)—as "verbal *mujahidin*," with their speech activities serving as alternative media sources narrating the beliefs and experiences of a "nation." Their very experiences, when verbalized, represent a discursive struggle against oppression. This struggle is not fought in the language of classical religious texts—it's fought in that sacred, steetified, slick-ass Black Language (BL). Here, I'm viewing BL not as a checklist of linguistic features, but as discourse itself, that is, as a potentially powerful weapon of mass culture (WMC). As Dyson (1991: 22) noted in a special issue of *Black Sacred Music: A Journal of Theomusicology*:

> The rap artist, as Cornel West has indicated, is a bridge figure, who combines the two potent traditions in black culture, preaching and music: the rapper appeals to the rhetorical practices honed in African American religious experiences and the cultural potency of black singing/ musical traditions to produce an engaging hybrid. In a sense rappers are truly urban griots dispensing social and cultural critiques, verbal shamans exorcising the demons of hiphopcrisy and a laissez faire orality that refuses to participate in the media of cultural exploration and social provocation. The culture of Hip Hop has generated a lexicon of life that expresses rap's b-boys/b-girl's Weltanschauung, a perspective that takes delight in the postmodern practice of demystifying high classical structures of language and celebrates the culturally encoded twists of phrases that communicate in their own idiom.

Initial questions and concerns

In this chapter, I am raising questions from multiple perspectives. From a historical perspective, can an exploration of the histories of Black American

Muslim Movements, and their contemporary presence in the Hip Hop Nation (HHN), move us toward a more in-depth understanding of the social, political, and cultural consciousness that is central to the philosophy of the Hip Hop Cultural Movement (see Chang 2005)? Clearly, there is more than an *aesthetic* continuity between the Black Arts Movement of the 1960s and 1970s and the Hip Hop Cultural Movement that immediately followed; there is also a profound *spiritual* continuity that contains but is not limited to Black nationalistic concerns (see Chapter 6 and Alim 2000).

Through ethnographic research, I explore issues of central concern to Religious Studies and anthropologists of religion, namely issues of *praxis* and *consciousness* in the believing subject. How has Islam served as a transformative force both in the personal lives and in the public roles of many Hip Hop artists as community-conscious agents? How has Islam helped to shape their identities and ideologies as human beings in process and practice, and their actions as socially and politically conscious Hip Hop beings involved in a movement for change in the world? Throughout this chapter, I will be highlighting the potential of Muslims in the Hip Hop Cultural Movement to create a counterhegemonic discourse that "threatens" the ruling class, and their ideas. In other words, we'll see how the Muslim verbal *jihad*, the discursive struggle against oppression, "threatens," as Chuck D and Flava Flav rapped years ago, "the powers that be."

Despite journalist Harry Allen's (1991) description of Islam as Hip Hop's "official religion," Islam's dynamic presence and central role in the HHN have been largely unexplored. I will be raising a number of issues and questions for further exploration in our on-going attempt to gain an increased understanding of the Global Hip Hop Nation and how it functions within a borderless Islamic nation. That is, Prophet Muhammad of Arabia did not speak of an "Islamic Iraq" or of a "Muslim Senegal"; he imagined a transglobal Muslim community, an *umma* where citizenship was predicated upon faith rather than contemporary nation-state distinctions, or rather, on how colonizing cartographers cut up the global landscape.

Given the fact that Islamic civilization has been "at once transnational and connective" (cooke and Lawrence 2005), how has this transnational connectivity been manifested within the Hip Hop Cultural Movement? Further, given the transglobal nature of the Hip Hop Cultural Movement (which developed at least two decades ago in the movement's early period; Spady and Eure 1991, and Mitchell 2001)—what Perkins (1996) referred to as "Youth's global village" and Osumare (2002) as the "Hip Hop Global 'Hood"—how has this cultural nation without traditional borders served the purposes of spreading Islamic knowledge, values, teachings, ideas, and ideals?

My use of "Islam" in this chapter is broadly conceived, encompassing a spectrum of ideologies and schools of thought. I will address the three most dominant forms of Islam in the HHN in the US (the Nation of Islam, the Nation of Gods and Earths, or the Five Percent Nation of Islam, and the Sunni Muslim community) paying particular attention to the Nation of Islam which has had and continues to have the most profound impact upon the HHN. While there are theological and terminological differences between these communities, all view Islam as a transformative force in the lives of its practitioners, and the data reveal similarities among the views of their adherents. These similarities are revealed through conversations with Hip Hop artists about the various creative processes involved in their craft.

Contextualizing the discussion: Controlling the discourse and flippin the script

It is useful to note that as Islam was having such a powerful effect on the HHN in the US, Islamic Studies itself was experiencing significant changes. As recent scholars have observed, "Islamic Studies—or the study of Muslim groups and their religion Islam—has been changing dramatically in the last decades. Until recently, Islamic Studies was largely the exotic focus of a relatively small group of academics who wrote books about it mainly for one another's consumption" (Ahmed and Donnan 1994). These significant changes in Islamic Studies are happening in an Islamic world that is itself experiencing dramatic changes and challenges. "The contemporary Muslim world is facing internal and external challenges. Entering the twenty first century, Muslim societies are struggling in their confrontation with enormous cultural dilemmas as they are rethinking, renegotiating and in some instances re-inventing traditional society but with unique modern tones" (Weiss 1994). The study of Hip Hop Culture In the early 1990s has given birth to several examples of what might be considered studies of Islam and popular culture, an area of Islamic Studies that has gained increasing attention in the past several years.

The first study of Hip Hop Culture to highlight the widespread practice of Islam in the HHN, its "unique modern tones," and how it has impacted the philosophy of key players within the Hip Hop Cultural Movement, was *Nation Conscious Rap: The Hip Hop Vision* (Spady and Eure 1991), which spawned the unique, French language film by Algerian filmmaker Bernard Zekri, *Rap et Islam* (1993). In preparing *Nation Conscious Rap*, the Black History Museum Committee consulted with some 57 representatives of the Hip Hop Cultural Movement— which they referred to as a "major cultural transformation of Western Civil- ization"—including Chuck D, Flavor Flav, Big Daddy Kane, Q-Tip, Sister Souljah, Poor Righteous Teachers, X-Clan, KRS-One, Sister Harmony, and many others. Conversations with artists ranged from 1 hour to 9½ hours in a single session. The results were 227 hours of taped interviews, 1,279 transcribed pages (some single-spaced), and invaluable insights into the histories and ideologies of the HHN (Spady 1994). This current research continues the work begun by the Black History Museum (Spady and Eure 1991, Spady *et al.* 1995, and Spady *et al.* 1999) and is part of a larger project that includes dozens of interviews with Muslim Hip Hop artists (see Spady *et al.* forthcoming).

A number of interesting articles on Hip Hop and Islam were published in the early 1990s. The British publication *The Face* (October 1991: 80) carried this headline on its cover page: "Louis Farrakhan and Muslim Rap." The article was written by David Toop, author of one of the pioneer books on rap music and Hip Hop culture (Toop 1984). Toop writes:

> Rakim, Lakim Shabazz, Isis, Hakeem X, Professor Griff, Brand Nubian, Poor Righteous Teachers, X-Clan, KRS-1, Afrika Bambaataa, Jungle Brothers, King Sun, Movement Ex, Big Daddy Kane, Gang Starr, 2 Black 2 Strong, The Jaz, Queen Mother Rage, Paris, Two Kings In A Cipher, Public Enemy, all of these rap artists have introduced some version of Afrocentrism, Black nationalism or Islam to Pop Culture.

Toop continues, pointing to what he saw as an Islamic shift in Black American music:

> African American singers used to dedicate their albums to God or their attorneys, now they give album sleeve credit to Minister Louis Farrakhan, the Honorable Elijah Muhammad, Malcolm X, Marcus Garvey, Clarence 13 X, Khalid Muhammad, the Five Percent Nation, The Nubian Islamic Hebrews and the Moorish Holy Temple of Science. The best popular music has always concealed a sense of mystery behind its open heart, but a growing section of rap is plunging into deep realms, that the inventors of rock n' roll could never have dreamed of.

The first Rapper Toop mentions is Rakim, one of the most influential Rappers in the history of Hip Hop. Rakim testified to the power of Islam in his life:

> I had a crazy childhood. I needed something to pick me up. I used to go to church but that was like looking up to something I couldn't see. The Nation of Islam taught me about myself, my history and everything under the Sun. I took the name Rakim Allah. Ra means Sun God. Kim [as in Kemet] was another word for Egypt, meaning "land of the burned-faced people." Once I got into Islam I had to speak on it. We reveal rather than conceal.

In a widely distributed article, Hip Hop journalist Charlie Ahearn (1991) writes plainly, "Rap's got religion and that religion is Islam." Ahearn, a Euroamerican who was vexed that "certain white teens across America seem to be craving contact with the metallic powers of Satan while their black brethren are busy digging the prophets of ancient scriptures," continued to show the influence of Islam on Hip Hop artists:

> On his track called, "The Universal Flag," King Sun flows with the funk while "elevating" on Five Percent doctrine. The video for Brand Nubian's "Wake

Up" shows lead Rapper Puba "rolling up on a cipher" before a massive posse of "gods" in front of Five Percent Headquarters—the School of Allah on 125th Street in Harlem. Another video, this time for "The Lost Tribe of Shabazz" finds Lakim Shabazz journeying to the Motherland and lip synching in front of the pyramids along the Nile.

Jeffrey Louis Decker (1993) provides useful historical background about the relationship between Hip Hop and Islam. He explains:

> In the 1970's, while the Nation of Islam reorganized after the death of Elijah Muhammad, the Hip Hop Nation was born largely through the efforts of one of rap music's pioneers, Afrika Bambaataa. Influenced partly by the release of a British feature film on the Zulu tribe of Southeastern Africa, Bambaataa summoned into existence the Zulu Nation in New York City's South Bronx in an attempt to bring about peace in a region increasingly prone to gang violence. It wasn't until 1983, when Brother D came out with "How We Gonna Make the Black Nation Rise," that an explicit nationalist message was heard in rap music. Later that same year, Tommy Boy Records released a collection of Malcolm X speeches officially endorsed by Malcolm's widow, Betty Shabazz. The Malcolm X album titled, "No Sell Out" was made relevant for a 1980's audience by Keith LeBlanc, a white drummer previously with the Sugarhill Label, who dubbed Malcolm's uncompromising voice over a hard driving beat.

Long before members of the HHN ever heard Malcolm on a beat box track, they'd heard Malcolm X, Louis Farrakhan (the former Minister of Mosque No. 7 in New York City, who was born in the Bronx long before the birth of Hip Hop in that same borough) and other Nation of Islam (NOI) members who lived in virtually every community where Hip Hop took root. In fact so popular was Hip Hop within the NOI that their newspaper, *The Final Call*, published a weekly column, "Muhammad Inside Rap."

Hip Hop music, from its inception, has been an active vehicle for social protest in the US and around the world. As Tricia Rose wrote in *Black Noise* (1994), its targets have been racism, discrimination, police brutality, miseducation, and other social ills. When Hip Hop pioneer Afrika Bambaataa launched the Muslim-influenced Zulu Nation in the US in the 1970s, and expanded the movement globally in places like France in the early 1980s (Prevos 2001, Meghelli 2004), he was networking to help spread socially and politically conscious ideas and ideals, to build a community of people who would actively resist social, political, and economic subordination. Bambaataa, inspired by Michael Craine's *Zulu*, formed the Universal Zulu Nation as a postcolonial resistance force in the streets of Black America and later the world (Toop 1984: 29). As a child, he had been influenced by the NOI and he continues to be influenced by them throughout his adulthood. As he recalled:

I first heard the Honorable Elijah Muhammad when I was real little. A lot of my family was a part of the Nation of Islam. Some uncles and aunts and cousins. I began hearing the speeches of Malcolm X and the Honorable Elijah Muhammad. I was there in 1975 when Wallace D. Muhammad took over and there was a shift in power. Mr. Muhammad [Elijah] wasn't the kind of speaker Minister Farrakhan and Malcolm were, but you heard everything that you needed to hear and he got right to the point. A lot of times now when I get lazy, like I've got to fix something in the house . . . It's not that I hear Minister Farrakhan's voice or Malcolm's voice speaking to me. I hear Elijah saying, "Brother, you better get up and do something for self." Sometimes his voice comes to me like an angel in the night . . .
(Bambaataa interview with Spady cited in Spady 2004)

This idea to have a Zulu Nation was formed early in Bambaataa's mind as a member of the Black Spades street gang, when he was also coming into contact with the teachings of the NOI and other Muslim groups. It was his interaction with the NOI, in particular, that enabled him to envision a *Universal* Zulu Nation.

The Nation of Islam has had a big impact on me and the Universal Zulu Nation for years. Starting from the time I was in the Black Spades we have always had our elder brothers who had concern for us and everybody's Mama was your Mama. We had the Nation of Islam speaking to us, the Ansaru Allah Community speaking to us . . . Having the Honorable Elijah Muhammad's teachings first made me realize that I should go and use those teachings and place it on a world basis. Take other teachings and add on to it. France was the first place we had the Universal Zulu Nation in the world besides the United States. In France, I encouraged them to write rap lyrics in their own language. That was back in the early 80s, 1982–1983. I told them to rap in your own language, speak to your own social awareness and address your own problems happening in your own country . . .

Other researchers (Nelson and Gonzales 1991, Perkins 1991, Stephens 1991) mention the impact of the NOI on the ideologies of the HHN, but few are in direct conversation with the Hip Hop artists themselves. Recent work has focused on the Five Percent Nation of Islam (Miyakawa 2005) and on the diverse spiritual sensibilities of Hip Hop Culture (Pinn 2003). Floyd-Thomas (2003) is a particularly relevant chapter that examines the co-evolution of Black American Muslim Movements and Hip Hop Culture. In this chapter, I build upon Floyd-Thomas' description of Malcolm X's "jihad of words" by going beyond lyrical production and engaging artists in ethnographic interviews in order to uncover the *jihad* of their lived experiences. Besides explaining *jihad* in greater detail and providing a reinterpretation of the Nation of Islam's teachings, I also explore the Believer's move from practical to discursive consciousness

(Giddens 1984), as well as internationalize the Muslim Hip Hop struggle by linking Black American Muslim Movements to the transglobal Hip Hop *umma*. There is a need to closely examine mass-based popular culture movements, such as the Hip Hop Cultural Movement, for their ever-present potential for disrupting the current, dominating social order, or to paraphrase Ludacris, "to disturb allayall's peace."

An uninformed viewer of mainstream media outlets may get the idea that there is nothing of significant cultural and social value in Hip Hop. However, many Hip Hop Heads' observations regarding the spiritual, socially conscious dimensions of Hip Hop Culture have been corroborated by recent work in the field, which states that "there is much of religious significance in Hip Hop Culture" (Pinn 2003: 2). It is incongruous for me to know of the many religious traditions in the Black American community and to assume that Hip Hop Culture is without spirit. Hip Hop artists, after all, represent the various religious traditions within which they were socialized (see Umum Hip Hop Trilogy: Spady and Eure 1991; Spady, Lee and Dupres 1995; Spady, Alim and Lee 1999). Given that Islam has been a normative practice in Black America for centuries since slavery, and that Black American popular culture from the Blues to Be Bop has always contained strong elements of social protest, the dynamic presence of Islam in the HHN should not come as a surprise. In fact, the lack of a Muslim presence in Hip Hop would represent an astonishing rupture from Black American popular cultural tradition.

Sista Souljah on the front lines: The discursive construction of Islam and Hip Hop Culture in the US

In a 1990 interview with Chuck D, the lead rapper of Public Enemy, a Swedish writer asked him how he felt about the fact that many White Americans feel "threatened" by his music. Chuck D didn't blame "White America" for feeling this way. As he put it, "They *should* feel threatened because they *are* threatened." As some scholars have pointed out, Hip Hop music represents a counterhegemonic discourse which comes from all up inside "the actual lived experiences in the corrugated spaces" of Black communities nationwide. Hip Hop artists *been* knowin the power of discourse; it can not only circumscribe activity, but virtually end resistive activity altogether (through what Pharoahe Monch calls "the brainwash of a people"). As the Rzarector (also known as the Wu-Tang Clan's Rza) asked the HHN, "Have you not heard that words kill as fast as bullets?" Killarmy, an affiliated group, entitled their debut album *Silent Weapons for Quiet Wars*, knowing that the war was not to be fought primarily with loud weapons of mass destruction, but with the relatively quieter, but equally insidious, weapons of mass deception. In other words, the battle for the hearts and minds of the people was to be won through the relatively quiet manipulation and control of discourse. Like other members of the Five Percent Nation of Islam, the Wu-Tang Clan sees the connection between discourse, power, and knowledge ("knowing the ledge") at least as clearly as Foucault, viewing language as a weapon of mass culture to be used in discursive combat.

One of the most effective rappers to use language as a weapon of mass culture is Sister Souljah, an important part of the Muslim-influenced rap aggregation, Public Enemy. In Decker's (1993) study of Sister Souljah and other Nation-conscious rappers (Spady and Eure 1991), he makes the following point:

> Black America, insists Sister Souljah, is in the midst of a war—and she is a revolutionary . . . The connection between her sixties-inspired political posture and the Hip Hop pseudonym, Sister Souljah, recalls the title character of Sonia Sanchez's militant play, Sister Sonji (1969) . . . In 1972, the same year that Sanchez joined the Nation of Islam, Sister Sonji was first produced on stage.

Decker perceptively sees the connection between Black Arts Movement poet-activist Sonia Sanchez and the convergence of a changing black female self in Hip Hop. How was she to know that two decades later, Sister Souljah would emerge with the transformative activism of the 1960s and the Hip Hop nation consciousness of the new millennium? Decker concludes,

> In Sister Souljah's solo rap music video, "The Final Solution: Slavery's Back in Effect," a snare drum keeps time to a military beat. Although the video is set in 1995 [the year of the Million Man March], urban America, Sister Souljah instructs the black community to "Remember the times when they bought and sold ya/ We are at war/ That's what I told ya/ Slavery's back in effect."

So influential was Sister Souljah's discursive power as a "raptivist" (rapper and activist) that her work came to the attention of those in the seats of power.

The discursive attack on the HHN came to a head in the national political arena in 1992 when then presidential candidate Bill Clinton attacked Sister Souljah. Again, her name begs the question: If you are a souljah ("soldier"), then whose army are you fighting in? Former President Clinton attacked the raptivist—who also happens to be a fiction writer, a graduate of Rutgers University, and has visited and lectured in several countries abroad, including the former Soviet Union, England, France, Portugal, Finland, Holland, and South Africa—for "racist" lyrics on her album, *360 Degrees of Power*, and comments she made in the national press. When Sister Souljah referred to a "war zone" in America, she was referring to the depressed state of many urban communities in America when, at the time, statistics reported that it was actually safer to be a *soldier* in Vietnam than to be a Black male between fourteen and twenty-four living in America. Her comments refer to what has been constructed as "Black-on-Black" crime in the US, and were posited after the Los Angeles insurrection which was set-off by the highly publicized police beating of Rodney King. In her statement to the press, Sister Souljah explained that she was responding to a journalist's question about whether or not she was surprised by the "L.A. Riots":

> "No, I was not, White people should not have been surprised either; they knew that Black people were dying everyday in the streets of Los Angeles to gang violence created by poverty and social chaos, but they did not care. If young Black men in L.A. would kill their own kind, their own Brothers and Sisters, what would make White people think they wouldn't kill them too?"
> (Gardell 1996: 299)

As a young college student and member of Public Enemy, Sister Souljah was heavily influenced by the Nation of Islam's Minister Louis Farrakhan. When she exclaims "We are at war!" the line between military and discursive action is blurred. She demonstrates her awareness of the discursive war on Black America, particularly as managed by the press, when she states: "When the white press tries to attack black leaders, we wind up loving those leaders even more" (Gardell 1996: 299). However, like many in the Black community, she is also aware that the struggle against oppression may have to come "by any means necessary," including force. The words of Minister Louis Farrakhan's "Stop the Killing" campaign were ringing loud in Sister Souljah's ears. On this tour, which also included the historic Million Man March in Washington DC in 1995, the Minister describes the media as implicated in setting up the pretext for the destruction of Black America:

> The press is part of the conspiracy to . . . paint black people as though we are all criminals, we are all animals, we are all drug-users, we are all gang-bangers, so that it justifies white police, white sheriff departments, coming into our community, treating us in any way they see fit—they got a license to kill . . . When they move on you, they've already created the climate.
> (Gardell 1996: 287)

The Minister's firm belief in this plot against Black Americans, and particularly the press's role in it, is based partly on the media's labeling of another Muslim leader, Muammar Qadhafi of Libya, as "the mad dog of the Middle East" as a pretext for military action against his nation. The Minister's critique can be extended to recent times, where we've seen military action, the deaths of thousands of human lives (soldiers, civilians, international contractors), and lengthy and resented military occupation against entire nations, as we've seen in the predominantly Muslim nation of Iraq, for example. Military occupation and war, in this case, were predicated upon the discursive construction of Saddam Hussein as being "linked with Al-Qaeda" and an "owner of weapons of mass destruction," neither of which have been proven.

Members of the HHN, particularly those involved in the S.T.O.P. Movement, a Hip Hop collective with an overt anti-war agenda led by Palestinian

DJ/producer Farid "Fredwreck" Nassar (producer and tour DJ for artists like Snoop Dogg, Nate Dogg, Xzibit, and Kurupt, among others) moved on behalf of their own political communities. In 2002, these artists produced a fierce, defiant track that interrogated President Bush and his administration's domestic and foreign policies, especially their decision to "free Iraq" by an unjust war for "oil, religion, and culture, big business dollars and family honor." They rapped about how they were "sittin back and watchin they plots and schemes" and how media reports were like the "tangled up strings to a puppet machine." In a telling line, referring to the discursive molding/morphing of Saddam Hussein into Osama bin Laden, they rap, "The media just turned Saddam into Osama/ Rock a As-Salaam Alaikum, peace be upon us!" The press, as the *New York Times* admitted two years later in a May 26, 2004 editorial, acted irresponsibly:

> We have found a number of instances of coverage that was not as rigorous as it should have been. In some cases, information that was controversial then, and seems questionable now, was insufficiently qualified or allowed to stand unchallenged. Looking back, we wish we had been more aggressive in re-examining the claims as new evidence emerged—or failed to emerge.

Hip Hop texts and the *Qur'anic* text: Structural and symbolic similarities

In response to the dominant discursive construction of Hip Hop and Islam, many Hip Hop artists have constructed Hip Hop lyrical production as a creative, artistic extension of central Islamic texts. Just as Mecca remains the metaphoric center of the global Muslim *umma*, so do the concepts of the *Qur'an* and its revelation to Prophet Muhammad remain at the core of Muslim beliefs. Diverse Muslim members of the HHN have independently observed that the very means by which the *Qur'an* was revealed to the Prophet—that is, orally and, in large part, through rhymed prose—exhibits parallels to the linguistic and literary mode of delivery found in Hip Hop lyrical production. The Black American oral tradition has rarely been interpreted in this way, yet Muslim artists have creatively conceptualized links between their mode of production and their Islamic faith. Muslim Hip Hop artists are forging new connections between Hip Hop lyrical production and the method and means by which *Allah* revealed the *Qur'an* to the Prophet. An important methodological point is that these connections unfolded during the course of ethnographic interviews about Hip Hop Culture generally, *not* Islam, underscoring the need for direct engagement with Hip Hop artists in order to uncover layers of meaning.

Engaged in a conversation about how Black youth, often as early as pre-school, are familiar with "rap language," rapper Wise Intelligent (a member of the Nation of Gods and Earths, and representing the rap group Poor Righteous Teachers) claimed:

You have to understand that the potency of the melanin in the black man makes him naturally rhythmic. So when he hears anything that has that rhythm he's going to become a part of that instantly. Anything that rhymes. Many of our ancestors were poets. Imhotep, who built the first step pyramid. The pharoah Akhenton, he was a poet. The Prophet Mohammed even wrote poetry. This is our blood.

(Spady and Eure 1991: 74)

Rapper Mos Def, who is a member of the Sunni Muslim community, discussed the reasons why he believes Hip Hop lyrics can be an effective medium in educational practice. In the midst of his animated description, he drew a bridge between Hip Hop poetics and the *Qur'anic* text as forms of poetry, each possessing a rhyme scheme and an ability to transmit "vital information" in a relatively short amount of time. His knowledge of the *Qur'an* and the Arabic language through which it was revealed were evident in his comments:

Alim: What do you feel the larger relationship between Hip Hop and education could be?

Mos Def: I mean, Hip Hop could be *phenomenal*. Hip Hop's relationship to education could be phenomenal. It could be extremely phenomenal, in the sense that Hip Hop is a medium where you can get a lot of information into a very small space. And make it hold fast to people's memory. It's just a very radical form of information transferal.

A: So, you see it as being a vehicle for transferring information?

M: Oh, hell, yeah! I mean, do you know how much information—vital information—you could get across in three minutes?! You know, and make it so that . . . I mean, the *Qur'an* is like that. The reason that people are able to be *hafiz* [one who memorizes the entire *Qur'an* through constant repetition and study] is because the entire *Qur'an* rhymes. [Mos Def begins reciting Islamic verses from the *Qur'an*] "*Bismillah Al-Rahman Al-Rahim. Al-hamdulillahi Rabb Al-Alameen.*" Like everything . . . Like, you see what I'm saying? I mean, it's any surah that I could name. "*Qul huwa Allahu ahad, Allahu samud. Lam yalid wa lam yulad wa lam yakun lahu kufwan ahad.*" It's all like that. Like, you don't even notice it. "*Idha ja'a nasru Allahi wal fath. Wa ra'aita al-nas yadkhuluna fi dini Allahi afwajan. Fa sabbih bi hamdi rabbika wa istaghfirhu innahu kana tawwab.*" Like, there's a rhyme scheme in all of it. You see what I'm saying? And it holds fast to your memory. And then you start to have a deeper relationship with it on recitation. Like, you know, you learn *Surat Al-Ikhlas*, right. You learn *Al-Fatiha*. And you learn it and you recite it. And you learn it and you recite it. Then one day you're reciting it, and you start to understand! You really have a deeper relationship with what you're reciting. "*A'udhu billahi min al-shaitan al-rajim . . .*" You be like, "Wow!" You understand what I'm saying? Hip Hop has the ability to do that—on a poetic level.

Bay Area Rapper JT the Bigga Figga also refers to the literary similarities between what young Black Americans are doing with language (what I refer to as Hip Hop Nation Language throughout this book) and the purposeful use of creative language by Allah as a pedagogical tool to reach the hearts and minds of mankind. In a discussion of the relationship between the "language of the streets" and the "language of Hip Hop," JT draws on his knowledge of the *Qur'an* and links it to his Bay Area comrade Rapper E-40's inventive and metaphorical use of language:

Alim: How does he [E-40] come up with all this different stuff, man?

JT: Just hangin out and just different people talkin. And, you know, "fo sheezy, off da heezy!" Me and you, what we doin right now, to him, it's called marinatin.

A: Yeah, I hear him say that.

J: Marinatin. We marinatin right now. We goin over . . . Like, it's almost like with *Allah* how he'll describe his prophets as moonlight. He'll describe his word that he speaks in a metaphoric phrasing. Where he'll say the clouds and when they swell up heavy and the water goes back to the earth, distilling back to the earth. The water's heavier than gravity so it distills back to the earth on dry land, producing vegetation and herbs comin up out the ground, you feel me? And results is happening, you feel me? And the Disbelievers, how they dry land and the sun's scorching it . . . [JT is paraphrasing well-known verses about *jihad* in the *Qur'an*, 25: 45–60. Verses 48–52 read:

48   *And He it is Who sends the winds as good news before His mercy; and We send down pure water from the clouds,*

49   *That we may give life thereby to a dead land, and give it for drink to cattle and many people that We have created.*

50   *And certainly We repeat this to them that they may be mindful, but most men consent to naught but denying.*

51   *And if We pleased, We could raise a warner in every town.*

52   *So obey not the disbelievers, and strive against them with a mighty striving with it.*

A footnote to verse 49 reads: "The mercy of Allah, which appears in the form of rain in physical nature, comes spiritually in the form of revelation. As the pure water from the clouds gives life to a dead land so does the pure water of revelation from Him raise the spiritually dead to life."]

A: So He's describing the Believers when things start growing, right.

J: Yeah, yeah. He describe the different conditions, you know what I'm saying? And it can be related to nature, you feel me? *Nature*. And what we see, how we conduct ourself, can be related to some aspect of nature . . . And that's kinda like what E-40 do when he take something and take a word and apply it, you feel me?

Whether engaged in conversations about young Black children's familiarity with "Rap language," or the pedagogical potential of Hip Hop music, or the inventive and innovative use of language by specific artists within the HHN, these Hip Hop artists invoke Islamic knowledge to accomplish diverse tasks. For Wise Intelligent, it makes sense that young Black children would be so attentive to "Rap language," because their ancestry, including the Prophet Muhammad (according to this strategically essentializing perspective), has always been attentive to poetry and rhyme, in particular. For Mos Def, Hip Hop's ability to function as what he calls a "radical form of information transferal" is similar to the poetic and pedagogical means by which Allah revealed the *Qur'an* to mankind through Prophet Muhammad. Finally, JT the Bigga Figga refers to Allah's use of "metaphoric phrasing" in order to clarify his description of E-40's lexical innovation and semantic expansion. Muslim Hip Hop artists' descriptions of their craft often recall the function of the *Qur'an*. In many of my interviews, I heard Islamic knowledge being invoked spontaneously in the flow of conversation (as often occurs in Muslim–Muslim conversations), pointing to the fact that members of the HHN are studying and applying Islam in their everyday lives as well as casting Hip Hop Culture and lyrical production in a uniquely Islamic light.

Verbal *mujahidin* and weapons of mass culture

In the introduction to this chapter, I wrote that I view Hip Hop artists, particularly those engaged in what I have called the "transglobal Hip Hop *umma*" (Alim 2005), as "verbal *mujahidin*," with their rhymes serving as alternative media sources narrating the beliefs and experiences of a generation of marginalized youth. Given that *jihad* is a central and fundamental concept in Islamic practice, and that Muslim Hip Hop artists are applying Islam in their everyday lives (as we read earlier), I will now provide a brief account of the concept of *jihad* in Islam in an effort to work toward a conceptualization of Muslim Hip Hop artists as verbal *mujahidin* (those who accept and undertake the struggle).

Many others have already noted that the *jihad* one hears about in many American media outlets is a grossly reductionist view of a far broader, more nuanced, multi-layered concept in Islam. As Cook (2005) explains:

Jihad is one of the most loaded and misunderstood terms in the news today. Contrary to popular understanding, the term does not mean "holy war". Nor does it simply refer to the inner spiritual strength . . . Jihad like other words taken from a religious context, has a long history, and a complex set of meanings. Conventionally it is translated as "Holy War", but this definition, associated with the medieval crusades is usually rejected by Muslims as too narrowly Christian. In Arabic, the word's literal meaning is "striving" or "exerting oneself" with the implication, on the basis of its usage in the *Qur'an*, with regard to one's religion.

Moreover, when most Americans hear the word *mujahidin*, if they are familiar with it at all, they think of such things as the formerly US-supported global network of militant Islamic freedom fighters that helped liberate Afghanistan in the decade-long struggle against the Soviet invasion (1979–1989). In a sense, those who hear "*jihad*" and jump to images of militant Islamic warriors are not wrong *per se*, but they should also be willing to contextualize these images within a broader, more widely accepted range of Muslims' interpretation of the concept (as all religions offer multiple levels of interpretation throughout varying contexts and histories). Those fighters in Afghanistan, Palestine, Iraq, and other occupied Muslim countries, are interpreting *jihad* by its secondary meaning. This meaning can be found in *Qur'anic* verses such as the following: "And fight in the way of Allah against those who fight against you but be not aggressive. Surely Allah loves not the aggressors. And kill them wherever you find them, and drive them out from where they drove you out, and persecution is worse than slaughter" (2: 190–191); and "Permission to fight is given to those on whom war is made, because they are oppressed. And surely Allah is able to assist them—Those who are driven from their homes without a just cause except that they say: Our Lord is Allah" (22: 39–40). *Jihad* here is clearly armed struggle, yet it cannot be ignored that it is one of self-defense and self-determination in the face of persecution, oppression, and occupation.

The primary meaning of jihad, sometimes referred to as the "greater *jihad*," is one that is found throughout the *Qur'an* (for example, in the verse that JT the Bigga Figga quoted above, 25: 48–52—*So obey not the disbelievers, and strive against them with a mighty striving with it.*). In this verse, according to most translations of the *Qur'an*, the sentence-final "it" refers to the Holy Book itself. A Muslim is to strive against the disbelievers with the *Qur'an*, that is, to make every effort (without compulsion) to make the Truth as revealed to the Prophet known. *Jihad's* primary meaning of "struggling" or "striving" occurs throughout the *Qur'an*, so it is not necessary to quote each verse. What *is* necessary to point out is that *jihad*, the struggle against evil, is left open to various possible levels of interpretation. After reviewing some of these interpretations, I will present the meaning of *jihad* from the widely misunderstood perspective of the Nation of Islam, the Muslim community that has most impacted the HHN.

Many Muslims rely heavily upon *Al-Hadith*, the "sayings of the Prophet," as they struggle with the controversial and hotly debated, yet undoubtedly central, concept of *jihad* (see Peters 1996 for pertinent *ahadith* and rulings from Muslim scholars and jurists). One *hadith*, in particular, has led to a widely accepted belief that *jihad* operates simultaneously on multiple levels. The Prophet is reported to have said: "He amongst you who sees something evil should change it with his hand; and if he is unable he should change it with his tongue; and if he is unable to do that he should at least hate it in his heart, and that is the weakest form of faith" (Saheeh Muslim, No. 79). Particularly relevant to our conceptualization of Hip Hop artists as "verbal *mujahidin*" is the *jihad* of the tongue, or *jihad bil lisaan*, which also includes *jihad bil qalam*, or *jihad* of the pen.

Recently, Congolese French Muslim rapper Abd Al Malik, who was a member of the New African Poets (NAP, very popular group in France in the mid-1990s), has picked up the *jihad bil lisaan* (tongue) or more appropriately, *jihad bil qalam* (pen), and published a book titled *Qu'Allah Benisse La France!* ("May Allah bless France!"). After moving through multiple Muslim communities, he writes about his understanding of *jihad* from a Sufi perspective:

> [This] conception of Islam [holds that] the most formidable struggle that one has to fight, the *jihad al-nafs*, "jihad of the soul" or the major jihad, [is] to be that carried out against one's own ego, which is the screen between the inner self and the divine: "He who knows his soul knows his Lord," says a *hadith* of the Prophet . . . I liked this idea that as opposed to pointing one's finger at someone else, it is ourselves that we ought to call into question.
>
> (Abd al Malik 2004: 148)

Just as relevant to the concept of "verbal *mujahidin*" is what some scholars describe as the dual essence of *jihad*. In this broad interpretation, *jihad bil nafs* (*jihad* of the soul) and *jihad fi sabil Allah* (*jihad* in the way of Allah) are used to refer to "internal" and "external" *jihad* respectively. That is, one must struggle against the evil within oneself to purify the soul and rid it of all evil desires in order to come closer to Allah. At the same time, since the self, or the soul, does not exist in isolation, but rather in a community of human beings, Believers are called to struggle in the way of Allah in order to improve the welfare of their immediate community, larger society, and humanity as a whole. I argue that this dual essence of *jihad* has been the fulcrum of the Nation of Islam's (NOI) teachings, and that this conceptualization of *jihad* has had a profound impact on members of the HHN.

Juan M. Floyd-Thomas (2003), in a thoroughly researched and insightful article, writes about the historical development of various modalities of Islam in Black American communities and the expression of these modalities in Hip Hop lyrical production. Although setting up Malcolm X as the initiator of a "jihad of words" that would later capture the Hip Hop imagination, it is of historical importance to note that the "jihad of words," as described by Floyd-Thomas, was an integral methodological aspect of Elijah Muhammad's pedagogy before Malcolm as well as a prime focus of the many Muslim poets (such as Sonia Sanchez, Amiri Baraka, and Marvin X) of the Black Arts Movement who influenced the streets of Black America (see Chapter 6). Further, as with many other scholars of religion, and Black American religious practice in particular, the NOI is erroneously presented as a static, non-evolving community of Believers whose teachings are out of touch with what is called "Sunni" or "orthodox" Islam. In addition, a more fluid definition of Islam is needed in order not to present an unnecessarily bifurcated view of Islamic communities *and* in order to be faithful to the lived experiences of many artists, who like many individuals, struggle, support, and move (and hardly ever linearly) through various Muslim communities.

The NOI, among the many Muslim communities in Black America, has had the most profound impact on the HHN's moral, cultural, and political consciousness (Spady and Eure 1991). Here, I am positing a new reading of the NOI—with a specific focus on the central concept of *jihad*—that aligns the NOI with the more traditional views and interpretations of the Sunni Muslim community. There is no doubt that there are differences in theology between these communities, but as we will see, it is the unity of the concept of *jihad* that drives the HHN (particularly those involved in the various modalities and expressions of Islam in Black America) to mobilize on various fronts.

In a widely overlooked, yet landmark, moment in NOI history, Minister Louis Farrakhan offered a reinterpretation of Elijah Muhammad's teachings to the community of Believers. This September 21, 1986 speech in Phoenix, Arizona, entitled "Self-Improvement: The Basis of Community Development," relies heavily on the dual essence of *jihad* in Islam and serves as the centerpiece of a life-long process in which Believers would engage in "self-examination, self-analysis, and self-correction" in order to become "morally awakened" and "spiritually resurrected." According to Minister Farrakhan, "Resurrection is that process that begins with the self-accusing spirit [*Qur'an* 75: 1–4] and does not end until we become one in perfect harmony or peace with Allah and His Creation." In this speech, the Minister stressed that "self-improvement" (what he referred to as "vertical growth") was a necessary precondition for "community development" ("horizontal growth"). In other words, how can one perform a proper and productive *jihad fi sabil Allah* if one has not first engaged in the "greater *jihad*," the *jihad* of the soul, or *jihad bil nafs* ("self-improvement")?

After discussing the importance of the soul (*al nafs*), the nature of struggle (*jihad*), and the desire for all Believers to become one with the essence of Allah, the Minister posits a reinterpretation of Elijah Muhammad's teachings regarding "the devil." This passage reveals that religious studies scholars have often neglected to examine the NOI as a community in *process*. Given that this speech was delivered two decades ago, and that misrepresentations of the NOI continue today, it is worth quoting this passage at length:

Now. This part of the lecture is really the heart of it. This is very difficult and I want you to pay attention . . . In this *Qur'an* as well as the *Bible*, Allah says, "I am going to place a ruler in the Earth." And the Angels say to Allah, "What will you place in it except that which will create mischief and cause the shedding of blood? . . . We celebrate Your Praise and extol Your Holiness." But, God says to them, "I know what you know not . . . I am going to place a ruler in the Earth and that ruler that I place in the Earth is going to create mischief and cause the shedding of blood." The Angels say, "You are Holy, why would you do a thing like this?" And God says, "I know what you know not." Listen carefully now . . . The Honorable Elijah Muhammad gave us a very clear interpretation of this *Qur'anic* passage. The interpretation dealt with a ruler who is over the nations of the Earth, who has created mischief and the shedding of blood. But God, Who knows best, said that even though a mischief-maker "has become the ruler by My permission, nevertheless, at the end of the mischiefmaking and bloodshed there is something that will wipe away the pain of his rule . . . I know what you know not." Tonight, I would like to advance another interpretation of that scripture . . . I would like to offer this interpretation to you as another way to look at scripture. Listen. "I am going to place a ruler in the Earth." Not *on* the Earth, but *in* the Earth. Where did you come from? Your flesh is from what? The vegetation of the Earth. Your bone is from what? The stone of the Earth. Your blood is from what? The water of the Earth. This lump of flesh and blood and bone has to have a ruler in it. Something that rules us; something that commands us; that dominates it. Is that right? . . . But the ruler that he puts in you has got to come through stages of development and on its way it is going to create mischief and cause the shedding of blood. I want you to follow me, because I want you to see yourself.

(Farrakhan 1986: 11–12)

The Minister then goes on to describe the devil as *not* "the White man", *not* "the Black man", *not* as "the Jew" or "the Arab" or any one people, and further, *not* anything that is external to the human being; but rather, when he states that he wants "you to see yourself," it is a message to all of humanity to observe and study what "you *become* when you abuse the God Force and use it for negative ends." The Minister makes a final point that integrates the concept of *jihad* of the soul with the reinterpretation that he has just given:

There is but one life. God gives you life. Now, how do you live it? If you live it in a negative way, under the influence of our own life force that you will not struggle to master, then you become a devil in your person. You become an opposer to the Will of God in your person. There is no devil outside of you giving you hell; it is you, the devil of yourself, raising hell with yourself and on the Earth. Does this negate what the Honorable Elijah

Muhammad taught? No! This bears witness to what he taught. The more you struggle to gain mastery over yourself, the closer you come to God. It is faith in God that stretches you towards Him. It is your faith in Him that makes you move closer to Him to connect with Him. And when you connect with Him, Heaven and Earth meet . . . You have to wrestle with the God Force in your own Self, in order to advance. If you do not wrestle and overcome it with an intelligent, enlightened, mature mind, you become a devil.

(Farrakhan 1986: 16)

In the NOI's teachings—which have greatly impacted the HHN and are more aligned with other modalities of Islam than one might think—self-improvement, the *jihad bil nafs*, is the basis for community development, *jihad fi sabil Allah*. When Muslim Hip Hop artists engage in community development, or what I have termed "nation-building practices and activities" (Alim 2005), they do so verbally, as verbal *mujahidin*, as well as physically, with the *jihad* of the hand. This raises an entirely new set of questions for further exploration, as we shall see later.

Narratives from the Nation-conscious members of the transglobal Hip Hop *umma*

Many of the artists involved in the global manifestations of the Hip Hop Cultural Movement—in places such as France, Brazil, Japan, Italy, South Africa, Cuba, and Palestine—resist the multifarious forms of oppression in global societies. Exploring what he refers to as the "transglobal Islamic underground," and writing in particular about England's Fun-Da-Mental and France's IAM, Ted Swedenburg states:

In both countries Muslims are attempting to construct cultural, social and political spaces for themselves as ethnic groups (of sorts), and are massively involved in anti-racist mobilizations against white supremacy. Hip-hop activism has been an important arena for anti-Islamophobic mobilization for both French and British Muslims.

(Swedenburg 2002: 16)

Many Hip Hop artists in the US, as we heard from pioneer Afrika Bambaataa, became acquainted with the NOI as a direct result of the Nation's work in Black communities. Once introduced to Islam through the Nation, many artists speak of reclaiming their Black identity and of regaining a "knowledge of self" that was stripped from their ancestors by European slavemasters. Once that identity is reclaimed, an ideology of nation-consciousness and nation-building shapes the actions of those involved in the HHCM. They can no longer see themselves as merely "artists," but as active laborers in the rebuilding of their Nation. How do the members of the HHCM become acquainted with Islam? What is that process like? What do they see as their role within the HHCM? What are their stories?

Flava Flav, a member of Public Enemy (perhaps the best-known NOI Hip Hop group), explains his involvement while attending the Nation's annual Saviors' Day event in Chicago:

> Let me tell you something man, I used to be in the Nation at one time, which I'm still a Muslim, you know what I'm sayin'. You know, which nothing will ever change. Which we're all Muslim by nature. But I used to also be in the Nation when I was in my younger days. I used to be in high school, I used to go to school with my *Muhammad Speaks* newspaper, my suit on, my bow tie, fresh cut, nice shoes, you know what I'm sayin', and those white teachers, man they couldn't stand me, because they knew that I was making progress. And they knew that I was a person that was going to lead other black people into a better way of life. This is back in the day when the Honorable Elijah Muhammad was still living. And after he died then the Minister was Farrakhan, he took over, so that was years ago.
>
> (Spady and Eure 1991: 311–312)

Flav's rhyme partner and Public Enemy frontman, Chuck D, describes the group's shift from giving live Hip Hop performances to contributing in a more practical way to nation-building:

> So this year I've dedicated my time to speaking not only at colleges, but in high schools, prisons, juvenile detention centers, corners, where I'm out trying to get brothers to put those 40 (oz.) bottles down. I work with the Nation of Islam in places around the world, especially in the United States, and I'm trying to get down to the nitty gritty . . . I'm trying to make the words count as much as possible. I think that's the responsibility of being an adult, not just in being a role model, but in being an adult . . . I try to set a precedent, and try to do some of the things I talk about, or try to get involved as much as I can. Try to clear up what I'm talking about and what should be done in our communities and neighborhoods. I think people say, "if he does it, I can do it too." I think that is how our communities and neighborhoods get built.
>
> (Spady and Eure 1991: 364)

The next generation of Hip Hoppers grew up listening to Rappers like Public Enemy and Ice Cube, and many of them became acquainted with Islam through their lyrics. In addition, many Hip Hop artists have direct contact with the NOI, and their narratives of spiritual transformation and moral responsibility are riveting. DJ Hi-Tek, hailing from Cincinnati, and one-half of Reflection Eternal with his Muslim rhyme partner Talib Kweli, takes the mic and describes how he became a "next generation soldier":

Hi-Tek: I went to the Mosque, you know what I'm saying? I wanted to be a Muslim.

Alim: This is in the Natti?

H: No doubt. Yeah, yeah. I was a Muslim, you know what I mean?

A: Where did you go?

H: I went to Mosque No. 5 at Avondale, at the firehouse, you know what I'm saying? That was real. That's really what got me to being the next generation soldier, you know what I'm saying? You know . . .

A: What was it about the No. 5 Mosque and the Nation that attracted you in the first place?

H: I think I was just introduced by somebody that I knew. Yeah, that's how it works.

A: You were invited, right.

H: Yeah, I was invited. And I was already into it, you know. Farrakhan and Malcolm X, you know, that's what I was into. And that's really what kept me focused, man. Knowing the realities of who I am as a Black youth, you know what I mean?

A: How did that impact your everydayness? How did the teachings impact you or guide you?

H: Basically, man, it's the Devil and God. Good and Evil. Good come from God and Evil come from the Devil. You gotta choose, man. It ain't really no in between. It's a in between, but it's like, if you live in between for too long, you gon fall victim to one of them, you know what I'm saying? I ain't saying I'm all good or I'm all bad. I'm still going through it. I'm only twenty-four. It just kinda taught me what's *right*, you know. And I choose, you know, if it was my last choice, I would choose right, you know what I'm saying? Not to say that I'm doing all right, you know what I'm saying, but I know what's right and what's wrong, man. And I know what I'm worth on this planet, you know what I'm saying? I was told a long time ago, you know what I'm saying?

A: If you had to take away maybe one or two of the most important points of Minister Farrakhan, what would they be for you?

H: At the time when I got into Farrakhan it was around the time when a lot of my peoples was dying and getting shot. You know, dying from crack, you know what I'm saying? He was just saying, "Stop killing ourselves! Stop killing," you know what I'm saying? [Minister Farrakhan launched a nationwide "Stop the Killing" tour in 1993–94.] And "Uplift the young Black youth." And that's what I was into. I kinda seen it. When I was young, everybody used to say I was a old man. I just kinda seen it like, "Yo . . ." You know, I wasn't no preacher, but I was living it, too. It was like, it was real, man, you know what I mean? Still, it ain't over yet, you know what I'm saying? It's still out here . . .

A: What are some of the stuff that you see that's still the same, and what would you like to see different?

H: Man, just the depression of my people, man, you know especially being from Cincinatti. I feel a lot of depression when I go back home . . . [Muslim rapper Common enters the backstage area and begins playing a mellow tune on the piano.] . . . A lot of people just talk a lot of depression talk, you know what I'm saying? I just want my people to see what they can do, you know what I'm saying? . . . That's my job, man. I wasn't given this position for no reason. So, I'ma take advantage of it, man.

A: You see a responsibility, don't you?

H: Yeah, no doubt, you know what I'm saying? I was blessed to make good music that people like that stands out, so I'ma take advantage of that. If I don't, God might punish me if I don't. So, you know, All Praises and Thanks to the Most High All the Time, man.

A: That's right

H: That's what got me here, man.

(Unpublished interview, Alim 2000)

There are many "next generation soldiers" with stories to tell, including Philadelphia's Ced Synatra who became involved with Mosque No. 12 in Philadelphia and Soldierz At War who are members of Mosque No. 2 in Chicago. Both groups heavily supported the NOI's efforts at the Million Family March on October 16, 2000.

   Another next generation soldier, who attended the March suited up as a member of the NOI, is the Bay Area's JT the Bigga Figga. While conducting a hiphopography of the Bay Area, we interviewed JT on six separate occasions resulting in over ten hours of audio and videotape. Like many who come to the Nation, JT tells of being caught up "livin that life" and then making the transformation into a righteous way of living. His transformation, once again, is not only manifested through moral change, but also through an ideology of nation-consciousness and an active involvement in the nation-building process. Before discussing when, where, why, and how he entered the Nation, JT first describes the scene at the Rapper's Summit, which was held at the National House of Minister Farrakhan on April 3, 1997 in an effort to quell the violence after the premature deaths of Tupac Shakur and Biggie Smalls. We join the conversation backstage in San Francisco's Maritime Hall:

Alim: Now what was he [Minister Farrakhan] saying? What did he start out with?

JT: I mean, he started out opening up the introduction, "In the Name of Allah, the Beneficent, the Merciful," you know what I'm saying? All prophets of God came from Him. In Allah name, first and foremost. Then he wanted to greet all the brothers and thank them for coming out, you know what I'm saying? And heeding the call. And, you know, he was talking about how powerful the brothers are, and he asked everybody to introduce themselves . . .

A: Okay, and everybody went around?

J: And everybody introduced themselves. Went around the table. I mean, it was about [counting to himself] one, two, three, four—five—table like sections, you know what I'm saying? And I was actually blessed . . . If you have a table, you know how the table's a rectangle, right? He was sitting at the head of the table and he had Russell Simmons sitting to his right. Barry Henkerson. The editor of *Vibe* magazine, a Black Man . . .

A: Keith Clinkscales?

J: Keith Clinkscales, he was sitting there. Then you had Kam. You had Shorty from the Lynch Mob. Then you had Snoop. You had Kurupt. Then you had Nate Dogg. And then it went around. Then you had the Goodie Mob coming up on the left side. Then you had Bone Thugs N Harmony. Not all of them, Bizzy Bone. You had Chuck D. You had Doug E Fresh. And then you had Captain Charles—either Captain or Lieutenant— Brother Charles Muhammad from Mosque No. 7. He was sitting there because he has a radio show on Hot 97 or one of them big stations out there on the East Coast. And then you had Minister Tony Muhammad from the West Coast Regional Headquarters. And then you had Brother Kwame Ture, formerly known as Stokely Carmichael, sitting right next to the Honorable Minister Louis Farrakhan. And then you had your *big brotha* . . .

A: [Laughter]

J: Brother Joseph Muhammad, JT the Bigga Figga! Sitting right there!

A: That's crazy, man.

J: You know, and it was a blessing. It was something unexpected. I just got a call two days before saying *be* . . .

A: And you went.

J: And I went, because I'm a member of the Nation of Islam. You know, so I'm a member.

A: How long have you been a member?

J: I been a member since January 4th, 1995.

A: What made you become a member?

J: What made me become a member of the Nation of Islam? Following and reading the *Final Call* newspaper, number one. The *Final Call* newspaper is a paper that the Brothers from the Nation of Islam, the FOI, go out to the communities and deliver the paper. And the Brothers was delivering the paper in my community, where I was involved in crime and, you know, a lot of evil things, basically. In San Francisco, the Fillmore District. And, you know, being out there livin that life, it really wasn't what I was looking for, you know what I'm saying? It really wasn't . . . Well, actually, it *was* what I was *lookin* for, let me change this . . . It was what I was looking for, but it was the wrong path. I was on the wrong path. And the *Final Call* newspaper was like a light in the community for brothers like us who were getting the paper. Buying it for a dollar from the brothers, supporting them, who just was out there doing what we was doing. And now they coming back as a savior, you know what I'm saying? They coming back to do a *work*. Sacrificing. You could see the work, you know what I'm saying? So, that inspired me to know, "Man, you was just stealing cars with me! Now you come selling a paper to me," you feel me? And they're like, "Brother, you know, I'm changing my life."

A: You knew *something* happened.

J: It *had* to be something, and I wanted to get it. I wanted to see what that was about. What caused that, you know what I'm saying? "I want to learn about what you learning that helped you get like this. Because I'm not strong enough to do that right now. I gotta sell you rocks, I gotta steal these cars," you know what I'm saying? So, getting them papers, that was the first thing. Then one day, Allah (God) just must have guided me to the Mosque. Because one of my potnas was like, "Man, I'ma go see what these Mooozlims talkin about."

A: [Laughter]

J: You feel me?! Because they was right on our turf, you feel me? Brother Christopher Muhammad in San Francisco, Mosque No. 26. You know, it was at the Community Center. This is like '92, you know what I'm saying? So, '91, that whole year I'm buying the papers. And '92, right after the riots had happened [the LA riots], I go into a Mosque meeting and he was talking about the whole thing about the riots and how the FBI and the government allowed it to happen to paint a picture of the Black Man, you know what I'm saying? So, all of that is going on, you know what I'm saying? I'm going through that. I'm hearing these new teachings about God and Allah and Muslims and, you know, we from the East and we not really from America, and we got stole and brought over here. Now, I knew we were slaves that came from Africa, but I didn't know the process, you know what I'm saying, or how that happened. But what I do know is that something wasn't right. And then here go a man name Minister Farrakhan that's teaching and sending Ministers of the Nation of Islam . . . He's a Representative of the Honorable Elijah Muhammad before him, you know. So, by him being the Representative of the Honorable Elijah Muhammad, and continuing the work of raising up the people, he missioned by God, you know what I'm saying?

(Unpublished interview, Alim 2000)

JT's initial involvement with the NOI leads him to reconsider his real purpose in life. Later in the same conversation, he states:

Eventually, I see myself being a Minister in the Nation of Islam in helping Minister Farrakhan take this message throughout the country, taking it throughout the world, you know. Being the first major rap artist to be a Minister, you know what I'm saying, for Minister Farrakhan. And to really do it, though, you know what I'm saying? And to inspire more people to come closer to the Nation of Islam. And one thing that he's teaching us is that even if you a Christian, if you white, if you Black, it don't even matter. It's about the human family coming together and getting the truth of these spiritual keys that Allah blessed the Honorable Elijah Muhammad with and now the Honorable Elijah Muhammad blessed him with it. And now he's carrying it on, you feel me, continuing the work. And I want to participate in that.

(Unpublished interview, Alim 2000)

Five months later in the same year, we resume the conversation on the corner of 3rd Street and Revere in the Bay View / Hunter's Point district. Now we're driving in JT's mobb (vehicle). We join the narrative and witness JT's evolving ideology and his evolving view of his role within the HHN. Like DJ Hi-Tek and Public Enemy before him, JT learns to view his position within the HHCM as one of increased responsibility and duty to himself, his people, and Allah:

Alim: You were saying that, you know, you feel that you were put in a certain position . . .

JT: Oh, yeah, I really was just talking about how, you know, how my whole life in terms of the life of crime and, you know, like every other young brother out there trying to do it your own way first and going through all the trials and tribulations. But I never would've thought I would've been in no position where I'm probably the number one artist . . . Maybe not because I rap the best, but just because of how I conduct myself, you know. I'm not just a regular rap artist. I got something positive to say, you feel me? The hardcore brothas respect me. A lot of people respect me for my business ethic, how I conduct myself in the business. I put it out there real heavy about being independent. All these different principles in the way that I conduct myself I'm learning at the Mosque, though. So, maybe how I was naturally really got brought up out of me *fully* by coming to the Mosque. Islam bring that up out of you, whatever's in you. So, over time I start seeing that, you know, Allah put me in this unique position to address the parents, to address the children. The parents is at me about doing these songs . . .

A: Yeah, you were saying the parents were coming . . . What kinds of things are they saying to you, man?

J: Well I had a talk with a Sister yesterday and she was saying how her son, he's rapping now. He's nine years old and he wants to be a *rapper* so bad. She's like, "My son just talk about you all day. JT! JT! JT! I seen

JT, mama. It was me and my friend, I seen JT!" And he's rapping but he's cussin, though. He's just cussin through the whole song, you know. And he's hiding his raps from his mother. She said she found them, and they was just full of cuss words, "Muthafucka, bitch, I'ma shoot you, kill you, ho . . ."

A: Dag!

J: All these different things because they think that that's how it's supposed to go. But they only mocking what they hearing being said on tapes, anyway . . .

A: At nine years old . . . He only nine years old.

J: Exactly. So, I look at it that I'm not supposed to be in this rap game like everybody else, just trying to please myself. I'm thinking about the impact it's having on my community, the impact it's having on the Nation, the impact that it just has on me, you know. I really started realizing it when I first started coming to the Mosque in '02. Now, it's 2000 and it's like now I can see it even more clearer that I got a bigger work to do through this music. And Minister Farrakhan confirmed it even more, too, when we was at his home on April 3rd, 1997—about who the rappers are, you know . . .

A: Do you remember what he said, exactly?

J: He said the rappers are the leaders, you know what I'm saying? He said we're like the "Pied Pipers." He didn't want to use that word, but the people respond to our tune. They listening to what we saying. White boys trying to imitate us, you feel me? They parents is mad at them! But they don't care; they want to be like us, you feel me? So, he was really just letting us know that we're put in this position for God's purpose, though, you know what I'm saying?

A: And he said, as far as the kids go, that the rappers . . .

J: The rappers are the number one teachers. The rappers have more influence over the people, really, than the teachers, preachers, politicians, the presidents, the mayors . . . He said with the exception of himself [laughing]. He made that real clear!

A: [Laughter] We all know that!

J: Yeah, he made that part real clear. So, it's really like, you know, to realize that maybe I was born to do *this*, you know. And how people always keep coming up to me—people that's like on the serious tip— like, "Man, you the one, I'm tellin you!" Sometime I look, "Oh, this guy, he just trying to make me feel good." But maybe they saying something that I might not really fully see. Because I could sit here and talk to you and tell you what I think I'm seeing, but to really know that in your heart mean you gon *act* on it now, even in a bigger way, you feel me? And have faith in yourself and in the God who brought you into existence to know that, "I'm behind you. Do the inspiring thing." Like what Minister [Christopher Muhammad] was saying how Minister Farrakhan act on inspiration, you feel me? I feel that sometime in the music I be inspired to try to do positive things. I see these visions of how I'ma help my people some kinda way. I don't know it all the way, but I know that dudes out here risking they life over a thousand dollars. Maaan, I could show all these dudes how to make a thousand dollars. I could show people how to make a hundred thousand dollars, you feel me? I don't want nothing for it. It's just that our people is caught up in selling dope, want to just get high everyday, want to just chase women everyday, you feel me? The different things that give us pleasure. The lowest things that's giving us pleasure—we at the bottom of the scale now. The real pleasure, the number one pleasure come from pleasing Allah, or God as you know him, you know what I'm saying? But we all caught up in going the other way. So, you know, now that my album is out, I tried to design my album according to . . . I kinda tried to design it as best I could to whereas Minister Farrakhan would be happy how I put it together.

(Unpublished interview, Alim 2000)

These brief but remarkable examples of nation-consciousness offer a range of sites for us to explore a fundamental question: How do the Muslim members of the HHCM make the move from practical to discursive consciousness? In other words, how do these agents go from, as some heads would say, "*talkin* about it, to *bein* about it"? What is it that makes Public Enemy's Chuck D "try to *do* some of the things that he *talks* about"? (Spady and Eure 1991: 191). When San Francisco's JT the Bigga Figga states, "Because I could sit here and *talk* to you and tell you what I think I'm seeing, but to really know that in your heart mean you gon *act* on it now, even in a bigger way, you feel me?", what is mediating the move to an active, discursive nation-consciousness? Clearly, from these narratives, these moves are predicated upon faith. JT continues: "And have faith in yourself and in the God who brought you into existence to know that, 'I'm behind you. Do the inspiring thing.'"

As verbal *mujahidin*, artists also engage in *jihad* of the hand and fight in the way of Allah (*jihad fi sabil Allah*) to help improve their local communities. My research reveals that not only are these artists studying Islam (as demonstrated by their ability to quote and vividly describe *Qur'anic* passages) and applying it to their everyday lives, but they are also operationalizing Islam, that is, acting upon what they have learned in order to help build a nation. Mos Def does not only rap about issues like consciousness and justice, he lives them. His Islamic consciousness moved him and partner Talib Kweli to rescue Nkiru Bookstore, a Black-owned bookstore in his home community of Brooklyn, from shutting down. It guided him to actively participate in the creation of a Hip Hop album (*Hip Hop for Respect*) dedicated to obtaining justice for police brutality victims and the immoral murder of Amadou Diallo, a Muslim immigrant from Guinea who was murdered by the NYPD in 1999. Mos paraphrased the *Qur'an* and expressed his faith in Allah at a public rally against the acquittal of the officers who fired 41 shots at the brother: "To people who seek justice, to the Amadou Diallo family, and to everyone who speaks against oppression, I say, FEAR NOT, Allah is the best of judges."

Similarly, Public Enemy front man, Chuck D's Islamic consciousness moved him from giving live performances in concert halls to giving talks about nation-building in the streets, prisons, and schools of Black communities. It is what moved him to become perhaps the best-known advocate for "cutting out the middle man" in the Hip Hop record industry by circumventing major record labels and distributors and building independent labels and engaging in e-commerce. JT the Bigga Figga not only realized that he "had a bigger work to do through this music," but he has also helped to revitalize his local communities of Fillmore and Bay's View / Hunter's Point through speaking engagements and providing business classes to youth. He not only actively supported and attended the Million Man March and Million Family March, and the many NOI-sponsored Hip Hop Summits since 1997, but also assembled a group of young Blacks, Latinos, and Pacific Islanders into a national cooperative business venture named Black Wall Street (in commemoration of the Tulsa Police Department's bombing of Oklahoma's Black Wall Street in 1921), thereby providing networking opportunities and economic growth to those traditionally excluded from such enterprises. JT's *jihad fi sabil Allah* is a prime example of how artists have become more than verbal *mujahidin* (fighting with their lyrics, speaking engagements, interviews, and other opportunities to dialogue). Although talk is itself a form of social action, Muslim Hip Hop artists are not only "speaking out against evil," but are actively engaged in "community development" in a direct effort to "stop that evil with their hands" (recall the Prophet Muhammad's *hadith* about *jihad* mentioned earlier).

I am currently conducting research to uncover more of these Islamic nation-building activities within the HHN. More attention needs to be directed at uncovering the role of Muslim female artists who are covering in the name of Allah. What do we know about Philadelphia rapper Eve's struggle and search for inner peace in a male-dominated recording industry? As she reminds us, "Heaven Only Knows." But we can start by engaging Eve, and other Muslim female artists, in familial conversation. Eve, who opened up the liner notes on her album *Eve of Destruction* with "All Praise Is Due To Allah," speaks on her relationship with Islam: "It's not strong like it should be. I'm striving. When I get to the point where I'm stable I definitely want to cover and go to the *masjid*. But now it's hard. It is really hard. But it definitely has a grip on me. I pray to Allah every night, every morning, all during the day, know what I'm saying? If it wasn't for Him I wouldn't be blessed" (unpublished interview with Spady, Alim 2000). What do we know about NYC's Egyptian female Rapper Mutamassik (meaning "tenacious" in Arabic)? What are her personal struggles, and how has she contributed to nation-building activities through and beyond her music (see Swedenburg 2001)?

Internationalizing the struggle: From Palestine to Paterson

What is the relationship between Black American Muslim Movements in the HHCM and the global Islamic World? Did Philly rapper Freeway (quoted in the opening of this chapter) meet any Muslim rappers when he took his trip to the Holy Land? What kinds of nation-building activities are occurring when Wu-Tang Clan's Rza visits with his Muslim brethren in Egypt, or when The Sunz of Man meet up with IAM in France? What happens when Palestinian rhymer and graffiti artist Masari writes a graff on the San Francisco city walls reading "Liberate Palestine" then spits these lines on the concrete streets of the US to note that "back in Ramallah, my brothers are straight strugglin":

> Those gone souls are in my soul
> So now my mission's to be plottin
> Let the evil rot in . . .
> And our people live forever, cuz souls are not to be forgotten.

Hip Hop's back-and-forth motion from the US to Palestine has moved one filmmaker to produce "Slingshot Hip Hop: The Palestinian Lyrical Front," a documentary that explores the daily lives of Palestinian rappers living in Gaza, the West Bank, and inside Israel. When a crew of American Hip Hoppers, including Sake 1 of Local 1200 and Samantha of Freedom Fighter Records, went to Palestine to get a first-hand view of the Palestinian–Israeli conflict, did they run into Palestinian rappers Zilzal (Arabic for "earthquake") and No Fear (displaying an AfroAmericanized fashion sense and throwin up hand signals to *rep they block*)? (Davey D, "Hip Hoppers Return from Palestine" December 5, 2002). Did they hear the Dearborn Michigan's Palestinian-American rapper Iron Sheik's chorus playin in the streets of Gaza:

> They exiled us and stole our homes
> Now all we have are old keys and new poems.

How is it that B-Dub and Ragtop, two Palestinian brothers growing up in East Tennessee, became involved with Hip Hop music, formed a crew called The Phillistines, and produced an album, *Self Defined*, all while they performed at benefit concerts from Guatemala to Jersey? What are we to make of the many sons and daughters of Palestinian immigrants to the US, like Masari and S.T.O.P. Movement founder Farid "Fredwreck" Nassar, who have been hiphopitized by this Black American cultural movement? Recognizing Hip Hop as a "weapon of mass culture" in the face of a sorely imbalanced military struggle, Palestinian rapper Tamer puts it succinctly: "Music can be a good weapon" (El-Sabawi 2005). Palestinian rappers are highly politicized and often view their involvement with Hip Hop Culture as one way to represent their struggle on an international level, serving as a site for what Osumare (2001) refers to as "connective marginalities". Maged's new offering, "My Struggle," represents a recent success story as the video is currently being played on heavy rotation on an international satellite station, Melody Hits, with Hip Hop Heads all over the world hearing him shout, "We in the struggle!"

Will academic centers like Duke University's Center for the Study of Muslim Networks or the American University in Cairo's American Studies Center begin examining the role that Hip Hop has played in networking Muslims around the globe from South Asia to South Philly, from South Africa to South Carolina, and from Shobra to Shaolin? Researchers are needed to study the trilingual verbal *jihad* (Arabic, Hebrew, and English) of Rappers in Palestine as they rail against what they perceive to be the tyranny of the Israeli state, to explore the struggles of Muslim rappers in Algeria as they wage war on what they believe are corrupt regimes (Rappers with Black American-inspired names like Ole Dirty Shame, MC Ghosto and Killa Dox), and to examine how Muslim artists in South Africa are critiquing what they perceive as the hypocrisy of their nation's "new democracy."

The *jihad* continues . . .

Through this work, I have sought to explore the influence and impact of both Islam and Hip Hop Culture on American society and the world, separately, together, and on each other. This work also expands and updates the already existing literature on Black American Islamic history, Black American popular culture, and Hip Hop Cultural Studies. Importantly, this project also addresses larger questions about the relationship between spirituality and popular culture, particularly the growing area of Islam and popular culture. Through the extensive use of primary sources, namely ethnographic interviews of members of the HHN found in the collective work of the Black History Museum Committee in Philadelphia (including my own work), it is my hope that I have contributed to research in Discourse Studies, Cultural Studies, Religious Studies, and Black Popular Culture Studies, particularly Hip Hop Cultural Studies and Black American Islamic history, and the newly formed Hip Hop Linguistics (HHLx).

This chapter has shown that Hip Hop artists from Palestine to Paterson, New Jersey, are creating, as Iron Sheik says above, "new poems" for a new day. As verbal *mujahidin* engaged in the "transglobal Hip Hop *umma*," their speech activities function as "weapons of mass culture" that narrate the marginalized experiences of a "nation." Their experiences, when verbalized, represent a discursive struggle against oppression and Hip Hop's engagement in a battle over the manipulation and control of discourse. Throughout the chapter, I have highlighted the potential of Muslims in the HHCM to create counterhegemonic discourses that threaten to overturn existing power relations. Hip Hop Culture, as evidence of Black American youth's agency, provides global youth culture with incredible resistive potential in what has become an uncertain and unsettling geopolitical landscape.

In this chapter, I have attempted to uncover the *jihad* of Hip Hop artists' lived experiences. By raising many questions about the nature of *jihad* as manifested in Hip Hop, I have also explored the Believer's move from practical to discursive consciousness. As verbal *mujahidin*, artists also engage in *jihad* of the hand and fight in the way of Allah (*jihad fi sabil Allah*) to help improve their local communities through nation-building practices and activities. Not only are these artists studying Islam (as demonstrated throughout the chapter) and applying it to their everyday lives, but they are also operationalizing Islam through both verbal and nonverbal means. Like JT the Bigga Figga said above, Muslim and Muslim-inspired Hip Hop artists feel they "got a bigger work to do through this music."

Chapter 3

"Talkin Black in this White Man's World"

Linguistic supremacy, linguistic equanimity, and the politics of language

> I mean, I think the thing that teachers work with, or *combat* the most at Haven High, is definitely like issues with standard English versus vernacular English.
>
> (Teacher at Haven High in Sunnyside, USA (2003))

Studies of intercultural discourse and communication, or intergroup communication, often examine communicative misunderstandings or conflicts that occur when speakers of different language backgrounds come into contact. These misunderstandings usually occur not because the languages have different syntactic structures, but because they have different rules of language use. For example, in the US, misunderstandings or conflicts may not occur between a native Arabic speaker learning English and a native speaker of English simply because Arabic does not use the copula (*is* or *are*) in sentences like "She excellent" for "She is excellent" (Bahloul 1993). However, misunderstandings or conflicts may occur between the same two speakers as a result of fundamental differences in their native speech communities' rules of language use regarding social distance, formality, and age, among other variables (Hussein 1995). Intergroup conflict can occur between speakers of the same language group (but perhaps different ethnicity, gender, social class, religious affiliation, regional background or other grouping) when speaker intent (illocutionary force) is misinterpreted by the hearer.

This chapter explores the politics of language, and Black Language in White public space in particular, in order to call for the eradication of the ideology of *linguistic supremacy*. In its place, I argue for *linguistic equanimity*—the structural and social equality of languages. Any study of Black–White intercultural communication must take into account the persistent racial tensions that exist between these communities in the US. Wolfram's (1974) paper on the controversial nature of Black–White speech relations begins with an observation that Black–White speech differences are "still interpreted by some" through the White ideological lens of Black inferiority. This is a point that has been understated in the literature and is now beginning to be newly interrogated by studies of "whiteness" (to be discussed shortly). Further, to my knowledge, no study of Black–White intercultural communication directly examines the multiple reasons—historic and contemporary—for interracial tensions between the two groups in a given community. The next section provides the community context as a necessary precondition for examining Black Language in White public space. It is within this context that the following sections are to be interpreted.

The gentrification of speech and speakers

The data presented in this chapter stem from a multi-year ethnographic study of Sunnyside, a diverse, working-class suburb of about 20,000, which has experienced a dramatic increase in ethnic diversity and economic development within the last decade. The community was once a thriving Black community that led the nation in Black consciousness and nationalism, establishing the nation's only independent Black preschool through college educational system in the 1960s and 1970s. Since the government's forced closure of the city's only high school in the 1970s, the Black community has experienced an increasing sense of displacement in what was once known as "a Black city," as the Latino population rises and Whites begin to move in slowly. For two decades, the community did not have a high school and Black students experienced a 65 percent drop-out rate in the schools of the neighboring suburbs, all of which were predominantly White and upper-middle-class. The gentrification of the community by White real estate developers is directly linked to educational concerns, since the city's new 28-acre, high-end shopping plaza (and several expensive hotels) stands on the grounds of the former high school. (Similar situations are occurring nationwide from Oaktown to Chi-town to H-town.)

While it is not possible to do justice to the community context in this chapter (see Alim 2004a for an in-depth account), it is helpful to present the perspectives of the current generation of Black youth juxtaposed with a perspective from the previous generation. The previous generation, after experiencing the rise and fall of Black nationhood, illegal real estate practices, land annexation, lack of job opportunities and a serious crack epidemic—all of which were debilitating—saw the interest shown by White developers as perhaps one of the only ways to save the city from a withering tax base. Below, we present two generations' views of this recent gentrification:

Male: C'mon, cele*BRATE*!
Female: Yeah, we gon celebrate this day!
Reporter: What are you celebrating?
F: We are celebrating the demolition of Raven High School.
M: We're celebrating hope for the city! That's right, a *major* milestone.

Bilal: This is the, the, the white part of Sunnyside now . . .
Researcher: Yeah, so what *is* all of this?
Yesmina: The *white* part!
B: This *bullshit* right here!
R: Is this Sunnyside?
B: Hell naw! This is, this is corporate America takin over . . .

It's the beginning of our economic independence, which we hope. That's what it seems like, a great opportunity for us.

F: Right. Right on!

[Clapping and cheering]

(50-year-old Black couple in Sunnyside, 1996)

Aqiyla: Yeah . . .

B: This is the sunnyside of Sunny-side . . .

Amira: This whole area, right here, where all this new, all these new buildings are, this useta be Raven High School . . .

(17-year-old Black youths in Sunnyside, 2002)

While one generation celebrates the demolition of the old, dilapidated structure of the city's only high school, another is lamenting the displacement of Black people from a city that no longer *has* a public high school. As the city continues to raise revenue through the continued development, rent control legislation is being overturned and more and more Blacks are being forced out of the area (the community is now less than 20 percent Black in 2006, and needless to say, the economic independence of Black people in Sunnyside has not been attained). Tensions between Blacks and Whites, and other ethnic groups, continue to rise in this small city, as well as distrust for Whites, as we see in the dialogue between me and several Black youths below. In this conversation, I commented on how the only place I see White people is in the newly developed area of Sunnyside, and I asked if Whites (drivin they fancy cars) have always been in Sunnyside:

Bilal:	*Hellll naw!*
Researcher:	. . . the Volvo station wagon . . .
Amira:	Never!
R:	. . . and the Mercedes and all that?
B:	Never . . .
R:	Never? Forreal?
A:	Mm-mm . . .
B:	*Ever!* Only time you . . .
A:	They scared or they buyin drugs . . .
B:	Only time you see them, only time you see them is when they crossin over the bridge, if they commute . . .
Yesmina:	Oh, yeah, the commuting . . .
B:	[suck-teeth] that's *all* they do . . .
A:	And they got they doors on *lock*! [Laughter] . . .
R:	Oh, yeah? [Laughter]
A:	Yep . . .
R:	How you know they got they doors locked? You can't see . . .
A:	They don't look—they don't look at you. They be like this [making a scared face] . . .

Y:	*Mm-hmm*!
A:	. . . and start flyyyin!
Voice:	. . . [suck-teeth]
R:	Man, that's crazy, so people just basically be ridin through . . .
Y:	Mm-hmm . . .
A:	Usin our streets . . .
B:	We should put a damn toll on *them*, *shiiitt*!
Y:	[Laughter] . . .
R:	[Laughter] . . . a toll every time you drive through . . .
B:	*Yeahhh*, I'll toll they ass two dollars [Laughter] . . .
Y:	We'd make a lot of money . . .

Whites are seen as outsiders ("usin our streets") who are "scared" of Blacks and who are only in Sunnyside to either commute to work or if "they buyin drugs." Also, one can see that Whites are also viewed as having the economic upper hand in the way that Bilal insists: "We should put a damn toll on *them*, *shiiitt*!"

In this context, Black youth in Haven High will often comment on how they only see their teachers (mostly White) when they are exiting or entering the community on the nearby freeway ramp. The fact that White teachers don't spend time in the community only reifies feelings of social distance and distrust between students and teachers, which can be a major source of tension in the schooling experiences of Black youth. As one student put it, "Man, they don't know what it's like here—they act like they know, but they don't know . . . they *can't* know."

Just as economic institutions are gentrifying and removing Black communities around the nation and offering unfulfilled promises of economic independence, one can also say that educational institutions have been attempting (since integration) to gentrify and remove Black Language from its speakers with similarly unfulfilled promises of economic mobility. In both cases, the message is: "Economic opportunities will be opened up to you if you just let us clean up your neighborhoods and your language." Most Blacks in the US since integration can testify that they have experienced teachers' attempts to eradicate their language and linguistic practices (see Morgan 2002 on "outing schools") in favor of the adoption of White cultural and linguistic norms. I'll return to this point at the end of the chapter.

Black Language structure and use

Turning our attention to language within this context, this chapter focuses on Black Language (BL, sometimes referred to in the literature as "Ebonics," "African American Language," "African American English," or "African American Vernacular English," among other labels) as a complex system of structure and use that is distinct from White Mainstream English (WME) in the US. While it is true that BL shares much of its structure with WME, there are many aspects of the BL syntactic (grammar) and phonological (pronunciation) systems that mark it as distinct from that variety. If we examine syntax alone, sociolinguists have described numerous distinctive features of BL, such as *copula absence* (as we saw in the Arabic example at the beginning of this chapter, Labov 1969), invariant *be* for habitual aspect ("He *be* actin crazy," meaning "He usually/regularly/sometimes acts crazy," Fasold 1972) and equatives ("We *be* them Bay boys" for "We are them Bay boys," Alim 2004a, 2004b), *steady* as an intensified continuative ("She *steady* prayin her son come home," meaning "She is intensely, consistently and continuously hoping her son comes home," Baugh 1983), *stressed BIN* to mark remote past ("I *BIN* told you not to trust that woman," meaning "I told you a long time ago not to trust that woman"), *be done* to mark future/conditional perfect ("By the end of the day, I *be done* collected $600!", meaning "By the end of the day, I will have collected $600!", Baugh 1983), aspectual *stay* ("She *stay* up in my business" meaning "She is always getting into my business," Spears 2000), *third person singular present tense -s absence* ("I know who run *this* household!", for "I know who runs *this* household," Fasold 1972), *possessive -s absence* ("I'm braidin Talesha hair," for "I'm braidin Talesha's hair"), *multiple negation* ("I ain't never heard about no riot big as the one we had in LA" for "I have never heard about a riot as big as the one we had in LA", Labov 1972a), *negative inversion* ("Can't nobody touch F-40!" meaning "Nobody can touch F-40!", Sells, Rickford and Wasow 1996), and several other features (see Rickford 1999). It is important to note that many of these distinct BL features are used in variation with WME features, as most speakers possess an ability to shift their speech styles, to varying degrees (not all BL speakers have the same stylistic range). I am conceptualizing BL to include the full range of styles, including WME, as speakers deem appropriate.

While much of the sociolinguistics literature has focused on distinctive phonological and syntactic features of BL, most researchers are aware that BL cannot simply be defined as a checklist of features that are distinct from WME (Morgan 1994). Aside from having an ever-evolving *lexicon* (Turner 1949, Major 1970, Dillard 1977, Folb 1980, Anderson 1994, Smitherman 1994, Stavsky, Mozeson and Mozeson 1995, Holloway and Vass 1997), speakers of BL may participate in numerous linguistic practices and cultural modes of discourse, such as, *signifyin* (and *bustin, crackin, cappin,* and *dissin,* Abrahams 1964, Kochman 1969, Mitchell-Kernan 1971, 1972, Labov 1972a, Smitherman 1973, 1977, Morgan 1996), *playin the dozens* (Abrahams 1970, Brown 1972), *call and response* (Daniel and Smitherman 1976, Smitherman 1977, Alim 2004b), *tonal semantics* (Smitherman 1977, Keyes 1984, Alim 2004b), *battlin* and *entering the cipher* (Norfleet 1997, Newman 2001, Alim 2004b), and the use of direct and indirect speech (Spears 1998, Morgan 1998), among others.

BL, then, refers to both linguistic features and rules of language use that are germane to Black Speech Communities in the US. In the following sections, we see how the richness of BL goes completely unnoticed and is regularly censored in White public space. We also see how speakers manipulate BL and how use of BL can often lead to misinterpretation and conflict for Blacks languaging in White public space, particularly educational institutions. While differing rules of language use are certainly part of what sometimes creates misunderstandings in intercultural communication, miscommunication often occurs in sociopolitical and sociohistorical contexts where communities (and their languages) are in conflict for economic, political, and social reasons as we touched on earlier (see Lippi-Green 1997).

Black Language in White public space

The racial segregation present in American society has led some scholars to use the term "American apartheid" to describe the deliberate isolation and exclusion of Blacks from educational, occupational, and social institutions in the US (Massey and Denton 1993). Perhaps centuries of persistent segregation between Blacks and Whites accounts for the dearth of significant studies of Black–White intercultural communication, with the notable exception of Kochman's (1981) *Black and White Styles in Conflict*. Additionally, when Blacks and Whites do interact, as Kochman (1981: 7) points out, "Black and white cultural differences are generally ignored when attempts are made to understand how and why black and white communication fails." One could argue that most Black–White intercultural communication occurs either in schools or on the job, where Blacks and Whites are "forced" into contact and Whites tend to be in the position of power. In this sense, I will draw on "White public space" as used by Page and Thomas (1994, cited in Hill 1998: 683): "a morally significant set of contexts that are the most important sites of the practices of racializing hegemony, in which Whites are invisibly normal, and in which racialized populations are visibly marginal and the objects of monitoring ranging from individual judgment to Official English legislation." Whites in educational and occupational settings may exercise their power in obvious ways (such as giving an order or firing an employee) and less obvious ways. As research on "whiteness" argues (Frankenberg 1993, Yancy 2000), Whites exercise power through overt and covert racist practices, which often reveal racist ideologies that even the "racist" may be unaware of (Hill 1998). In our case, WME and White ways of speaking become the invisible—or rather inaudible—and unmarked norms of what becomes glossed as "communicating in academic settings." Further, White public space in this chapter not only refers to physical space, but also to most interactional spaces in which Blacks encounter Whites, particularly White strangers or Whites in positions of power over them. In both cases, Blacks work to maintain a social face (Goffman 1967)—or the "mask," as poet Paul Laurence Dunbar described in his 1895 poem and rappers The Fugees rhymed 101 years later—"the image and impression that a person conveys during encounters, along with others' evaluation of that image" (Morgan 2002: 23).

The fact that it is the language and communicative norms of those in power, in any society, that tend to be labeled as "standard," "official," "normal," "appropriate," "respectful," and so on, often goes unrecognized, particularly by the members of the dominating group. The following dialogue with a teacher from Haven High in Sunnyside serves as the entry point to our discussion of how BL (and its speakers) are viewed in American educational institutions. We enter the dialogue as the teacher describes the "communication" goals of the school, and the language and communication behavior of her Black students. We will return to some of the key words and phrases underlined in this passage:

Teacher: They [Haven High] have a lot of presentation standards, so like this list of, you know, what you *should* be doing when you're having like an oral presentation—like you should speak slowly, speak loudly, speak clearly, make eye contact, use body language, those kinds of things, and it's all written out into a rubric, so when the kids have a presentation, you grade on each element. And so, I mean, in that sense, they've worked with developing communication. I mean, I think the thing that teachers work with, or *combat* the most at Haven High, is definitely like issues with *standard* English versus *vernacular* English. Um, like, if there was like one of the few goals I had this year was to get kids to stop sayin, um, "he was, she was . . ."

Alim: They was?

T: "They was. We be." Like, those kinds of things and so we spent a lot of time working with that and like recognizing, "Okay, when you're with your friends you can say *whatever you want* but . . . *this is the way it is. I'm sorry, but that's just the way.*" And they're like, "Well, you know, it doesn't make sense to me. This sounds right." "She was." Like, and that's just what they've been used to and it's just . . .

A: Well, "she was" is right, right? You mean, like, "They was"?

T: "They was."

A: And "we was" and that kinda thing . . .

T: Yeah, "we was." *Everything is just "was."*

A: [Laughter] . . .

T: And like, just trying to help them to be able to differentiate between what's *acceptable* . . . There's a lot of "ain't", "they was," "we ain't not . . ."

A: [Laughter] . . .

T: And *they can't codeswitch* that well . . .

A: Uh-huh . . .

T: Um, and I have to say it's kind of *disheartening* because like despite *all that time that's been spent focusing on grammar*, like, I don't really see it having helped enormously. Like, if I stop them in class and they're like, you know, "The Europeans, they was really blah-de-blah . . ." and I'd be like, "*Oh, they was*?" And they'd be like, "they were," like they'll correct themselves, but it's not to the point where it's *natural* . . . They're like, "Why does it matter?"

A: "You knew what I said, right?"

T: Yeah . . . I'm not sure they understand *why* it's necessary . . .

A: Do you have any other ideas about language at the school, like maybe the way the kids speak to themselves versus they way they speak in class, or do you notice . . .

T: Well, I mean, of course, they're not gonna be as *free* as when they're speaking to each other when they're speaking to me. I mean, I guess the only thing is not so much spoken language as it's like unspoken language, like tone, like a lot of attention is paid to like tone and body language, in terms of *respectful attitudes* . . . For a lot of kids, they don't see the difference. They're like [loud voice and direct speech] "Yeah, I just asked you to give me my grade. Like, what's the big deal?" And I'm like, "You just ordered me. I mean, you talked to me like that." Like, it's like, [loud again] "You didn't give me a grade!" like that, it's very *abrasive*, but they don't realize that it's abrasive. And so, I mean, it's just like, I guess, teaching them like the nuances of like when you're talking with people, what's *appropriate*? Should you be sitting up, or should you be kinda be leaning over [and she leans in her chair] . . .

A: [Laughter] . . .

T: Like that your body language and your facial features like speak just as loudly if not *more* loudly than what you *actually* say . . . I mean, just even bringing awareness to that, like, it's upsetting to them and it's like shocking to them that we'll comment on that, like, *maybe their parents let them get away with that and speak to them that way* and having to be like, "Hey, you know what, like, maybe your parents let you, but here that's never acceptable." Like, there's just so many—I mean, thinking about it, it's just, it's asking a lot of them to do, not only to speak standard English but to know all these other like smaller nuances that they've never experienced before and never had to think about. Like, it's probably on some level pretty overwhelming to them to have to deal with all of these things at once. Because, I mean, their parents say "they was" . . .

A: Yeah, is there any talk about what they're being expected to do, and what they do ordinarily, in the community, in the home, or anything?

T: Um, I mean, not officially or regularly, but I'll always be like, "I know you might speak this way at home, but in an academic setting, or if you're interviewing for a job, or if you're applying to college, and you talk to someone like that, they will like not even give you the time of day". . . .

A: Do they ever ask why?

T: Yeah, they're just like, you know, "Why?" and I'm like, *"I don't know!"*
        [Laughter!] "You know, that's just the way that it is! You have to learn
        how to play the game guys! I'm sorry."
A: Right, and I can see that being such an inadequate answer for a
        student who doesn't care about "they was" or "they were," being
        like, "What's the difference? What's the big deal? Like what's the
        overall picture?"
T: Right, and *I don't know how to provide that . . .*
A: Yeah . . .

After two years of ethnographic research as a teacher-researcher at Haven
High, and several years of experience as a teacher-researcher in Philadelphia
schools, I marvel at how remarkably consistent teachers' ideologies of language
are, particularly in response to the language of their Black students. The
language of the Black child is consistently viewed as something to eradicate,
even by the most well-meaning of teachers. In fact, this particular teacher is
genuine about her commitment in seeing as many of her students attend four-
year colleges as possible. And when she states, "I have to say it's kind of
disheartening because like despite *all* that time that's been spent focusing on
grammar, like, I don't really see it having helped enormously," one gets the
sense that she is actually disheartened and saddened by her lack of results.

What teachers like this one are probably not aware of is how they are
enacting whiteness and subscribing to an ideology of *linguistic supremacy*
within a system of daily cultural combat. It is revealing that the teacher
describes the language of her Black students as the thing that teachers at
Haven High "*combat* the most." In fact, her attempt to eradicate the language
pattern of her Black students has been "one of the *few* goals" she has had
throughout that academic year. The teacher not only works to eradicate the
language pattern of her Black students, but responds negatively to what she
calls "unspoken language," or the students' "tone." Black students and their
ways of speaking are described with adjectives like "abrasive" and not
"respectful." This attribution of negative characteristics due to cultural
differences has been noted frequently in studies of intercultural communication
(Gumperz 1982a, 1982b).

Interestingly, the teacher notes her students' failure to speak "standard
English"—particularly in the case of what's known as the generalization of was
to use with plural and second person subjects (Wolfram 1993)—while she fails
to make several linguistic distinctions herself (her own language being only
marginally "standard"). Not only does the teacher erroneously point out "he was"
and "she was" as cases of BL (this is actually WME) and imply that BL has a
random system of negation ("we ain't not" is actually not found in BL or any
other language variety in the US), but she is clearly not aware of the stylistic
sensitivity in the use of was and were. When the teacher says, rather
exasperatedly, "Everything is just 'was'," she is not recognizing the subtle stylistic

alternation of *was* and *were* that is employed by BL speakers, where speakers alternate their use of *was* and *were* based upon various contextual and situational factors, including the race of the person with whom they are speaking. In fact, the teacher goes as far as to say that her Black students do not have the ability to "codeswitch." Somehow, despite the vitality of BL, teachers continue hearing what's not said and missing what is (see Piestrup 1973 and Smitherman 1981).

We will return to the teacher's comments at the end of this chapter, but for now we take up her claim that her Black students do not possess stylistic sensitivity in speech (what she calls "codeswitching," and I will call "style-shifting"). The next section reveals how Black youth shift their speech style when speaking with Whites and Blacks, and the following section reports on mis-understood Black linguistic practices and the resulting conflicts with Whites. These sections report on findings from a larger ethnographic and sociolinguistic study of styleshifting in Sunnyside (Alim 2004a).

Black stylistic flexibility

Contrary to the teacher's comments that her Black students could not styleshift—that is, shift their speech style according to various contextual and situational factors—sociolinguistic research at Haven High reveals that Black youth possess a wide range of linguistic styles. Following Labov's (1969) research on Black teenagers in New York City, Baugh's (1979, 1983) research on the styleshifting of Black adults in LA and other urban centers, and Rickford and McNair-Knox's (1994) reporting of the styleshifting of one 18-year-old Black female, I designed a sociolinguistic study of style to determine what factors influenced the speech style of Black youth. Focusing on the impact of the interlocutor's identity characteristics, I recorded conversations between youth in Haven High (Sunnysidaz) and unfamiliar interlocutors from a university (Stanfordians). In this study, I asked the question: How do Black youth vary their speech style based on the race, gender and level of Hip Hop cultural knowledge of their interlocutors? Figure 3.1 presents a grid that identifies the characteristics of the participating interlocutors.

The grid shows that there are only two types of Sunnysidaz, Black Male Hip Hoppers and Black Female Hip Hoppers. It also shows that the Stanfordians vary based on race, gender, and Hip Hop cultural knowledge. Within these three factor groups, there are two factors each, allowing for eight different types of Stanfordians ($2^3 = 8$ possible combinations). So, each Sunnysida speaks to 8 different Stanfordians, making for 16 conversation types as shown in Figure 3.2. So, the total corpus for this portion of the study consisted of 4 Sunnysidaz— 2 Black Male Hip Hoppers and 2 Black Female Hip Hoppers—and 8 Stanfordians for a total of 32 conversations (4 Sunnysidaz × 8 Stanfordians = 32 conversations).

		Stanfordians		
		Race	*Gender*	*Hip Hop*
Sunnysidaz	*Black Male Hip Hopper*	Black/White	Male/Female	Hip Hop/ No Hip Hop
	Black Female Hip Hopper	Black/White	Male/Female	Hip Hop/ No Hip Hop

Figure 3.1 Interlocutor characteristics of Sunnysidaz and Stanfordians.

The 32 conversations averaged 40 minutes per interview for a total of approximately 1,280 minutes of talk, or over 21 hours. All transcripts were transcribed verbatim, resulting in approximately 1,300 pages. In addition to these 32 conversations, I have recorded the speakers' peer, in-group talk, which will serve as an additional point of comparison.

All three identity characteristics proved to be significant factors in the styleshifting of Black youth in Sunnyside. One student, for example, shows a remarkable range of stylistic flexibility. Figure 3.3 shows Bilal's varying rates of copula absence across each Stanfordian interlocutor and for his peer group.

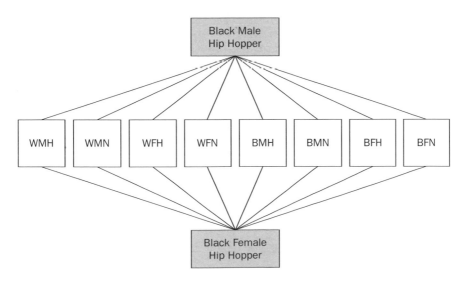

Figure 3.2 16 conversation types, total of 32 conversations.

In this remarkable case of styleshifting, Bilal displays an *extremely* broad stylistic range of copula absence. He goes from exhibiting 0 percent absence when talking with the WFN Stanfordian to 88.37 percent absence in his peer group! (Δ 88.37%).

Black linguistic practices

Not only do Black youth possess and deploy a variety of sociolinguistic styles, but there are numerous Black linguistic practices that are misunderstood and misinterpreted in White public space. As part of my experience as a teacher-researcher in Sunnyside, I trained students to become "hiphopographers"—that is, ethnographers of Hip Hop Culture and communication. As such, they were responsible for documenting and describing the linguistic practices of the most recent instantiation of Black American expressive culture, that is, Hip Hop Culture. Several examples of the linguistic practices that they described follow. Terms in small caps indicate other practices and lexical items also described by the class. The first practice is *battlin*, a form of Black verbal dueling associated

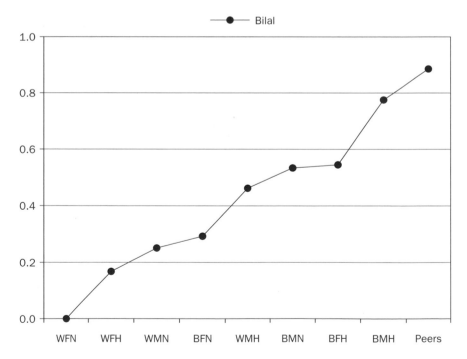

Figure 3.3 Frequencies of copula absence for Bilal across eight Stanfordian interlocutors and his peer group.

with Hip Hop Culture and the verbal art of rhyming (Spady, Alim, and Lee 1999). The second is *hush mode* and *scratch that green off yo neck*, two phrases associated mostly closely with Black female interaction, argumentation, and play. Both of these entries highlight the value placed on verbal creativity and competition in the Black speech community. The third is *rogue*, a localized example of semantic inversion (where the negative meaning proscribed by the dominating group is flipped on its head) used *only* within the 2.5 square miles of Sunnyside. All of the examples that follow are taken from student writing that is part of a larger project where students describe and document their own linguistic practices.

BATTLIN *(noun)(verb)* and FLOW *(noun)(verb)*

Battlin involves more than one person. A FREESTYLE rapping contest is when a group of people take turns rapping lyrics. They don't write the lyrics; they say them as they think of them off the top of their heads. As they take turns rapping back and forth, they're actually competing. In the end, the judges or the people watching the competition vote who won the competition and who had the better lyrics. It is also judged by who had the better meaning behind his/her words. Sometimes it is just obvious to the contenders who won by who DISSED/CLOWNED the other better.

> *Example:* JT and T-Reezy were battlin in the grass last week; they got on each other. JT got on T-Reezy's braids and face and T-Reezy got on JT about his height and women/girls.

The term comes from the idea of fighting with words. A battle is set up like a fight. One contender takes one side and the other takes the other. They rap at each other (in turn, though) until one *gives up* or a specific winner is announced. Usually done by males—those who tend to be street affiliated. Males talk about guns, women and SETS (areas of affiliation) and other topics. Done at clubs, social events, on street corners, etc. Takes the place of actual fights at parties where people FLOW—to have a smooth current of rap lyrics. If a person messes up their rap lyrics while saying them, then they ain't flowin. Flowin does not necessarily have to rhyme, as long as your words go good together.

HUSH MODE *and* SCRATCH THAT GREEN OFF YO NECK *(phrase)*

Hush mode is when you get CLOWNED (to get talked about rudely) and not have a remark or comeback for that person. To be dumbfounded. Usually used when instigating or talking about a fight or argument.

Example 1:

Aisha: Shut up, Tee!
Tee: [doesn't say anything]
Tereese: She got you on hush mode!

When somebody get CAPPED ON, and that person don't have anything to come back with, then the person who capped on them would say, "I got you on hush mode."

Example 2:

For example, say Shahira and Bibi are capping on each other and Shahira says to Bibi, "Yo mamma so old she used to gang bang with the Hebrews." If Bibi can't come back with something, then Shahira would say to her, "I got you on hush mode."

While we were defining the word, Jamal got on Tereese nerves and she said she was gon hit him . . .

Example 3:

Tereese: I'mma bust you in yo mouth.
Jamal: [silent]
Aisha: Oooh, Jamal, she got you on hush mode.
Jamal: She ain't got me on hush mode.
Tereese: I'mma hit you in yo mouth.
Jamal: I WISH YOU WOULD.

Females use this phrase a lot because they tend to instigate more than males. Males sometimes use it when they want to start something. Someone might tell you to "scratch that green off yo neck" after you been hush moded. I'm not sure of the origin of this phrase, but it's used after someone has been proven wrong.

Example 4:

For example, say two people are arguing and one of them got proven wrong, then someone would say to them, "Oooh, scratch that green off yo neck."

ROGUE (noun)

A word that people use as a substitute for another person's name. Originated in Sunnyside, California and mainly used in Sunnyside. JT uses it a lot to say hi to people. "What's up rogue?"

Example 1:   Waz up rogue?
Example 2:   Dang, rogue, what you doing?!
See DOGG, HOMIE, PATNA

Males use it more, but females do often use it. Used by all races in Sunnyside. Used mainly with the younger generation.

Example 3:

Aisha was CONVERSATIN with Shahira on the phone and at the end she said, "alright, rogue." Then her mom asked her why they call each other rogue.

All of these linguistic practices can be misunderstood by Whites not familiar with Black culture and language. For example, while Black youth place extreme value on the verbal inventiveness and competition involved in *battlin*, teachers broke up the biggest rhyme battle in the school because, as one student relayed, "Whenever they see a group of Black folks they automatically think it's a fight!" One teacher described the event in these words, "Whatever they were doing, it wasn't appropriate on school grounds." If teachers were more aware of the verbal creativity of Black youth and their penchant for verbal games, perhaps their linguistic practices would not be so misunderstood. Rather, they would be utilized for pedagogical purposes. As Labov (1972a: 212–213) wrote plainly decades ago:

> The view of the black speech community which we obtain from our work in the ghetto areas is precisely the opposite from that reported by Deutsch or by Bereiter and Englemann [verbal deprivation]. We see a child bathed in verbal stimulation from morning to night. We see many speech events that depend on the competitive exhibition of verbal skills—sounding, singing, toasts, rifting, louding [and battlin]—a whole range of activities in which the individual gains status through his use of language. We see the younger child trying to acquire these skills from older children, hanging around on the outskirts of older peer groups, and imitating this behavior to the best of his ability. We see no connection between verbal skill in the speech events characteristic of the street culture and success in the schoolroom.

The incident previously described is not merely a matter of communicative misunderstanding. An issue that is often not taken up by studies of intercultural communication, but is certainly central to them, is the fact that Black verbal competition is interpreted as *violence*. This interpretation must be understood in relation to the White racist view of Blacks as violent, despite the fact that it is Whites who commit most of the violent crimes in American society. This misunderstanding is particularly poignant when the students' definition of *battlin* includes the notion that it often "takes the place of actual fights at parties."

Several questions for studies of Black–White intercultural communication remain: Why is it that, despite ample evidence from sociolinguistic studies and theory that different speech communities possess different, yet theoretically equivalent, linguistic rules and rules of language use, BL and linguistic practices continue to be denigrated and underappreciated by Whites, particularly in educational institutions? What is at the *root* of this denigration and misinterpretation? How is it that the ideology and practice of *linguistic supremacy*—the unsubstantiated notion that one set of linguistic norms are inherently superior to the linguistic norms of other communities, and the practice of mapping White norms, in this case, onto "the language of school," "the language of economic mobility," and "the language of success"—persist, even *within* the subjugated group? What is the role of communicative misunderstanding in maintaining and perpetuating tensions between communities? How do we understand communicative differences not as the source of tensions but as a means of perpetuating and reinforcing those tensions? How do we move beyond searching for communicative mismatches to explain intercultural tensions and conflicts that already exist due to the larger and systemic social, political, and economic subjugation of a group? Or worse yet, will greater knowledge of communicative differences be used *for* or *against* justice (see Eades 2005)? As overt forms of racism begin to be more publicly censured in some areas of the US, linguistic differences are currently being used to exclude Blacks from full participation in society in a number of ways (see Baugh 2003 on *linguistic profiling* in housing discrimination based on "Black-sounding" voices, and Bertrand and Mullainathan 2004 on differential access to employment based on "Black-sounding" names). Studies of intercultural communication need to address these questions if the field is to remain relevant to dominated populations. Such studies are essential since the problem with BL has more to do with Black *people* than Black *language*. Given the emerging studies addressing the role of BL in various forms of discrimination, more scholars are beginning to see the BL "problem" as one that is part and parcel of a sociostructural system of White racism in the US (Hill forthcoming).

For this population of Black youth, how do we avoid explanations of Black academic failure as the result of Black "opposition" to formal schooling and begin interrogating the daily cultural combat (conscious or unconscious) against Black language and culture in White public space? How do we go beyond the oft-heard and inadequate teachers' response to Black resistance to White cultural and linguistic norming: "I don't know!" [Laughter!] "You know, that's just the way that it is! You have to learn how to play the game guys! I'm sorry"? Responses of this type are enactments of whiteness that put the onus on the oppressed group at the same time as they alleviate the dominating group of any responsibility. In this case, when pushed, the teacher is willing to admit that she is not equipped to provide an answer for the underlying reasons of what I have called the gentrification of BL—this is a start. The continued gentrification of BL is the cultural analogy to the physical removal of Black communities by White developers. As one of my students so passionately expressed her resistance to the gentrification of the community in which she was born and raised, "I mean, that's takin part of our heritage outta there, cuz I mean, we, we, that's where people was *raised* and stuff! [She pauses for a brief second, glaring over the freeway ramp, and adds] . . . and now the hotels."

While Blacks around the nation continue to be removed from their communities, BL persists despite every attempt by Whites to eradicate it. The community continues to resist these efforts to "renew" its language for reasons so clearly articulated by Black writers and artists.

> The language, only the language . . . It is the thing that black people love so much—the saying of words, holding them on the tongue, experimenting with them, playing with them. It's a love, a passion. Its function is like a preacher's: to make you stand up out of your seat, make you lose yourself and hear yourself. The worst of all possible things that could happen would be to lose that language . . . It's terrible to think that a child with five different present tenses comes to school to be faced with books that are less than his own language. And then to be told things about his language, which is him, that are sometimes permanently damaging . . . This is a really cruel fallout of racism.
> (Toni Morrison 1981 cited in Rickford and Rickford 2000: 4–5)

A Black teacher in Philadelphia provides a different perspective: "The reason why Black students continue to speak their language is because, really, if you think about it, it's the *one thing* that they own in this world. It's the one thing that *noooobody* can take away from them. NO-body."

Facing and fighting the challenge

By this point, if the responses to my teacher workshops are any indication, there are probably many of you who are asking a "philosophical" question: "What are you saying, Alim—are you proposing that teachers should not teach 'standard English'?" Here's what I'm proposing. First and foremost, we must begin with an understanding that there is nothing *standard* about "standard English." Standard simply means that this is the language variety that those in authority have constructed as the variety needed to gain access to resources. What we have, then, for a "standard" in the US is nothing short of the imposition of White linguistic norms and ways of speaking in the service of granting access to resources to Whites and denying those same resources to as many others as possible, including poor Whites (*linguistic supremacy* operates similarly for *varieties* of a language as well as languages other than the dominating language, whatever that may be).

Secondly, I take the statement that I've heard from so many teachers, linguists, and scholars—"Well, fair or unfair, that's just the way the world works"—as a *starting* point for the discussion that we need to be having, not as an *end* point. This is truly where philosophical interrogation begins. Rather than agreeing, for one reason or another, that we *have* to provide "these students" with "standard English," I ask: By what processes are we all involved in the construction and maintenance of the notion of a "standard" language, and further, that the "standard" is somehow better, more intelligent, more appropriate, more important, and so on, than other varieties? In other words, how, when, and why are we all implicated in *linguistic supremacy*?

Thirdly, many well-meaning teachers and scholars who insist on the teaching of "standard English" to Black youth are under the assumption that BL is a monostyle, that is, that BL can be described as one style of speaking that is identifiably Black. As these data have shown, Black youth possess a broad range of speech styles (review Bilal's stylistic flexibility when talking with a White female non-Hip Hopper and in his peer group, for example, in Figure 3.3). It makes more sense, that is, it is more in line with the data on Black stylistic variation, to consider BL as the whole range of styles within speakers' linguistic repertoires. Part of speaking BL is possessing the ability to styleshift in and out of in-group ways of speaking. This is not astonishing. But somehow, when it comes to Black youth, some are under the impression that they are mired in this monostylistic linguistic ghetto (this is certainly a contemporary strain of "linguistic deprivation" thinking). But the ghetto can be a beautiful thang—that is, speakers such as Bilal, who have had a full range of experiences as Black youth, naturally (and quite obviously) vary their speech styles in different situations and contexts. Any time spent in Black communities would reveal that Bilal speaks to his Minister and the Nation of Islam mosque in one way, to his White teachers in another, to his grandmother in another, to his girlfriend, father, brothas on the block in yet another. And certainly, since he's forced to look for employment outside of his community, as a sporting goods store employee he will speak to White customers and non-English speaking customers in yet another style. And why should we expect him not to? The question is: If the Black speech community possesses a range of styles that are suitable for all of its communicative needs, then why the coercion and imposition of White styles?

Lastly, while it may be true that many Blacks would resist a pedagogical approach that did *not* focus on "standard English," it is *also* true that there are many Blacks who view access to White ways of speaking as part of "playing the game" (Urrieta 2004). That is, as one of my informants put it, "If you livin in the White man's world, you gotta play by the White man's rules. At least as long as *they* runnin shit." As is often the case, subjugated populations develop survival strategies that seem antithetical to linguistic emancipation. This does not mean that it is futile to attempt to develop ways to eradicate *linguistic supremacy*. This means that scholars dedicated to *linguistic equanimity*—the structural and social equality of languages—have to work equally as hard among the oppressors and the oppressed. This is the challenge—and it is one worth fightin for.

Chapter 4

"Bring it to the cypher"

Hip Hop Nation Language

Four hundred years ago, when black slaves were brought to America, Africans who spoke the same language were separated from each other. What we're seeing today, with this insane campaign to intimidate rappers and rap music, is just another form of separating people that speak a common language.

(Ice Cube, June 25, 1990; cited in Sexton 1995)

The centrality of language to the HHN is evident in such song and album titles as "New Rap Language" (Treacherous Three, 1980), "Wordplay" (Bahamadia, 1996), "Gangsta Vocabulary" (DJ Pooh, 1997), "Project Talk" (Dobby Digital, 1998), "Slang Editorial" (Cappadonna, 1998), *Real Talk 2000* (Three-X-Krazy, 2000), "Ebonics" (Big L, 2000), *Country Grammar* (Nelly, 2000), *Project English* (Juvenile, 2001), "Dangerous Language" (Afu-Ra, 2002), and many more. In numerous ethnographic interviews, I have found that language is a favorite topic of discussion in the HHN, and its members are willing to discuss it with great fervor—and to defend its use.

In the previous chapter, I examined Black Language in White public space. In this chapter, we enter a Black Language Space as we take a journey through Hip Hop's linguistic landscape and explore the anatomy of language and language use within the HHN, providing a thorough description of Hip Hop Nation Language (HHNL). My research on the language and linguistic practices of the Hip Hop Nation Speech Community examines how HHNL both builds upon and expands the Black American Oral Tradition. In what I consider this book's central chapter, I outline several Hip Hop discursive practices and cultural modes of discourse—*call and response*, *multilayered totalizing expression*, *signifyin* and *bustin* (*bussin*), *tonal semantics* and *poetics*, *narrative sequencing* and *flow*, *battlin* and *entering the cipher*.

In exploring the development of nation language in Anglophone Caribbean poetry, Caribbean historian, poet, and literary and music critic Kamau Brathwaite (1984: 13) writes: "Nation language is the language which is influenced very strongly by the African model, the African aspect of our New World/Caribbean heritage. English it may be in terms of some of its lexical features. But in its contours, its rhythm and timbre, its sound explosions, it is not English." Concerned with the literature of the Caribbean and the sociopolitical matrix within which it is created, Brathwaite used the term "nation language" in contrast to "dialect." Familiar with the pejorative meanings of the term "dialect" in the folk linguistics of the people, he writes that while nation language can be considered both English and African at the same time, it is an English which is like a "howl, or a shout, or a machine-gun or the wind or a wave." Then he likened it to the blues. Surely, nation language is like Hip Hop (as rapper Raekwon spits his "machine-gun-rap" (on *Wu-Tang Forever*, 1997)). HHNL is, like Brathwaite's description, new in one sense and ancient in another. It comprises elements of orality, total expression, and conversational modes (Brathwaite 1984).

Rapper Mystikal, known for having a unique, highly energetic rhyming style highlighted with lyrical sound explosions, provides a perfect example of nation language when he raps: "You know what time it is, nigga, and you know who the fuck this is/ DAANNN-JAH!!! [Danger] DAANNN-JAH!!! [Danger]/ Get on the FLO' [floor]!/ The nigga right, yeaaahhHHH!" (2000). Mystikal starts out speaking to his listener in a low, threatening growl, asserting his individuality ("you know who the fuck this is"), and then explodes as if sounding an alarm, letting everyone know that they have entered a dangerous verbal zone! "Get on the FLO'!" has a dual function—simultaneously warning listeners to lie down before the upcoming lyrical "DAANNN-JAH!" and directing them to get on the dance floor. When rapper Ludacris (2001) commands his listeners to "ROOOLLLL OUT!" and raps: "Oink, Oink, PIG! PIG! Do away with the POORRK-uh/ Only silverwuurrr [silverware] I need's a steak knife and FOORRK-uh!", he stresses his words emphatically, compelling one to do as he says. In that brief example, he is in conversation with Black American Muslim and Christian communities currently dialoguing about the eating of swine flesh (which Muslims consider unholy).

When we speak of "language," we are defining the term in a sense that is congruent with the HHN's "linguistic culture" (Schiffman 1996). Wideman (1976: 34) situates HHNL in the broader context of Black American speech:

> There is no single register of African American speech. And it's not words and intonations, it's a whole attitude about speech that has historical rooting. It's not a phenomenon that you can isolate and reduce to linguistic characteristics. It has to do with the way a culture conceives of the people inside of that culture. It has to do with a whole complicated protocol of silences and speech, and how you use speech in ways other than directly to communicate information. And it has to do with, certainly, the experiences that the people in the speech situation bring into the encounter. What's fascinating to me about African American speech is its spontaneity, the requirement that you not only have a repertoire of vocabulary or syntactic devices/constructions, but you come prepared to do something in an attempt to meet the person on a level that both uses the language, mocks the language, and recreates the language.

On her single recording "Spontaneity" (1996), Philadelphia rapper Bahamadia validates Wideman's assertion. She raps about her "verbal expansion" in a stream of consciousness style: "Everybody's on it cause eternal verbal expansion keeps enhancin brain child's ability to like surpass a swarm of booty-ass-no-grass-roots-havin-ass MC's." The verbal architect constructs her rhymes by consciously stretching the limitations of the "standard" language. In describing her lyrical influences, she cites Rappers Kool Keith of the Ultramagnetic MCs, De La Soul, and Organized Konfusion as "masters at what they do in that they explore the English language and they try to push the boundaries and go against the grains of it, you know what I mean?" (Spady and Alim 1999: xviii).

Wideman continues: "It's a very active exchange. But at the same time as I say that, the silences and the refusal to speak is just as much a part, in another way, of African American speech." Rapper Fearless of the group Nemesis exemplifies the point: Envisioning rappers, including himself, among the great orators and leaders in the Black community, he says:

> I always looked up to great orators like Martin Luther King, Malcolm X. Anybody who could ever stand up and persuade a group of young men or a nation . . . Just the way they were able to articulate. The way they emphasized their words. And the way they would use pauses. They would actually use *silence* powerfully . . . Just the way they made words cause feelings in you, you know what I'm saying? Just perpetuate thought within people, you know.
>
> (Spady and Alim 1999: xviii)

So, "language" in HHNL obviously refers not only to the syntactic constructions of the language but also to the many discursive and communicative practices, the attitudes toward language, understanding the role of language in both binding/bonding community and seizing/smothering linguistic opponents, and language as concept (meaning clothes, facial expressions, body movements, grafilti, and overall communication—"cuz as Beanie Sigel knows, '85% of communication is non-verbal'").

In addition to the preceding, HHNL can be characterized by ten tenets.

1 HHNL is rooted in Black Language (BL) and communicative practices (Spady and Eure 1991; Smitherman 1997; Yasin 1999). Linguistically, it is "the newest chapter in the African American book of folklore" (Rickford and Rickford 2000). It is a vehicle driven by the culture creators of Hip Hop, themselves organic members of the broader Black American community. Thus HHNL both reflects and expands the Black American Oral Tradition.
2 HHNL is just one of the many language varieties used by Black Americans.
3 HHNL is widely spoken across the country, and used/borrowed and adapted/transformed by various ethnic groups inside and outside the US.
4 HHNL is a language with its own grammar, lexicon, and phonology as well as unique communicative style and discursive modes. When an early Hip

Hop group, The Treacherous Three, rhymed about a "New Rap Language" in 1980, they were well aware of the uniqueness of the language they were rappin in.

5   HHNL is best viewed as the synergistic combination of speech, music, and literature. Yancy (1991) speaks of Rap as *musical literature* (or rhythmic-praxis discourse)." Henderson (1973) asserts that the Black poetry of the 1960s and 1970s is most distinctly Black when it derives its form from Black speech and Black music. HHNL is simultaneously the spoken, poetic, lyrical, and musical expression of the HHN.

6   HHNL includes ideologies of language and language use (see Pharcyde dialogue later).

7   HHNL is central to the identity and the act of envisioning an entity known as the HHN.

8   HHNL exhibits regional variation (Morgan 2001). For example, most members of the HHN recognize Master P's signature phrase, "Ya heeeaaard may?" (for "You heard me?") as characteristic of a southern variety of HHNL. Even within regions, HHNL exhibits individual variation based on life experiences. For example, because California Rapper Xzibit grew up in the Hip Hop-saturated streets of Detroit, New Mexico, and California, his HHNL is a syncretization of all these Hip Hop Nation Language varieties.

9   The fundamental aspect of HHNL—and perhaps the most astonishing to some—is that it is central to the lifeworlds of the members of the HHN and suitable and functional for all of their communicative needs.

10 HHNL is inextricably linked with the sociopolitical circumstances that engulf the HHN. How does excessive police presence and brutality shift the discourse of the HHN? How do disproportionate incarceration rates and urban gentrification impact this community's language? As Spady (1993) writes: "Hip Hop culture [and language] mediates the corrosive discourse of the dominating society while at the same time it functions as a subterranean subversion . . . Volume is turned up to tune out the decadence of the dominant culture."

Rappers are insightful examiners of the sociopolitical matrix within which HHNL operates. Discussing the role of HHNL in Hip Hop lyrics, Houston's Scarface concludes that HHNL functions as a communal "code of communication" for the HHN:

It's a code of communication, too . . . Because we can understand each other when we're rappin. You know, if I'm saying, [in a nasal, mocking voice] "Well, my friend, I saw this guy who shot this other guy and . . ." I break that shit down for you and you say, "Goddamn, man! Them muthafuckas is going crazy out where this dude's from." You know what I'm saying? It's just totally different. It's just a code of communication to me. I'm letting my partner know what's going on. And anything White America can't control they call "gangsters." *Shit!* I get real. Politicians is gangsters, goddamn. The presidents is the gangsters because they have the power to change everything. That's a gangster to me. That's my definition of gangster.

(Spady *et al.* 1999: xix)

Members of Tha Pharcyde actively debated the concept of HHNL:

Booty Brown: There's more than just one definition for words! We talk in slang. We always talk basically in slang. We don't use the English dictionary for every sentence and every phrase that we talk!

Pharcyde: No, there's a lot of words out of the words that you just said which all . . .

Booty Brown: Yeah, but the way I'm talking is not the English language . . . We're not using that definition . . . We're making our own . . . Just like they use any other word as a slang, *my brotha*! Anything. I'm not really your brother. Me and your blood aren't the same, but I'm your brother because we're brothas. That's slang . . . We make up our *own* words. I mean, it depends whose definition you glorify, okay? That's what I'm saying. Whose definition are you glorifying? Because if you go by my definition of "Black", then I can say "a Black person." But if you go by the *Webster Dictionary's* . . . You have your own definition. It's your definition.

(Spady, *et al.* 1999: xix)

Sociolinguistically, so much is happening in the exchange above. The HHN continues to "flip the script" (reverse the power of the dominant culture). Scarface is reacting to the media's labeling of reality-based rap lyrics as "gangster." By redefining gangster, he effectively turns the tables on what he believes is an oppressive state. If the presidents have the power to change everything, why ain't a damn thing changed?

In Tha Pharcyde conversation, when the *brotha* says the way he is talking is not the English language, he is talking about much more than slang. He asks pointedly, "Whose definition are you glorifying?" By making up your own words, he attests, you are freeing yourself of linguistic colonization (Wa Thiongo 1992). In an effort to combat the capitalistic commodification of Hip Hop culture, and to "unite and establish the common identity of the HHN," KRS-One refined the definition of Hip Hop terms and produced a document known as "The Refinitions" (2000)—putting the power of redefinition to action. KRS defines the language of Hip Hop Culture as "street language," and proposes that "Hiphoppas" speak an Advanced Street Language, which includes "the correct pronunciation of one's native and national language as it pertains to life in the inner-city." KRS is reversing "standard" notions of correctness and appropriateness, realizing that the HHN has distinct values and aesthetics that differ from the majority culture. Clearly, members of the HHN would agree that the use of BL stems "from a somewhat disseminated rejection of the life-styles, social patterns, and thinking in general of the Euro-American sensibility," as the writer of the first BL dictionary outside of the Gullah area put it (Major 1970: 10).

The relationship between HHNL and BL: Lexicon, syntax, and phonology

"Dangerous dialect/ Dangerous dialect/ I elect . . . to impress America." That's it, that's what it was about . . . Dangerous dialect, dangerous wording, you know what I mean? "I elect," that I pick, you know. "To impress America." That's what I pick to impress America, that dangerous dialect, you know.

(San Quinn, 2000, Alim and Spady, unpublished interview)

The relationship between HHNL and BL is a familial one. Since Hip Hop's culture creators are members of the broader Black American community, the language that they use most often when communicating with each other is BL. HHNL can be seen as the *submerged area* (Brathwaite 1984: 13) of BL that is used within the HHN, particularly during Hip Hop-centered cultural activities, but also during other playful, creative, artistic, and intimate settings. This conception of HHNL is broad enough to include the language of Rap lyrics, album interludes, Hip Hop stage performances, and Hip Hop conversational discourse. Black Americans are on the cutting edge of the sociolinguistic situation in the US (as evidenced by the preponderance of recent sociolinguistic research). HHNL, thus, is the cutting edge of the cutting edge.

A revised edition of the lexicon of "Black Talk" (Smitherman 1994 (2000)) begins with a chapter entitled, "From Dead Presidents to the Benjamins." The term "dead presidents" (meaning "money" and referring to American notes with images of dead presidents) has been in use in the Black American community since the 1930s. In the late 1990s, Hip Hop group dead prez both shortened the term and made explicit its multivariate meanings (within the revolutionary context of their rhymes and philosophy, they are surely hinting at assassination—a form of verbal subversion). The "benjamins", referring to Benjamin Franklin's image on one hundred dollar bills, is a term from the late 1990s popularized by Rapper Sean "Puffy" Combs (P. Diddy).

While several scholars and writers have produced work on the lexicon of BL (Turner 1949; Major 1970; Smitherman 1994; Dillard 1977; Anderson 1994; Stavsky, Mozeson and Mozeson 1995; Holloway and Vass 1997), it is important to note that Hip Hop artists, as street linguists and lexicographers, have published several dictionaries of their own. Old School legend Fab Five Freddy (Braithwaite 1992, 1995) documented the "fresh fly flavor" of the words and phrases of the Hip Hop generation (in English and German). Atlanta's Goodie Mob and several other artists have published glossaries on the inside flaps of their album covers. Of course, as lexicographers Hip Hop artists are only continuing the tradition of Black musicians, for many jazz and bebop artists compiled their own glossaries, most notable among them Cab Calloway (1944), Babs Gonzales, and Dan Burley.

Vallejo Rapper E-40 discusses the genesis of *E-40's Dictionary Book of Slang, Vol. 1* (forthcoming):

> I feel that I *am* the ghetto. The majority of street slang . . . "It's all good." "Feel me." "Fo' shiiiiiziiie," all that shit come from 40. "What's up, folks?" As a matter of fact, I'm writing my own dictionary book of slang right now . . . It's a street demand [for it]. Everywhere I go people be like, "Dude, you need to put out a dictionary. Let them know where all that shit come from," you know what I mean?
>
> (Spady *et al.* 1999: 290)

E-40 is credited with developing a highly individualized repertoire of slang words and phrases. If he were to say something like, "What's crackulatin, pimpin? I was choppin it up wit my playa-potna last night on my communicator—then we got to marinatin, you underdig—and I come to find out that the homie had so much fedi that he was tycoonin, I mean, pimpin on some real boss-status, you smell me?", not too many people would understand him. ("Crackulatin" = happening, an extended form of "crackin"; "pimpin" is sometimes used as a noun to refer to a person, like "homie"; "choppin it up" = making conversation; "playa-potna" = partner, friend; "communicator" = cell phone; "marinatin" = a conversation where participants are reasoning on a subject; "underdig" = understand; "fedi" = money; "tycoonin" = being a successful entrepreneur; "pimpin" = being financially wealthy; "boss-status" = managing things like a CEO; "you smell me?" = you feel me? Or you understand me?)

In HHNL, "pimp" refers not only to one who solicits clients for a prostitute, but also has several other meanings. One could be suffering from "record company pimpin" (the means by which record companies take advantage of young Black artists lacking knowledge of the music industry), engaging in "parking lot pimpin" (hanging around the parking lot after large gatherings), "pimpin a Lex" (driving a Lexus while looking flashy), or "pimpin somebody's ride" (custom designing a car; see Xzibit in MTV's *Pimp My Ride*). As we also saw earlier, "pimpin" can also refer generally to an individual, or specifically to one who sports a flashy lifestyle. The word "politickin" can refer to the act of speaking about political subjects relevant to the Black community, simply holding a conversation, or trying to develop a relationship with a female. One might catch "frostbite" or get "goose-bumps" from all of the "ice" they got on ["ice" = diamonds]. In the HHN, "rocks" can be a girl's best friend (diamonds) or a community's silent killer (crack cocaine), while "to rock" can mean to liven up a party, to wear a fashionable article of clothing, or to have sexual intercourse. If you really wanna liven up a party, you would "lean widdit, rock widdit" (like Dem Franchize Boyz) or get "crunk" (like Lil Jon 'nem boys down Souf be doin), or get "hyphy" (like how E-40, Keak da Sneak and dem Bay Boys be gettin down).

Given the fluidity of HHNL, speakers take a lot of pride in being the originators and innovators of terms that are consumed by large numbers of speakers. Rappers, as members of distinct communities, also take pride in regional lexicon. For instance, the term "jawn" emerged in the Philadelphia Hip Hop community. "Jawn" is what can be called a *context-dependent substitute noun*—a noun that substitutes for any other noun, with its definition so fluid that its meaning depends entirely upon context. For instance, one can say, "Oh, that's da jawn!" for, "da bomb!" if they think something is superb; "Did you see that jawn?" for "female" when an attractive female walks by; "I like that new Beanie jawn"; for "song," when the song is played on the radio, and so on. Recently, Philadelphia's Roots have handed out T-shirts with "JAWN" written on the front, advocating the use of the distinctive Philly Hip Hop term. Placed in a broader context, the meaning of the distinct lexicon of HHNL can be nicely summed up: "Slick lexicon is hip-hop's Magna Carta, establishing the rights of its disciples to speak loudly but privately, to tell America about herself in a language that leaves her puzzled" (Rickford and Rickford 2000: 86).

Several scholars have written that the syntax of HHNL is essentially the same as that of BL (Remes 1991; Smitherman 1997, 2000; A. Morgan 1999; Spady and Alim 1999; Yasin 1999; Rickford and Rickford 2000; M. Morgan 2001). This is true. We must also examine the syntax of HHNL closely enough to elucidate how the language users are behaving both within and beyond the boundaries of BL syntax. What is happening syntactically when Method Man gets on the air and proclaims, "Broadcasting live from the Apocalypse, it be I, John Blazzzazzziiinnnyyyyy!" (KMEL 2001)? What is happening when Jubwa of Soul Plantation writes in his autobiography: "Jubwa be the dope mc, freestylin' to the beat deep cover" (cited in Alim 2001)? An important question is, How does HHNL confirm our knowledge of BL syntax—and how does it challenge that knowledge?

Probably the most oft-studied feature of BL is *habitual* or *invariant be* (see Green 2004). Early studies of BL syntax (Labov *et al.* 1968; Wolfram 1969; Fasold 1972) noted the uniqueness of this feature and were in agreement that it was used for recurring actions (*We be clubbin on Saturdays*) and could not be used in finite contexts (*She be the teacher*). Building upon this research, we see that HHNL provides numerous examples of what I have called *be3* or the "equative copula" in BL. (Alim 2001b, 2004a). Some examples of this construction (Noun Phrase *be* Noun Phrase) follow:

"I be the truth."—Philadelphia's Beanie Sigel
"Dr. Dre be the name."—Compton's Dr. Dre

"This beat be the beat for the street."—New York's Busta Rhymes
"Brooklyn be the place where I served them thangs."—New York's Jay-Z
"I be that insane nigga from the psycho ward."—Staten Island's Method
Man

These are but a few of countless examples in the corpus of Hip Hop lyrics, but this equative copula construction can also be found in everyday conversation, as in these examples:

"We be them Bay boys." (Bay Area's Mac Mall in a conversation with James G. Spady)
"It [marijuana] be that good stuff." (Caller on the local Bay Area radio station)
"You know we be some baaad brothas." (Philadelphia speaker in conversation)

It is possible that speakers of BL have begun using this form only recently, and that it represents a recent change in the system. Alternatively, the form may always have been present in the language but escaped the notice of investigators. Certainly it is present in the writings of Black Arts Movement poets of the 1960s and 1970s, most notably in Sonia Sanchez's We De Word Sorcerers. We also find the form being cited in one linguistic study of Black street speech ("They be the real troublemakers"; "Leo be the one to tell it like it is") (Baugh 1983). It is possible that members of the HHN, with their extraordinary linguistic consciousness and their emphasis on stretching the limits of language, have made this form much more acceptable by using it frequently.

The HHN's linguistic consciousness refers to HHNL speakers' conscious use of language to construct identity. Addressing the divergence of BL from "standard English," Baugh and Smitherman (in press: 20) write:

> Graffiti writers of Hip Hop Culture were probably the coiners of the term "phat" (meaning excellent, great, superb) . . . although "phat" is spelled in obvious contrast to "fat," the former confirms that those who use it know that "ph" is pronounced like "f." In other words, those who first wrote "phat" diverged from standard English as a direct result of their awareness of standard English: the divergence was not by chance linguistic error. There is no singular explanation to account for linguistic divergence, but Hip Hop Culture suggests that matters of personal identity play a significant role.

This conscious linguistic behavior deals with matters of spelling and phonemic awareness. (See Morgan 2001 and Olivo 2001 on "spelling ideology.") One case—one of the more controversial uses of language in Hip Hop culture—is the term "nigga." The HHN realized that this word had various positive in-group meanings and pejorative out-group meanings, and thus felt the need to reflect the culturally specific meanings with a new spelling ("nigger" becomes "nigga"). A "nigga" is your main man, or one of your close companions, your homie.

Recently the term has been generalized to refer to any male (one may even hear something like, "No, I was talkin about Johnny, you know, the white nigga with the hair") though it usually refers to a Black male. And even more recently, one might hear the term being used by females of all ethnicities in the San Francisco Bay Area to refer to each other in much the same way that males do, as this example from a conversational exchange between White and Black female teenagers shows:

Black female: Call me, nigga!
White female: Yeah, nigga, you know wassup. I'ma call you.

Tupac Shakur, showing Hip Hop's affinity for acronyms, transformed the racial slur into the ultimate positive ideal for young Black males—**N**ever **I**gnorant **G**etting **G**oals **A**ccomplished.

As with the highlighting of regional vocabulary, HHNL speakers intentionally highlight regional differences in pronunciation by processes such as vowel lengthening and syllabic stress (Morgan 2001). When Bay Area Rappers JT the Bigga Figga and Mac Mall announced the resurgence of the Bay Area to the national Hip Hop scene with "Game Recognize Game" (1993), they did so using a distinctive feature of Bay Area pronunciation. The Bay Area anthem's chorus repeated this line three times: "Game recognize game in the Bay, man (mane)." "Man" was pronounced "mane" to accentuate this Bay Area pronunciation feature. Also, as fellow Bay Area Rapper B-Legit rhymes about slang, he does so using the same feature to stress his Bay Area linguistic origins: "You can tell from my slang I'm from the Bay, mane" (2000).

When Nelly and the St. Lunatics "busted" onto the Hip Hop scene, they were among the first Rappers to represent St. Louis, Missouri on a national scale. Language was an essential part of establishing their identity in the fiercely competitive world of Hip Hop Culture. For example, in a single by the St. Lunatics featuring Nelly they emphasize every word that rhymes with "urrrr" to highlight a well-known (and sometimes stigmatized) aspect of southern/midwest pronunciation (here → *hurrrr*, care → *currrr*, there → *thurrrr*, air → *urrrr*, and so on). By intentionally highlighting linguistic features associated with their city (and other southern cities), they established their tenacity through language, as if to say, "We have arrived." Since then, many other rappers, even some not from that region, have played and experimented with this phonological aspect of BL.

Nelly and the St. Lunatics are conscious not only of their pronunciation, but also of their syntax. On his platinum single "Country Grammar" (2000), Nelly proclaims, "My gramma bees Ebonics." Clearly, HHNL speakers vary their grammar consciously. An analysis of copula variation in the speech and the lyrics of Hip Hop artists concluded that higher levels of copula absence in the artists' lyrics represented the construction of a street-conscious identity—where the speaker makes a linguistic-cultural connection to the streets, the locus of the Hip Hop world (see Chapter 5). John Rickford has suggested (in a conference comment made in 2001) that the use of creole syntactic and phonological features by many rappers supports the ability of HHNL speakers to manipulate their grammar consciously (see Eve's reported use of Creole in Spady *et al.* 1999 and Lil Kim's 2005 street anthem, "Lighters Up"). Like San Quinn (see opening quotation in this section) HHNL speakers elect dialects to demonstrate their high degree of linguistic consciousness and in order to construct a street-conscious identity.

Hip Hop cultural modes of discourse and discursive practices

Keyes (1984: 145) applied Smitherman's (1977) Black modes of discourse to HHNL. Working in Hip Hop's gestation period, she wrote that "Smitherman schematized four broad categories of black discourse: narrative sequencing, call-response, signification/dozens, and tonal semantics. All of these categories are strategically used in rap music." We know that rappin in and of itself is not entirely new—rather, it is the most modern/postmodern instantiation of the linguistic-cultural practices of Africans in America. Rappers are, after all, "postmodern African griots" (a class of musicians-entertainers who preserved African history through oral narratives) (Smitherman 1997). This section will demonstrate how the strategic use of the Black modes of discourse is manifested in HHNL and how the new ways in which these modes are practiced generate correspondingly new modes of discourse. This section is based on various forms of HHNL data—rap lyrics, Hip Hop performances, and Hip Hop conversational discourse.

Call and response

Here is perhaps the most lucid definition of call and response:

> As a communicative strategy this call and response is the manifestation of the cultural dynamic which finds audience and listener or leader and background to be a unified whole. Shot through with action and interaction, Black communicative performance is concentric in quality—the "audience" becoming both observers and participants in the speech event. As Black American culture stresses commonality and group experientiality, the audience's linguistic and paralinguistic responses are necessary to co-sign the power of the speaker's rap or call.
> (Daniel and Smitherman 1976, cited in Spady 2000a: 59)

The quintessential example of the HHN's use of call and response grows out of funk performances and is still heard at nearly every Hip Hop performance today: "[Rapper] Say 'Hoooo!' [Audience] 'Hooooooooo!' [Rapper] Say 'Ho! Ho!'

[Audience] 'Ho! Ho!' [Rapper] Somebody screeeaaaaammm! [Audience] 'AAAHHHHHHHHHHHHHH!!!'" Anyone who has ever attended a Hip Hop performance can bear witness to this foundational call and response mechanism.

A description of a Hip Hop performance by Philadelphia's Roots paints a picture of a scene where lead MC Black Thought senses that there is a communicative schism developing between him and his Swiss audience (Jackson *et al.* 2001: 25). The rapper says, "Hold it, hold it, hold it!" and stops the music abruptly. What follows is "impromptu instruction" in the call and response mode of Black discourse:

> Y'all can't get the second part no matter what the fuck I say, right . . . I wonder if it's what I'm saying . . . A-yo! We gonna try this shit one more time because I like this part of the show.

Providing more explicit instruction, Thought slows it down a bit:

> Aight, Aight this is how I'm gonna break it down. I'm gonna be like "ahh," then everybody gonna be like "ahhh." Then—I don't know what I'm gonna say second but y'all gotta listen close cause then y'all gotta repeat that shit—that's the fun of the game!

Thought is not only providing instruction but he is also administering a challenge to his European audience: either *git sicwiddit* [get sick with it] *or git hitwiddit* [get hit with it]! (in this context meaning, "Become active participants in this activity or get caught off guard looking culturally ignorant!").

Call and response mechanisms are so pervasive in HHNL that talented MC's (Rappers, Masters of Ceremonies) have taken this mode to new heights. Mos Def describes one of the elements that made Slick Rick a legendary rapper:

> Slick Rick is one of the greatest MC's ever born because he has so many different facilities that he would use. Style. Vocal texture. The way he would even record. Like, he was doing call and response with himself! He would leave four bars open, and then do another character, you understand what I'm saying?
>
> (Alim 2000, unpublished interview)

The individualized uses of call and response in the Hip Hop cultural mode of discourse deserve more attention. Also, as is evident from Mos Def's comments, HHNL speakers can be cognizant of the fact that they are operating within and expanding upon the Black American Oral Tradition. The linguistic and communicative consciousness of the HHN also needs further exploration.

Multilayered totalizing expression

Beyond the explicit instruction, one can witness the multilayered nature of the call and response mode at Hip Hop performances where both performer and audience are fully conversant with Hip Hop cultural modes of discourse. At the first Spitkicker Tour (2000) in San Francisco's Maritime Hall, I observed this multilayered, multitextual mode. Here's an excerpt from my fieldnotes:

> Maaan, all performers are on stage at once—[DJ] Hi-Tek, Talib [Kweli], Common, Biz [Markie], De La [Soul], Pharoahe [Monch]—and they just kickin it in a fun-loving communal-type Hip Hop atmosphere! Common and Biz are exchanging lines from his classic hit . . . The DJ from De La starts cuttin up the music and before you know it, Common is center stage freestylin. The DJ switches the pace of the music, forcing Common to switch up the pace of his freestyle [improvisational rap], and the crowd's lovin it! "Oooooooohhhhh!" . . . Hi-Tek and Maseo are circling each other on stage giving a series of hi-fives timed to the beat, smilin and laughin all along, as the crowd laughs on with them. Common, seizing the energy of the moment, says, "This is Hip Hop music, y'all!" Then he shouts, "It ain't nuthin like Hip Hop music!" and holds the microphone out to the crowd. "It ain't nuthin like Hip Hop music!" they roar back, and the hall is transformed into a old school house party frenzy . . . Gotta love this Hip Hop music.

What is striking about this description is that there are multiple levels of call and multiple levels of response, occurring simultaneously and synergistically, to create something even beyond "total expression" (Brathwaite 1984: 18). This is a *multilayered totalizing expression* that completes the cipher (the process of constantly making things whole). We witness a call and response on the oral/aural, physical (body), and spiritual/metaphysical level. My final note ("Gotta love this Hip Hop music") captures a moment of realization that meaning resides in what I've just witnessed—in the creation of a continuum beyond audience and performer. We hear varied calls made by the DJ and responded to by a freestylin MC; by the two MC's exchanging lines and by their impromptu leading of the audience in celebration of Hip Hop; by the physical reaction of performers to each other and the audience (who were also slappin hands with the performers); and by the spirited and spiritual response created during the climax of the performance. Like Common say, "Find heaven in this music and God/ Find heaven in this music and God/ Find heaven in this music and God" (cited in Jackson *et al.* 2001).

Signifyin and bustin (bussin)

Scholars have studied signification or signifyin—or, in more contemporary, semantically similar Black terms, *bustin, crackin,* and *dissin* (Abrahams 1964,

Kochman 1969, Mitchell-Kernan 1971, 1972, Smitherman 1973, 1977). Signifyin has been described as a means to encode messages or meanings in natural conversations, usually involving an element of indirection (Mitchell-Kernan 1972). Ironically noting the difficulty in pinpointing a dictionary definition for the speech act, Rickford and Rickford (2000: 82) cite Mitchell-Kernan's (1972: 82) attempt:

> The black concept of *signifying* incorporates essentially a folk notion that dictionary entries for words are not always sufficient for interpreting meanings or messages, or that meaning goes beyond such interpretations. Complimentary remarks may be delivered in a left-handed fashion. A particular utterance may be an insult in one context and not in another. What pretends to be informative may intend to be persuasive. Superficially, self-abasing remarks are frequently self-praise.

In Scarface's comments and Tha Pharcyde dialogue given earlier, we see evidence of this folk notion that "standard" dictionaries are insufficient to interpret Black language and life. But looking more closely at Tha Pharcyde dialogue, we witness an extremely sly (skillful and indirect) signification in Hip Hop conversational discourse. In the dialogue, Booty Brown is advocating the Black folk notion described by Mitchell-Kernan earlier. He implies that his partner is glorifying a Eurocentric meaning-making system over a meaning-making system that is African-derived. This does not become clear until Brown chooses his examples—carefully and cleverly. "Just like they use any other word as a slang, *my brotha!*" He emphasizes the "slang phrase" *my brotha*, as it is usually used as a sign of cultural unity and familial bond between Black American males (females will use *my sista* in a similar way).

Then he proceeds to ask the direct question, "Whose definition are you glorifying?" which is, in fact, a statement. Finally, as if to *really* lay it on thick (add insult to injury), he chooses to use the word "Black" to show that *Webster's Dictionary* is inadequate. The heat is diffused when "P" says, "I'm sayin, I'm sayin, that's what I'M sayin!" and they—and others around them—break into laughter. This dialogue is an example of how language is used to remind, scold, shame, or otherwise bring the other into a commonly shared ethic through signification.

We see an example of signifyin in Rapper Bushwick Bill's (of Houston's Geto Boys) description of the ever-changing, fluid, and flexible nature of "street slang" and the dangers of not "keepin your ear to the street" (being aware of what's happening around you at all times). In this case, Bushwick is referring to the rapidly evolving street terminology for law enforcement officials. He takes us deep into the locus of Hip Hop linguistic-cultural activity:

> You lose flavor. You lose the slang. You lose the basic everyday kickin it, you know, knowing what's going on at all times, you know what I'm saying? Knowing the new names for "5-0s". They ain't even 5-0s no more. They

call them "po-pos". That means everything changes. And they call them "one-time", you know what I'm saying? But you got to be in there to know that the police might know these words already. So they got to change up their dialect so that way it sounds like Pig Latin to the police.

(Spady *et al.* 1999: 308)

Bushwick's comment refers us directly to tenet 10 above. He is describing the changing nature of the various terms for "police" in the streets—from "5-0s" to "po-pos" to "one time." At one time, bloods referred to the "one-time" as "black and whites" (Folb 1980), while currently Young Jeezy refers to federal agents as "dem alphabet boys" (referencing the various acronyms of these agencies, such as the FBI, CIA, DEA, ATF, etc.). As I write this, brothas up in Harlem and Washington Heights got a new name for the po-po—squalie. Juelz Santana, operating like a street journalist, captures the multiple uses of the term, including its use as a general lookout call that's shouted when them cops is comin—squal-ayyyyyyyyyy! As New York-based Hip Hop historian Meghelli (personal communication 2005) notes, it is the sociopolitical context of many depressed and oppressed Black neighborhoods that necessitates these speedy lexical transformations.

Even though the police are not present in the dialogue above, Bushwick signifies on them with a clever one-liner that *also* serves to buttress his point. After runnin down all of the various terms (which have gone out of style as quickly as the police have comprehended them), he concludes, "So they got to change up their dialect so that way it sounds like Pig Latin to the police." "Pig Latin" is chosen here, rather than Greek, Chinese, Swahili, or other unfamiliar languages, to echo the fact that at one time police officers were called "pigs." Bushwick is not only signifyin on the police, but he is also demonstrating yet another term for police that has gone out of fashion! In addition, he is referencing an old form of Afroamericanized Pig Latin that employs innuendo, wordplay, letter and syllabic shifting, rhyming, and coded language designed to communicate with those in the know.

Like call and response, signifyin is ubiquitous in Hip Hop lyrics. In an example of male–female urban verbal play, in "Minute Man" (2001) with Missy Elliot and Ludacris, Jay-Z signifies on female R&B group Destiny's Child. Some insider knowledge is required to fully understand this speech act. Earlier that year, Destiny's Child had released "Independent Women," in which they asked a series of questions of men who dogged ("treated poorly") females. For example, they introduced each question with the word "Question" and then proceeded, "How you like them diamonds that I bought?" (to demonstrate to such men that they had their own income). Being that one of Jay-Z's many personas is the "playa-pimp"-type (one who uses women for sex and money), he rhymes to the listeners (including Destiny's Child): "I'm not tryin to give you love and affection/ I'm tryin to give you 60 seconds of affection/ I'm tryin to give you cash, fare and directions/ Get your independent-ass outta here, Question!" The signification doesn't become clear until the last line, or really, the last word, when Jay-Z borrows the word "Question" from their song (saying it in such a way as to completely match their prosody, rhythm, and tone). The only thing left to do is say, "Oooohhhhhh!"

We also witnessed signification in the call and response section of the Black Thought performance described above. As Jackson *et al.* (2001) note, Thought appears to be signifyin on the audience by highlighting their lack of familiarity with Black cultural modes of discourse: "I wonder if it's what I'm saying . . . A-yo!" The Roots have been known to signify on audiences that are not as culturally responsive as they would like them to be. During a recent concert at Stanford University, they stopped the music and began singing theme songs from 1980s television shows like "Diff'rent Strokes" and "Facts of Life," snapping their fingers and singing in a corny (not cool) way. The largely White, middle-class audience of college students sang along and snapped their fingers—apparently oblivious to the insult. After the show, the band's drummer and official spokesman, Ahmir, said: "Like if the crowd ain't responding, we've done shows where we've stopped the show, turned the equipment around, and played for the wall, you know" (Alim 1999). In this sense, the Roots remove any hint of indirection and blatantly *bust on* the unresponsive audience. The examples above make clear that HHNL speakers readily incorporate *signifyin* and *bustin* into their repertoire. Whether Hip Hop heads are performing, writing rhymes, or just "conversatin," these strategies are skillfully employed.

Tonal semantics and poetics

Black American tonal semantics can be thought of as the creative force that drives Hip Hop lyrics. As such, I've added the category *poetics* to the discussion. Smitherman (1977: 134) describes tonal semantics as the "use of voice rhythm and vocal inflection to convey meaning in black communication," and depicts the voice as instrument. Black American tonal semantics consists of talk-singing, repetition and alliterative word play, intonational contouring and rhyme. In their lyrical production, Hip Hop artists have capitalized on all of these categories and have taken them to "da next level" ("to a higher level of creativity").

Like the preachers in Smitherman (1977), rappers also believe that word-sound (which places emphasis on *how* words are said, in addition to *what* words are said) can move people. Rappers call upon the use of repetition at will and use it to perform a variety of functions, such as: to tell cautionary tales, to drive important points/themes home, to elicit laughter, and to display their lyrical skillz. Several examples of repetition in Hip Hop lyrics demonstrate the effective use of this semantic category (see Table 4.1).

Alliterative wordplay also appears in various forms. For instance, Pharoahe Monch uses alliteration in this verse to flex his phat phonetic skillz ("impressive phonetic skills"):

Table 4.1 Effective use of repetition

(A)
Never take a man's life cuz you hate yours
Never become so involved with something that it blinds you
Never forget where you from someone will remind you
Never take for granted what's been given as a gift
And **never** sleep on a nigga, less that nigga stiff . . .
Never say **never**, cuz I **never** thought this *clever* thought **never**

In "It's On," DMX begins 15 lines in this verse (most aren't shown) with the word "never." In the last line, he uses the word four times while interspersing clever rhymes like "never thought" and "clever thought" and punctuating the verse with a period in the form of "never." DMX is offering a tale of caution to young bloods in the streets. His repetition of the word "never" captivates his listener, making sure that his fans do not miss his point. He also makes sure to let them know that his repetition is "clever."

(B)
Nigga the **truth**, every time I step in the booth/ I speak the **truth**, y'all know what I'm bringin to you/ I bring the **truth**, muthafuckas know who I be/ I be the **truth**, what I speak *shall set you free*/ Nigga the **truth**!

In "The Truth," Beanie Sigel wants to be sure he is well understood. In an effort to convince others of his street credibility (authenticity) he wants to make sure listeners know that he speaks the truth, brings the truth and bees the truth! He also capitalizes on an oft-repeated Biblical phrase in the Black community, "The truth shall set you free."

(C)
I been around this block, **too** many times
Rocked, **too** many rhymes, clocked, **too** many nines, **too**
To all my brothas, it ain't **too** late **to** come **together**
Cause **too** much black and **too** much love equal forever
I don't follow any guidelines cause **too** many niggaz ride mines
So I change styles every **two** rhymes . . .

In "22 Two's," Jay-Z exploits the homonymy of "to/too/two" and also the letters "to" (together) to place "22 Two's" in a sequence. Jigga's main mission is to demonstrate that he's one of the most gifted rhymers in the game. In his undeterred confidence, he adds, "That's 22 two's for y'all muthafuckas out there, ya nahmean? Shall I continue?" Jigga is also driving the point home that he's learned lessons from the streets and "it ain't too late for brothas to come together."

(D)
That's what I ain't gon do
See the 5-0 and swing a tight donut
Uh-uh, that's what I ain't gon do
Be the nigga at the bar talkin shit but outside throwin up
Uh-uh, that's what I ain't gon do
Let baby tell me what I'm doin with my weekly check
Uh-uh, that's what I ain't gon do
Try hard to be the man and hit the club with a fake Rolex

In "Ain't Gon Do," Richie Rich is clearly using repetition for the purpose of humor. He is able to punctuate the listeners' laughter each time, lettin them know that's what he "ain't gon do."

F-f-f-f-f-f-f-f-f-follow me for now/ for no formidable fights I've been formed to forget/ For **Ph**aroahe **f**ucks **f**amiliar **f**oes **f**irst/ Befo fondling female MC's fiercely/ Focus on the fact that facts can be fabricated to form lies/ My **ph**onetics alone forces feeble MC's into defense on the fly/ **F**eel me, forreal-a

As a street linguist, Pharoahe knows that his phonetics alone will "force feeble MC's into defense on the fly." His linguistic sophistication ("skillz" in HHNL) is evident in this verse.

   The effective use of repetition and alliteration are often found in combination with complex rhymes. Rhyme is such an essential aspect of HHNL that one almost need not mention it, but we need a deeper exploration of Hip Hop poetics. Hip Hop Heads ("aficionados") are constantly evaluating rhymes, and what makes a perfect rhyme. Rapper Kurupt describes what makes a *dope* ("excellent") rhyme:

> Perfection of the rhymes. Like Perfection. Selection. Interjection. Election. Dedication. Creation. Domination. Devastation. World domination. Totally, with no Hesitation, you know what I mean? These are perfect rhymes . . . Really. Silly. Philly, you know. These are perfected rhymes. Where you could take a word like *we will* and you connect that with a full word like *rebuild*, you know what I mean? You got two words in *we will*. One word in *rebuild*. But perfect rhyme connection is the key to writing when you write your rhyme. And meaning too. When you're saying something that makes sense. Them are the keys to writing a rhyme. Perfect rhyme connection. And *style*.
>
> (Spady *et al.* 1999: 550)

A close examination of one verse from Talib Kweli on "The Truth" (1999) reveals multiple layers of complexity and creativity:

1 Ch<u>e</u>ck it, on my n<u>e</u>ck I still got marks from **the nooses**
2 The truth it **produces** fear that got niggaz on the run like Ca-**arl Lewis.**
3 **The truth is my crew is the smoothest** spittas of saliv<u>a</u> **juices** like **the roots is**
4 More organic than **acoustics**
5 H<u>ea</u>venly . . . s<u>e</u>t you free and kill you in the same br<u>ea</u>th
6 That shit you gotta g<u>e</u>t off your ch<u>e</u>st before your d<u>ea</u>th and r<u>e</u>st
7 The way you speak is lighter than a pamphlet
8 Cuz the truth give the words the weight of a <u>planet</u> god<u>dammit</u>
9 I <u>ran wit</u> what God <u>planted</u> in my heart and I under<u>stand</u> <u>it</u>
10 To be to **bring the light to the dark, breathe some life in this art**
11 This must be the truth ("why?") cuz we keep marchin on ("true")
12 The truth lay the foundation of what we rockin on ("true")

13 You can't see it if you blind but we will always prevail ("true")
14 Life is like the open sea, the truth is the wind in our sail
15 *And in the end*, our names is on the lips of *dying men*
16 If ever crushed in the earth, we always *rise again*
17 When the words of *lying men* sound lush like the sound of a *violin*
18 The truth is there, it's just the heart you gotta *find it in*

In examining Talib's *multirhyming* skillz (the ability to produce multilayered rhymes by employing multiple rhyme techniques synergistically), we'll begin with Line 1 where we see the beginning of a recurring assonance with the short /e/ vowel. This short /e/ is repeated several times in Lines 1, 5, and 6. Line 1 is also the starting point for a series of triple rhymes that follow the pattern: /a—oo—is/. In Line 3, we have a series of five triple rhymes, three of which are *back-to-back chain rhymes* (see Alim 2003 and Chapter 6). **Tha truth is** rhymes with **ma crew is**, **tha smoothest**, and **tha roots is**. These rhymes also match perfectly with two unexpected rhyme matches: (1) the last syllable in "saliva" and the word "juices,"—**a juices**, and (2) Talib splits the name "Carl" into two syllables, "Ca-arl" and uses the last syllable to continue the triple rhyme pattern with **Ca-arl Lewis**.

Talib continues with a series of feminine rhymes pairing up some unlikely suspects with: planet, goddammit, ran wit, planted, understand it. If you notice, all of these rhymes follow the pattern: a nasal (either n or m)—it. In Line 10, Talib blesses us with a rare sextuple rhyme as he describes his Hip Hop mission to be to: "bring the light to the dark, breathe some life in this art." This sextuple rhyme is accomplished by the use of parallel phrasing in which the poet matches up like categories across the parts of speech. For instance, the parts of speech in this rhyme flow like this: verb—modifier—noun—prep—modifier—noun. The sound pattern of the rhyme is near perfect: /br—reduced vowel—long-i—reduced vowel—th—ar/.

Lines 15 through 18 contain another set of triple rhymes that follow the pattern of: /long i—reduced vowel—in/. What makes this verse even more complex, as far as tonal semantics are concerned, is that Talib begins Line 15 with "And in the end," which serves multiple functions. Not only does this phrase refer to a final moment in history, "the end," but it is also cleverly signifies the beginning of the end of the verse. In addition to this, Talib says "in the end" in such a way as to almost prepare us for the triple rhymes that are to follow. The intonation is what glues this phrase to the triple rhyme series.

Talib also exhibits wordplay in Lines 4 and 5. "The truth is my crew is the smoothest spittas of saliva juices like the roots is more organic than acoustics." The Roots is a Hip Hop group from Philly who released an independent LP entitled *Organix* (1993). So, not only are roots considered organic in the dictionary definition of the word, but the phrase here is complimenting The Roots for their strong musical production. The word "organic" is also used here in a play on "organ" and "acoustics."

In Line 16, Talib references a famous line from *Battlefield*, a poem by William Cullen Bryant (1794–1878), which reads: "Truth crushed to earth shall rise again/ The eternal years of God are hers/ But Error, wounded, writhes with pain, And dies among his worshippers." The first line of this stanza has been utilized by many Black American religious leaders, including Minister Louis Farrakhan and Reverend Jesse Jackson, although the phrase is most associated with Rev. Dr. Martin Luther King. Talib has taken this line, and through semantic extension, refers to him and his crew (and by extension, his people). "If ever crushed in the earth, *we always rise again*." The collusion of "truth" with "we" brings the truth that much closer to heart.

Given all of this intricacy and poetic complexity, it is remarkable that the meaning of the verse is retained. Talib is giving us his understanding of "the truth," which, of course, means different things to different people. "The truth" to Talib is the pure unbridled power of Hip Hop. The beats, the rhymes, the content, the vibe. "The truth lay the foundation of what we rockin on." The truth will always remind one of one's own history (in this case, the days when Black Americans were lynched for the enjoyment of Whites—see *100 Years of Lynching* by Ralph Ginzburg, 1962), as well as protect one's own history (truth must be protected from the "words of lying men"). Talib uses the phrase "the truth" several times, invoking new meanings each time. And in classic Hip Hop call and response fashion, we see that the theme of "the truth" is reaffirmed by the clever and also classically Hip Hop affirmation—"True" (as sung by Talib's crew in Lines 11, 12, and 13).

Talib, by exploiting the use of tonal semantics and poetics, demonstrates the multilayered and multitextual complexity of HHNL. By employing talk-singing, repetition and alliterative wordplay, intonational contouring and extremely complex multirhyming, HHNL users have truly taken this Language Thang to newer heights and deeper depths of discursive activity.

While scholars usually turn to Rap lyrics, or perhaps music videos, to analyze the discourse of the Hip Hop community, few have turned to the Hip Hop conversational discourse of the very agents who create and recreate Hip Hop Culture—particularly those who display superior skill and staying power in a record industry that has always been *shady* ("ruthless and not trustworthy"). Spady (2001), writing on the link between Black American expressive culture and the dynamics of HHNL, provides an excellent analysis and theoretical frame for us to begin closely examining Hip Hop conversational discourse:

> A close examination of Kurupt's lyrical and musical *ouevre*, as well as his conversational narratives and overall communication practices reveal a highly sophisticated playa in the Hip Hop Nation Speech community. Kurupt's speech acts, witty, sardonic and satirical verbal exchanges, wordplay and play on words, ritualized speech and an assortment of distinct African American discourse markers single him out as a skilled member of

this speech community. Contrary to the popular myth perpetrated and perpetuated by critics of mass based black core culture, the Hip Hop Nation is not outside of the Black tradition. Kurupt and his confreres both maintain and expand that tradition in meaningful ways.

(Spady 2001: 18)

Contrary to the belief that Hip Hop artists lack the awareness and knowledge of the art form's cultural and linguistic foundations, Kurupt demonstrates his cognizance of Hip Hop's historical background in a memorable remark:

> I think Black Language is an essential part of Hip Hop—period. Hip Hop is a Black culture influenced art form of music . . . "EEEEEEEEEEE Tidleee Wop/ This is the Jock and I'm back on the scene/ With the record machine/ Sayin Ooh Bop Da Boo/ How do you do?" That's rap. Ahhh, man! My stepfather been hit me upside my head, "Boyyy, rap ain't new. People *been* rappin, *years ago*, son. Years ago!!! Jocko, he's one of the first rappers, son."

(Kurupt in Spady 2001: 18)

An extraordinary repertoire of speech devices and constructions (both verbal and nonverbal) is found in Kurupt's extensive conversational narrative in *Street Conscious Rap* (Spady *et al.* 1999). In our analysis of Kurupt's Hip Hop conversational discourse, we offer an evidential treatment of Spady's comments just quoted. His use of hyperbole, metaphor and simile, narrative style, and dialoguing others (doublevoicing or inserting other voices into the dialogue), the many features of tonal semantics and poetics—talk-singing, repetition, wordplay, freestylin (free rhyming), word creations, and word pictures—offer us deep insight into the complexity of Hip Hop conversational discourse. Kurupt's narratives also serve as metacommentary on several relatively unexplored Hip Hop discursive practices, such as *battlin* and *entering the cipher* (to be discussed later).

Kurupt masterfully uses metaphor, simile, and hyperbolic language to paint word pictures and animated verbal images that allow us to visualize what is being said. The more outrageous the description, the clearer the image. Kurupt's narrative strategies—dialoguing other voices, imitating referential voices, talk-singing, word explosions, kinesics, and strategic use of key summarizing statements that highlight main points—can be seen in this discursive passage. The passage (annotated for this discussion) begins with Kurupt responding to a question about whether he ever asked Tupac for advice on writing lyrics:

> I wasn't askin anything. I just sat around him, you know. Game [metaphor for knowledge of the music industry; also used for knowledge of other things such as women, business, sports, etc.] is learned from viewing rather than

questioning. Questioning, you take the person off their focus, meaning they don't go naturally, because they go and try to show something and that's not natural. But when you just let them go natural and you peep [observe], and you got to just *learn*. It's certain things to look at, man. You can tell when you see it. He's in there. He writes a song. He gets behind the booth. His energy splits the room in half! [metaphoric word picture; hyperbole] You feel like jumpin off the top of the roof [hyperbole] . . . You ain't feel it?! You know, when he's speakin, I mean, just, "RAAAH!" [word explosion] . . . You could have the greatest words in the world, but you must have the emotion and feeling that people can just walk down the street and feel that sound wave [motioning with his hands as if to make a tidal wave]. They're walkin and just—booosh! [word explosion; kinesics—tossing his body to the side, signaling the impact of the wave word explosion]. You're like, "What's that?" [dialoguing other voices] Next thing you know, you hear the song as they rollin by, "AAAH-AH-AAAH!" [word explosion] It's that energy—bam! [kinesics—slapping his hands together; word explosion] You're like, "Yo! What's goin on?!" [dialoguing other voices] "I'm gonna run it down/ Runnin clown!" [imitating referential voices—any member of the HHNSC would recognize DMX's lines by the vocal texture and timing Kurupt employs] The feeling strikes you and at that second is when you decide on whether it's a good song to you or whether it's not. [key summarizing statement] . . . But just like Master P, P is not the most poetical, the most lyrical, but he has *feeling* with music that smashes the board [hyperbole]. And so when the music is kickin—bam! [word explosion] "Oh, my goodness!" [dialoguing other voices] "I'm a No Limit Soldier/ That's what I told ya!" [imitating referential voices—using Master P's characteristic vowel lengthening and New Orleans phonology; kinesics—waving hands up and down]—boom, boom, boom, pshhh! [word explosions as referents to musical sounds in Master P's song]. Then you like, "Wow!" Then you hear his lyrics and it's, "Aww, he's alright." [dialoguing other voices] But then the delivery pulls you back in. You be like, "Woah! Okay!" Because you're startin to listen to things that he's sayin. Music is the first thing they catch. Then it is lyrics and delivery and the emotion for the situation. Then there's subject matter. Musical keys of making a hit: the music, the delivery and the lyrics that you spittin, and what you're talkin about, the subject matter. [key summarizing statement]

(Spady *et al.* 1999: 542–543)

Kurupt's use of metaphor and hyperbolic language in this passage is representative of the vast body of his Hip Hop conversational discourse. He does not merely describe Tupac as being energetic—rather, "his energy splits the room in half!" and makes one "feel like jumping off the top of the roof." In responding to a question about the changing demands made of him as an artist, he responds with a unique, witty series of metaphors and similes rooted in the oral tradition of Black American folklore:

You got to be hungry [eager, ambitious]. It's like seventy thousand other people, man, that's hungry as fifty five slaves with no food for seven years! [simile, hyperbole] . . . So, while you lolly-gaggin. See a penny, pick it up, "I don't need a penny." He'll sneak up right behind you, pickin up all the pennies, "I'll take it." Hungry! [word explosion]. And then come the next thing you know, he just zippin right by you! You're like the tortoise, "Do-dum-do-do." And this boy is like the hare, "Trrrrrrrrrrrrrr!" Gone! [word explosions; similes; word pictures] You know, you can't lapse. You have to treat everyday like it's the first day. [key summarizing statement].

(Spady *et al.* 1999: 543)

He continues to describe the industry as a "race" where one has to "*stay* hungry, *stay* wantin to smash the game" (aspectual *stay* in BL is an emphatic habitual that expresses the frequency or intensity of events and states, see Spears 2000), because if you don't, "it's seventy thousand people right behind you, man, that's on they way!" (Spady *et al.* 1999: 543).

Besides key summarizing statements, Kurupt, much like Black religious leaders, also uses repetition of key words to drive important points home. These next two passages are illustrative:

I have kids. I have things I have to take care of, *man*. That's what I'm talking about, about "out here" [California], teaching you how to be a **man**. To let you know that you're a **man** before anything, *man*. A **man**! A hardworking **man**, before anything. You see what I'm saying? And you can't do it sittin around, *man*." [notice the strategic and oft-repeated use of both **man** as a noun, and **man** as a discourse marker]

(Spady *et al.* 1999: 539)

We're all under the same situation that we been under from day one, even though it looked like we was havin a ball. **Pressure** comes in all forms. **Pressure**. Huge forms of **pressure**, small forms of **pressure**, you know. But it's all **pressure**, you know. Basically, **pressure** can push you to do things you don't want to do, say things you don't mean to say. **Pressure** can make you act out of character. **Pressure** can make you crumble, you know what I mean?

(Spady *et al.* 1999: 545)

As in the previous discussion of the use of repetition in Hip Hop lyrics, Kurupt often combines repetition with other forms of figurative language. In the conversation, he describes himself using metaphor: "I'm a arsonist on the mic. I make it burn!" In this next passage, Kurupt narrates how he connected with other rappers (Ras Kass, Canibus, and Killah Priest) to form a group called the Four Horsemen. Notice his use of figurative language as he depicts each member of the crew:

Well, me and Canibus and Ras, we've always been folks. And I told them, man, we're gonna make a group called the Four Horsemen. The Horsemen was one of the most dangerous, deadliest, out of the wrestling people. They didn't play no games. The Four Horsemen wreak havoc, you understand what I'm saying? So, that was a great thing to label ourselves after. We're the Horsemen in this Rap game. We're here to chop everybody heads off! You don't have no groups that's strictly for choppin heads off. Me and Canibus, we're strictly MC's that love to battle. We love to rhyme. Ras Kass is our connection with the West. That's my boy and Canibus' boy. And he's the assassin with the mic when it comes to the pen. We look at it like when a person want to freestyle, we got me. And I'm choppin every last one of their heads. Everyone! When it comes to the written, we got Canibus and we got Ras. They're written experts. And Killah Priest plays no games when it comes to assassinations on the mic. And he has a camp of assassins behind him and that's Killah Priest's situation in there. And that's Canibus' main nigga, you feel me? And Ras and Canny is my main niggas. So, Canibus felt like we need to bring Killah Priest into this to detonate all the rest of the fools, you know what I mean? Canibus and Ras and Killah Priest will decide which one of them is gon chop they heads off. Anybody freestyling, that's when I come into the picture. I'm the Headless Horseman, you know. We all got aliases.

(Spady *et al.* 1999: 551)

In this passage, Kurupt turns to his *freestylin* abilities. His explanation of a perfect rhyme (earlier in this section) demonstrated *freestylin* ("improvisational rhyming") or what Henderson (1973) called *virtuoso free-rhyming*. Henderson identifies several features found in Black Arts Movement poetry of the 1960s and 1970s that have correspondences in Rap lyrics. What Henderson described as *virtuoso free-rhyming* was usually in the context of a rhyme couplet, or where a rhyme served as a witty punch line. In HHNL, this witty free rhyming is expanded and exploited to create a new form called *freestylin*. In *freestylin*, one is expected to *sustain* witty and clever improvisational rhymes for extended periods of time (skilled freestylers can rhyme until they literally run out of breath). Kurupt, in describing his lyrical writing process, explains:

I think in freestyle, I'll kick a rhyme right now, you see what I'm saying? That's like my whole thing. That's where I get my rhymes from. I might freestyle and say something that I just think is so catty [cool]. So, then I just sit down and write the freestyle rhyme I said, but then I calculate it more, you see what I'm saying? I put more brain power to it when I just sit and write it because I can think more about how I can word it, you see what I'm saying?

(Spady *et al.* 1999: 538)

Kurupt claims that he not only freestyles, but he *thinks* in freestyle (Jay-Z and other Rappers claim to have never written a rhyme on paper in their lives). Adding support to his claim to a freestyle mode of thinking, he *busts* ("Raps") a spontaneous freestyle in the middle of conversation. The passage begins with him speaking: "That's where Philly and Darby Township kick in, you know. Rhyming against others and outlasting, and lasting through the wars, you know. That's the key to building up that confidence . . ." Then the freestyle begins dramatically: "Yo, check this out! I expose 575 flows, in the inkling of a second/ expecting to disassemble these in less than two verses/ I'm able to disengage mics and chew emcees up like Mike and Ikes when I recite/ Daylight's eclipsed/ I sink MC's like ships" (Spady *et al.* 1999: 550).

Clearly, Kurupt is a skilled user of language by any standard. Still unexplored are his word creations ("multimusical," describing someone who has a wide range of taste in music, a wide range of musical abilities, and the tendency to incorporate various musical forms into one), his unique phrasing (in describing his album, "I see it as being the East, West, North, and South. Upper East, upper West, upper North, upper South, downer East . . . [Laughter]"), and his varied and diverse discourse markers ("woo-woo-woo"—used to provide structure in Black American oral narratives, common in the West Coast, along with, "woompty-woomp-woomp" and "woopty-woo-woo"). It is important to note that while Kurupt is a highly skilled user of language, his Hip Hop conversational discourse shares many elements with that of JT the Bigga Figga, Sohoolly D, Beanie Sigel, Eve, Busta Rhymes, Mos Def, and other members of the HHN.

Narrative sequencing and flow

Narrative sequencing includes both ritualized story-telling and narrative speech as a frequently occurring genre in Black American discourse (Smitherman, 1977). Storytelling is highly valued in the HHN. In the 1980s and 1990s, Slick Rick dazzled Hip Hop Heads with humorous narratives (*The Great Adventures of Slick Rick*) that quite often concluded with a lesson for the listener. Skilled storytellers, such as Slick Rick, have influenced the next wave of Hip Hop artists, and they in turn influence the next wave—and the narrative torch is passed on. In a prime example of the HHN's love for the art of storytelling, and the passing of the narrative torch, Outkast (coming onto the scene waves after Slick Rick) produced "The Art of Storytelling (Part 1 and 2)" (1998). Recognizing Slick Rick as the baaadest ("best") storyteller, they joined him on his album *The Art of Storytelling* (1999) on the single, "Street Talkin." The last four lines of the song capture the point:

> Slick Rick and Outkast is on this jam
> Tryin to help raise all youth to men
> Slick the Ruler Rick his space to slam
> The reputation of this man.

Slick Rick's innovative, pioneering story raps have influenced many rappers. In a conversation with Raekwon, a member of the Wu-Tang Clan, he explains Rick's (and other rappers) influence on him, as well as how the narrative torch is passed down:

R: I'm from the 21st Century Rhymers . . . I grew up listening to Old School shit such as, you know, '89 and '90 with Kane and Slick Rick, Rakim. All of them niggas was doin it, you know. So, I'm like a replica of them, you know what I mean? And I'm a combination of them, as well as bein around my way in the projects, the [Wu-Tang] Clan . . . It's like, Rick is a storyteller to me. He know how to put words together to perfection. Kane was a hardcore lyricist, which Kane would keep it street, too. You got G Rap . . .
A: You said Slick Rick bein a storyteller. Do you see yourself that way, in that tradition?
R: Definitely, you know what I mean? Definitely. I know how to make vivid pictures come up from just experience and bein through a lot of shit. And like I said, bein able to watch some of the best do it, such as brothas like Slick Rick, Rakim and them, you know what I mean? I'm just them niggas in a younger generation, you know what I mean?

(Alim 2000, unpublished interview)

Smitherman (1977) states that narrative sequencing may be found in these forms: preaching and testifying; folk stories, tall tales, and Toasts. While all of these forms are present in today's Hip Hop lyrics, Rickford and Rickford (2000) point to Toasts as a way to understand the "wicked self-aggrandizement" found in Hip Hop. In Toasts, much like many Hip Hop lyrics, the hero is "fearless, defiant, openly rebellious, and full of braggadocio about his masculinity, sexuality, fighting ability, and general badness" (Smitherman 1977: 157). Rickford and Rickford (2000: 85) make the link: "Remember, no creation in the Spoken Soul universe emerges from a vacuum. LL Cool J . . . is as much a son of Rudy Ray Moore as he is of Muddy Waters."

On "How Many Licks" (2000), Lil Kim proves that she is also their daughter, puttin a sexual twist on the famous Tootsie Roll commercial. In one verse, she is all of what Smitherman describes in the previous paragraph and then some (but from a female perspective):

If you drivin in the street, hold on to your seat
Niggaz, grab your meat while I ride the beat
And if you see a shiny black Lamborghini fly by ya
Zooooooooooom! . . . that's me the Night Ridaaa
Dressed in all black with the gat in the lap
Lunatics in the street—gotta keep the heat
Sixty on the bezel, a hundred on the rings

Sittin pretty, baby, with a Cash Money bling
12 A.M., I'm on my way to the club
After three bottles I'll be ready to fuck
Some niggaz even put me on their grocery lists
Right next to the whip cream and box of chocolates
Designer pussy, my shit come in flavors
High class taste, niggaz got to spend paper
Lick it right the first time or you gotta do it over
Like it's rehearsal for a Tootsie commercial.

When Lil Kim says "while I ride the beat," she is talking about what is known as *flow* in HHNL. *Flow* relates directly to narrative sequencing because it impacts the telling of the story to a great degree. Flow can be defined generally as the relationship between the beats and the rhymes in time. In discussing the concept of flow with Raekwon, I asked him directly what he meant by flow, in order to develop an understanding from the artist's perspective. His definition provides useful insight:

Flow is like, *how* you say it. Flow is like poetry goin to the beat, but you makin it connect like a bridge, you know what I mean? It's like buildin a bridge with your rhymes [see *bridge rhymes* in Chapter 6]. You want to be able to let everybody know that, "Yo, I could rhyme like this, but off of this type a beat. But when it comes to another beat, I could switch it up," you know what I mean? And make it still flow, but just a different way of usin it, you know what I mean?

(Alim 2000, unpublished interview)

In discussing the relationship between Rap and poetry, Pharoahe Monch provides additional insight with his definition:

P: I mean, poetry is a awesome art form in itself. I dabble in it before I write some of the songs that I do. I try to be poetic with some of the songs. Hip Hop is based upon a mixture of that, but more writing musically. Points and timing, you know. So is poetry. But on a level where it's based upon the music, you have to be more rhythmatically connected with your listener and crowd, in terms of rhythm, you know. And *how* are you ridin that beat. You know, you could do the same thing with poetry without any music at all, you know what I'm saying? Get a response rhythmatically. So, I'm not disrespecting that. I'm just saying, Hip Hop, it's about where you are on that fourth bar, where you are on that first bar . . . You got to have flow, and I think that's something that just comes natural.
A: What exactly do you mean by that, by flow?
P: I mean, how the person rides the beat, you know. Some MC's ride the beat soulfully 100% like Slum Village, and they're funky with it. Some MC's go

against the grain of the beat, but they're so on point and you understand what they're doing, you know.

(Alim, 2000, unpublished interview)

Keyes (1984: 145) provided an interesting analysis, which needs updating (due to the pioneering nature of her work, rather than any shortcoming on her part): "In Rap music, the bass line functions as a time line. The rhythmic structure and the rhymed couplets weave around a two-bar melodic bass line . . . [The Rap is] superimposed on a four-beat bass melodic structure." The real challenge, as Keyes notes, is "synchronizing the rhyme couplets in a narrative form with the rhythmic pulse of the music" (p. 146).

The preceding accounts by Pharoahe and Raekwon indicate that a rapper need not always stay on the beat to have a good flow. The key is that there must be something recognizable in the pattern of one's timing, and it must be fresh and innovative to capture people's attention. Missy Elliot is skilled in rhyming off-beat, or "against the grain of the beat," and she sometimes describes her style as a "crazy flow." Superfast rhymers like Mystikal, E-40, Twista, Gift of Gab, and Pharoahe Monch are masters at alternating sequences where they are directly on beat, with stretches of rhymes where they may appear oblivious to the bass line. The remarkable thing is that they somehow land right back on the beat! A Hip Hop Head once described Method Man's rhyming talent as his ability to "dance all around the beat and decorate the beat with his rhymes."

Chuck D, in describing the relationship between Rap and poetry, touches on something very relevant to this discussion:

C: Poetry makes the beat come to *it*, and Rap pretty much is subservient to the beat.
A: What do you mean by that?
C: Well, you know, if you have a beat, you have to pretty much follow that beat in some kind of way. I think where you have the beginning of the meshing of the two (Rap and poetry) began with KRS-One, where they actually slowed the beat down to themselves. A poet would actually come around and do his or her particular thing and the beat had to ride to them.

(Alim 1999, unpublished interview)

Chuck's comments allow us to deduce that if rhythm is one's ability to stay on beat, then flow is one's ability to exploit the rhythm, rhyme around the rhythm, and yet be able to faithfully return to the rhythm on time.

Although it is extremely difficult to reproduce rhythm in print, Wood (1999) provides perhaps the most intricate analysis of the issue. While the analysis is preliminary, he bridges musicology and poetics in a way that is both refreshing and revealing. He states that "the primary rhythmic force of rap is to negotiate the varieties of possibilities set up by the sixteenth-note backbeat" (Wood 1999: 9). He explains: "The simplest place to start a phrase when rapping is on the

ONE of a four-beat measure, and the easiest place to drop the rhymes is on the TWO and the FOUR" (1999: 8). In this insightful piece, Wood goes on to demonstrate the differences between Chuck D, Snoop Dogg, and various other rhymers in the way they exploit the relationship between the rhymes and the beat—the *flow*.

Entering the cipha and battlin

> You think you all that, son?
> BRING IT TO THE CYPHER!
> You holdin down platinum?
> BRING IT TO THE CYPHER!
> You think you got props, son?
> BRING IT TO THE CYPHER!
> You livin Hip Hop, son?
> BRING IT TO THE CYPHER!

(Truck Turner and KRS-One 1999)

The Hip Hop cultural modes of discourse are at their peak in the communal and competitive *cipha* (sometimes spelled "cypher/cipha/cypha"). As noted in the introduction to this book, HHNL is both a communal and competitive discourse, with the cipher being the height of community and competition within the HHN. The cipher is where all (or some combination) of the Hip Hop cultural modes of discourse and discursive practices—call and response, multilayered totalizing expression, signifyin, bustin, tonal semantics, poetics, narrative sequencing, flow, metaphoric and hyperbolic language use, image-making, freestylin, battling, word-explosions, word-creations, word-pictures, dialoguing other voices, talk-singing, kinesics—converge into a fluid matrix of linguistic-cultural activity. The cipher is the height of linguistic creativity and is not for the faint of heart. Lyrical battling, which often occurs in the cipher, is a highly animated engagement where the Rap lyricist's skillz are sharpened and presented to a critical circle of Hip Hop conscious beings. When Truck Turner and KRS-One order their opponents to "bring it to the cypher," they are issuing the ultimate challenge.

Despite the centrality of the cipher to Hip Hop linguistic-cultural activity, this discursive speech event remains almost entirely unexplored by scholars. Rickford and Rickford (2000: 87) refer to the cipher as "the supercharged circuit of rap knowledge and creativity (something not dissimilar—in the vein of highly communal responsive rituals—to the ring shout)." Battlin in the cipher is also comparable to the competition among choirs in gospel music, "exchanges" in doo wop music, jam sessions in jazz music, and streetdancing (breakdancing) battles. The criteria in each one of these artistic endeavors are very high.

Addressing an audience at the University of Pennsylvania's conference on "Islam and the Globalization of Hip Hop," Peterson (2001) offers some insight:

The use of the term cipher in the Hip Hop vernacular is important. Ciphers are marvelous speech events. They are inviting and also very challenging. They have become a litmus test for modern day griots. Ciphers are the innovative formats for battles (the ritual of rhyming is informed by the physical arrangement of Hip Hop) . . . The concept of the cipher is essential to Hip Hop Culture and to its vernacular. It indicates an epistemology that is non-linear.

California's Ras Kass supports Peterson's definition of the competitive nature of the cipher and offers some further insight:

It's kinda like a training field, you know what I'm saying? It teaches you delivery, you know what I'm saying? You got to react under pressure, because it ain't even really fans in the cipher. I mean, everybody's a Hip Hop fan, but they ain't YO fan. They a fan of themselves. So, you spittin! It's gladiators! It's jousting. I call it jousting. Joust from the mouth. So, you know what I'm saying, it's a necessity.

(Alim 2000, unpublished interview)

The cipha is seen as a linguistic training field for MC's. Several skillz are developed in the cipha—Rap delivery, reacting under pressure, verbal battling, or "jousting from the mouth." The cipha is like Hip Hop's classroom, where one studies to learn the tricks of the trade, so to speak. Raekwon alludes to the pedagogical nature of this discursive speech event and highlights the communal aspect:

You know, it's everybody enlightenin they skills with the next person, and you know, you learn off of the best, you know what I mean? It's like training. It's like basic training. It's like, sparrin, you know what I mean? So, you know, that makes a better MC, bein able to know that he can express hisself amongst people that can teach him as well as he teach them. Everybody's teachin each other, you know, because they say experience the best teacher. So, when people listen to famous artists . . . they acquire what they learn from them and what they got, and they put it together, and that makes them a better person. It's like, its' like how you got Reverends out there right now that's a replica of Martin Luther King, you know what I mean? They got the same goals, the same ways of thinkin as that man. And, you know, that's all a part of being able to be a great man, is to be able to learn from the best, you know.

(Alim 2000, unpublished interview)

Whereas Raekwon highlights the communal and pedagogical nature of the cipha (see Newman 2001), others speak about the intensely competitive nature of some Hip Hop ciphas. Kurupt discusses the importance of the cipha as a pivotal stage of development for an MC. His experience is one of fierce competition and verbal battling, where each MC is at war with the members of the cipha. The MC's are required to *spit* freestyle rhymes that will lead them directly to their next opponent, and the MC who outlasts everyone in the cipha, emerges victorious. Kurupt's story is especially interesting due to the fact that he battled Snoop Dogg in the early stages of his career. Due to his impressive performance in the battle cipher, they became recording industry partners. Kurupt explains how he and Snoop formed their relationship on the West Coast:

> We both bust freestyles . . . At this club called the Roxy. We was just bustin with each other and all that and we was against each other at first. It's like our freestyles was so tight, you know what I mean, that he was bustin in his rhyme. He was like, you know, "We ain't gettin paid for this. If you tight, then I'm tight. Why don't we just bust together, you know what I'm saying? Let's kick some rhymes."
>
> (Spady *et al.* 1999: 536)

Kurupt explains that he learned his battlin and freestyle skills as a youngster in the East Coast ciphas of Philly. He begins his narrative about his early days in the cipha with the classic Hip Hop frame, "back in the day":

> Back in the day, I was like thirteen. A circle of ten or twelve people, ages of like thirteen and below, one might have been twenty, twenty one. And when it came down to the last two [rhymers], I was always there. And I've always been number one. Always. I never lost them type battles. You bust and it's like you don't say the next person's name, and you're out of there. I've always been in there. I just sit back and bust rhymes and I used to spell things on people's shirts. Like he'd have a shirt that says "Walk" on it. I'd break it down like the "W" is for this, the "A" is for that, the "L" is for this, and the "K" is for that. And they be like, "What?!" That's my style. Nobody else was doing that. That's something I created . . . Like, he could have a soda can, "Pepsi." Once, I spelled Pepsi for this nigga. The "P" is for punctuating rhymes and woo-woo-woo. "E" is for executing. And they're like, "God!" And I'm like what—thirteen, fourteen. C'mon now. They called me "The Kid." That was my rappin name because I was the youngest nigga that would always make it into the cipher.
>
> (Spady *et al.* 1999: 539)

What stands out so strongly in this reflective narrative on the cipha experience is the fierce intensity and the desire to be number one. HHNL is an extremely competitive discourse space. As John Wideman (1976: 34) noted:

> What's fascinating to me about African American speech is its spontaneity, the requirement that you not only have a repertoire of vocabulary or

syntactic devices/constructions, but you come prepared to do something in an attempt to meet the person on a level that both uses the language, mocks the language, and recreates the language.

The Rapper must come prepared to *do something* with this language. Kurupt describes the rules and rituals of this practice in Philly (as they varied in different cities). In his experience, the rhymer had to name the next person entering the cipher, which required the participants to always be on alert. Even those who are not called on are interacting with the rhymers by providing critical feedback, approval or rejection (see Jooyoung Lee's (2005) study of freestyle battlin in Los Angeles and Woods (2005)). Kurupt's language game of picking apart the words on other rhymers' articles of clothing demonstrates his creativity and inventiveness—"That's something I created." A deep sense of pride is communicated with regard to one's witty, inventive use of language and ability to outlast others in this linguistic competition.

As Rickford and Rickford (2000) suggested, the cipher has roots deep in the Black American and African Oral Tradition. Smitherman (1977: 82) cites H. Rap Brown's (Black leader in the 1960s and Muslim Imam today) experience with the dozens, which is remarkably similar to Kurupt's description above:

> what you try to do is totally destroy somebody else with words. It's the whole competition thing again, fighting each other. There'd be some 40 or 50 dudes standing around and the winner was determined by the way they responded to what was said. If you fell all over each other laughing, then you knew you'd scored.

Recently, Sonia Sanchez, Black Arts Movement poet—professor of the 1960s and 1970s (and still rappin strong today), was a participant in a Hip Hop cipher on June 23, 1999 in Philadelphia to celebrate Hip Hop Week. The cipher was led by Xzulu, formerly the prime time DJ of Philly's major Hip Hop station and producer of a nightly freestyle competition called "The Ultimate Cipher Challenge." About 50 or 60 people were involved in the cipha, along with two DJ's and various graffiti artists. The competition was fierce. MC's would take the mic and bust a freestyle rhyme while others evaluated their performance with shouts, hand clapping, and other affirmations. Some MC's stood back with their heads cocked to one side and one eyebrow raised as if to say, "That's all you got?" Others walked right up to the rhymer and faced directly in the opposite direction with the coolest, most disinterested look on their face—only to snatch the mic and rip their own freestyle! These facial expressions and acts of indirection are common in the cipher. You want to evaluate the other rhymer while maintaining a cool, calm, and confident exterior that lets the present rhymer know, "You got competition!"

In the heat of the moment, Sonia Sanchez entered the cipher and dropped a lyrical bomb on all those in attendance. With many Hip Hop artists on the scene like Parry P, Lady B, Da Fat Cat Clique, Legacy, Ehsan Jackson, and Supreem Da Regulata, Sonia stepped up and roc'd the mic right (*yeahhh*)! She described what moved her to do so:

> Well, I heard everyone before I got up in that circle. And, initially, I stood and watched it. And I watched not only the energy, but I watched the respect that people had for each other. And then I watched the young Brothas and Sistas, you know, rappin . . . And it reminded me a great deal of when we also got up on the stages . . . You could not go up and go [making a weak attempt] . . . you had to hold your own. And so when I see those young Sistas holdin their own, you know, I smiiile . . . It was not an alien circle. It was like, as I said, I belong there . . . We used to go out a lot in California. We used to go with Ed Bullins and Baraka and Marvin X and Sarah Fabio. We used to go out and do our poetry and our plays in the streets of Oakland.
>
> (Alim 2000: 21)

As Sonia Sanchez makes clear, the cipha is not alien to Black communicative and discursive practices. It is important to note, however, that while the cipher and other Hip Hop discursive practices are most certainly tradition-linked, they are not tradition-bound. What I mean by that is, HHNL is rooted in the Black American Oral Tradition, but also extends and expands that tradition in multiple ways to include new forms and styles of discourse. HHNL will continue to evolve and take it to "da next level."

Black Language Space, the power of the word, and the Hip Hop Nation Speech Community

HHNL exists within a Black Language Space (BLS)—a discursive space where Black Language is the culturally dominant language variety, and the power of the word is the overriding force of attraction. The Hip Hop Nation Speech Community (HHNSC) is driven culturally and linguistically by young Black males and females who are adept at language use in the Hip Hop-saturated streets of America. But who comprises the HHNSC? Hymes (1974) informs us that:

> Membership in a speech community consists of sharing one or more of its ways of speaking—that is, not in knowledge of a speech style (or any other purely linguistic entity, such as language) alone, but in terms of knowledge as well as appropriate use. There are rules of use without which rules of syntax are useless.

Membership in the HHNSC, then, hinges on having knowledge of HHNL and Hip Hop cultural modes of discourse.

This definition is suitable for defining the HHNSC because it is as catholic as the HHN's philosophy of race, ethnicity, and culture. Norfleet (1997), Cutler

(1999) and Newman (2001) have demonstrated the HHN's strong anti-racist ideology—this ideology has lead to the development of a multiracial, multiethnic, and multicultural speech community. Due to Hip Hop Culture's overwhelming influence on popular culture in America and the world, HHNL is influencing the far corners of the globe, creating what is perhaps the *illest* global speech community. Certainly there are differences in speech communities from city to city (and sometimes block to block), but the unifying elements of the HHNSC deserve attention. Spady (1994: 26) touches on this topic: "The Philly Hip Hop Language of Schooly D is preeminently modern [spreading beyond localized boundaries]. It shares common elements with Ice Cube, Snoop Doggy Dogg, Kool Keith, Ice T, Chuck D and Scarface," Rappers from various regions in the US.

Black Language Space (BLS)

Members of the HHN often refer to themselves as speakers of a common language. Ice Cube considers this notion, and roots this common language in the historical plight of Africans in America:

> Four hundred years ago, when black slaves were brought to America, Africans who spoke the same language were separated from each other. What we're seeing today, with this insane campaign to intimidate rappers and rap music, is just another form of separating people that speak a common language.
>
> (Ice Cube June 25, 1990; cited in Sexton 1995)

The common elements that unite people who "speak a common language" have been described earlier. But given the high value placed on individuality and originality in HHNL, the HHN, speakers of the many regional HHNLV (HHNL Varieties), are constantly shaping and reshaping existing language norms. These language norms exist and evolve in what we have termed a Black Language Space (BLS). It is the existence of a BLS that enables HHNL to come to life in full effect. By BLS, we mean a discursive space where Black Language is the prestige variety, where Black linguistic and communicative norms are the standard, where one cannot engage in meaningful conversation unless they are fully equipped to handle linguistic combat and competition. One has to come prepared to do battle, to hold their own, to enable the free flow of conversation. This is a space where language is the central focus, and the key element to maintaining and sustaining dialogue, as well as the primary site of authentication (Bucholtz 2003).

Spady's hiphopographic (1991) studies in the Umum Hip Hop Trilogy (*Nation Conscious Rap* (1991), *Twisted Tales in the Hip Hop Streets of Philly* (1995), and *Street Conscious Rap* (1999)) offer a key source of primary data in considering the concept of a Black Language Space. Several recent unpublished interviews will demonstrate how Spady, as an interlocutor who is fully conversant with HHNL, creates a BLS with a central focus on enabling the narrative. First, we hear from South Philly's Beanie Sigel, as he recounts the story of how he and Black Thought (from The Roots) used to be in the same grade school class:

S: Who was that 4th grade teacher who used to be tellin you and Tariq [Black Thought] to stop talkin in the back of the class?

B: Hah. Hah. Hah. [Beanie just laughin, as a challenge]

S: Who was that, man? Were you talkin or were you rhymin?

B: Tariq, he used to be in ah . . .

S: What elementary school was that?

B: Ah man!

S: You don't remember it. You've forgotten it. [Returning the challenge]

B: Wow! What was her name?

S: You remember her don't you? [Pushing the interlocutor to remember]

B: Wow. McDaniel School. Me and Tariq was in that school.

S: Were y'all writin rhymes in her class or what?

B: Yeah actually.

S: She said y'all were disturbing her class. [He-said, she-said talk, reporting what others have said]

B: All the time. Actually. See, what it was, Tariq . . .

S: On the real now. [Again, challenging, and enabling the truth]

B: On the real. Tariq was in a higher grade than me. He was one grade in front of me. [Recognizing the challenge to the truth]

S: He wasn't even called Black Thought at that time?

B: Nah. He was just Tariq. He was in my sista's class. They was in the 4th grade and I was in the 3rd grade.

S: You used to go to their room all the time.

B: I used to go to they fourth grade reading.

S: Oh. Reading?

B: I used to go fourth grade to read cause I was in a higher level than the kids in the third grade.

S: They were too slow for you? [Affirming and commenting on the narrative]

B: Ah. Ah. Well yeah. And that was all through elementary. When I was in kindergarten I used to go first grade and read. When I was in the first grade I used to go in the 2nd grade reading class. So that's how I was always in class with Tariq. And we used to be in the back just rappin, repeatin old Sugar Hill Gang Records and all that . . .

(Spady 2001, unpublished interview)

What one does not see from the printed page is the rapid spit-fire rate of some of these exchanges. The story unfolds in a fluid interactive space where the interlocutors fully expect what some might view as "interruptions." Spady is constantly commenting on the narrative and challenging the speaker. He is also freely using terms and phrases rooted in HHNL, and Black Language in general, such as "on the real now," which highlights the listener's desire for *real talk* ("talk that is both factual and sincere"). The result is a previously unheard narrative about how Beanie Sigel and Black Thought used to rhyme and rap together in grade school.

The following sequence between Spady and Oakland's Saafir exhibits how both interlocutors are highly competitive. Throughout the conversation, they have been discussing Saafir's days as a young buck ("adolescent") growin up in "the town":

S: Lookin back on school, man, are there any particular teachers that you can recall . . .
SA: Hell, naw! Hell, naw!
S: C'mon, man! I didn't finish the question yet . . .
SA: Hell, naw! Hell, naw!
S: Get outta here, man?!
SA: Hell, naw! No teachers. None.
S: Why was school a turn off for you, man?
SA: School wasn't a turn off. I love to learn, but the teachers is assholes. A lot of the teachers bring a lot of their personal attributes to the fuckin classroom, you know what I mean?
S: What do you mean by bringing their personal attributes?
SA: As far as their emotional problems and the ills they're havin at their house, you know what I mean? They take the shit out on the kids and fuck the kids on a certain level, psychologically fuck them up, you know what I mean? Depending on the caliber of teacher. I have experienced some fucked up ones, but I ain't mad at them, you know what I'm saying? In actuality, it made me understand them and the people around them a lot more.

(Spady 2000, unpublished interview)

We can see that Saafir anticipates Spady's question and immediately cuts him off with, "Hell naw! Hell naw!" Spady, also fiercely competitive, responds, "C'mon, man! I didn't finish the question yet . . ." Again Saafir cuts him off, "Hell naw! Hell naw!" Spady replies with "Get outta here, man?!" [said in a manner to mean something like, "Are you serious, man?"] These exchanges occur so quickly that they are difficult to separate line-by-line, as the speakers are speaking over and under each other. This creates a BLS where Saafir is then freed up to testify about his school experiences, which obviously still hold a lot of painful memories for him.

Spady's knowledge of HHNL and Black communication in general allows him to gain great insight from his interlocutors. In the following interaction, Spady's knowledge of the Black Oral Tradition (specifically Black DJ's and Jocko

Henderson, who produced *The Rocketship* six months before Sugar Hill Gang's release is key). Kurupt, who grew up in Philadelphia, is the interlocutor:

K: I think Black Language is an essential part of Hip Hop—period. Hip Hop is a Black culture influenced art form of music.

S: So the discussion about Ebonics and other Black Language expressions was not new to you when it became a hot issue in 1997–98? I guess you'd always known Ebonics.

K: Since the 70's. The 40's. The 30's and the 20's. Jock! [Referring to famous Black DJ of the 1960s and 1970s, Jocko Henderson, and even further back in history]

S: Jocko, Jocko? [Recognition of the reference to Jocko by repeating the introduction to one of his raps, "Jocko, Jocko"]

K: "EEEEEEEEEEE Tidleee Wop/ This is the Jock and I'm back on the scene . . ." [Spontaneous break into Jocko's rap]

S: With the record machine. [Finishing Kurupt's Jocko rendition]

K: Saying Ooh Bop Da Boo. [Continuing the Rap]

S and K: How do you do? [Said at the same time, completing the Rap]

S: How do you know that shit man? [Said In Black American falsetto, characteristic of Black male speech (Alim 2004a)]

K: Heyyyyyyyyyyyyyy!!! [Elongated "hey," to confidently express his knowledge of tho rap] No, please believe it, man [Common phrase heard particularly in the Bay Area, California] I'm from Philadelphia. [Cementing himself in the place where Jocko's raps are best known, establishing authenticity] Listen to that: "E Tiddlee Wop. This is the Jock and I'm back on the scene with the record machine. Saying Ooh Bop Do Boo. How do you do?" That's rap. Ahhh, man! My stepfather been hit me upside my head, "Boyyy, rap ain't new. People *been* rappin, *years ago*, son. Years ago!!! Jocko, he's one of the first rappers, son." Ah Hah Hah! [Kurupt laughs].

S: So you knew rap was within the Black tradition?

K: Oh, Fo Sho. (Said slowly for emphasis in that hip, urbane North Philly way).

S: From the Get-Go, right? ["Get-Go", Black term meaning from the very beginning]

K: Oh, Fo Sho. [Meaning, "for sure," "certainly." Associated largely with California, though used elsewhere. Similar to the phrase associated with the East Coast, "No doubt."]

(Spady 2001, unpublished interview)

Needless to say, the narrative would have taken a completely different turn (or maybe would not have even been expressed at all) if Spady did not recognize what Kurupt meant by "Jock!" The spontaneous break into Rap opens up the discursive BLS and allows the interlocutor to know that he is speaking to someone who is conversant with these language practices. Too often, members of the HHNSC are depicted as being unable to communicate. For example, many hold the belief that members of the HHNSC cannot express their thoughts through language (which should be clearly seen as erroneous by now). Sentiments I have often heard, in reference to this speech community, are, "They can't put two sentences together when they are talking," or, "They can't say two words without cursing" (see Spears 1998, for a discussion of *uncensored mode*). As Spady (2001: 18) writes: "Many people who interview Kurupt and/or comment upon his work in or out of the Dogg Pound, are simply not prepared as worthy interlocutors. Black American expressive and competitive behavior is very complex." Kurupt expresses his views on the challenge of rappin in Philadelphia:

> It's just so much talent around that you really have to concentrate on your skills. We're a perfectionist city . . . It's the word-connection. It's the type of words that either artist choose to use. It's the way you put those words together.
>
> (Spady 2001, unpublished interview)

In a Black Language Space, the word is the overriding force of attraction. HHNL is rooted, philosophically and ideologically, in the power of the word, or *Nommo*. As Smitherman (1994: 7–8) writes:

> The African American oral tradition is rooted in a belief in the power of the Word. The African concept of *Nommo*, the Word, is believed to be the force of life itself. To speak is to make something come into being. Once something is given the force of speech, it is binding—hence the familiar saying "Yo word is yo bond," which in today's Hip Hop Culture has become WORD IS BORN. The Hip Hop expressions WORD, WORD UP, WORD TO THE MOTHER, and similar phrases all stem from the value placed on speech. Creative, highly verbal talkers are valued.

The force of speech is expressed poetically by Mos Def in "Hip Hop" (1999), as if co-signing and bearing witness to the truth in Smitherman's statement. In one of the most oft-quoted opening lines of Hip Hop, he begins: "Speech is my hammer bang the world into shape now let it fall—HUH!" When asked directly about the genesis of this line, Mos explains:

A: You say in "Hip Hop," "Speech is my hammer bang the world into shape."
M: That's just something that came to me. It's my relationship to the way I'm using language in Hip Hop. You do build your world with language to a large degree. You build your world with what you say. Affirmations. "I'm gonna do this." "Things are gonna change." Then you start to act out those things. If you tell your children that you love them and that they're special to you,

then they start to feel that way about themselves and they start to treat themselves that way. If you tell your children the opposite of that, then they start to live that out.

(Alim 2001, unpublished interview)

Speech here is an agent of change. What does it mean to build your world with language? Linguistic anthropologists, much like Hip Hop artists have theorized, understand that we construct our realities, identities, and social worlds through language (Duranti 1997, 2004). The power of the word, of speech, is mos def ("most definitely") a driving force in HHNL. Many artists believe that their words have the power to change not only their lives, but the lives of members of their community as well. When Tupac joined Scarface on the memorable collaboration "Smile for Me Now" (2001), in which they lovingly expressed and assuaged the struggle of Black people in America—realizing that "through all the pain" you *got* to smile to remain sane in an insane world. Near the end of the song, Tupac speaks on the power of the word with a brief one-liner, "Embrace my words, make the world change."

Raekwon, in describing the power of the Rap, provides an added perspective on the phrase "word is life" (or "word life"):

R: We talk about things that involve life. Meaning that, we got joints that attack emotional spirits, you know what I mean? Meaning that, if we talk about—how could I say it?—if we talk about the streets or whatever showin you how shit be goin down in the streets, that's only one side of it, you know what I mean? Then we talk about emotional shit that make you want to cry, that make you flash back to your family, that make you go check out your moms and be like, you know, "We probably goin through some rough shit, mom, but you know how I feel about you." It's like, we make songs to be able to make you think about what's goin on in your life.

A: That's powerful shit right there.

R: Yeah, and that's what makes a great MC.

(Alim 2001, unpublished interview)

In Raekwon's moving testimony, we also see a spiritual dimension to the word, and to the power of the Rap. As more and more Black Americans continue to accept Islam, *Nommo* is being expressed through that spiritual experience. As we saw in Chapter 2, Mos Def made a link between the power of the word/rhyme and the way that the *Holy Qur'an* was written. Rapper JT the Bigga Figga also made links between the way Rappers use metaphoric language and rhyme to "the way Allah be teachin us in the *Qur'an*."

Black religious leaders have long understood the power of the word. In this example, Nation of Islam leader, Minister Louis Farrakhan (perceived by many as the HHN's primary teacher, and he would add, student), placed the power of the word in a uniquely spiritual context as he addressed the Hip Hop Summit in New York City on June 13, 2001 (see also Spady, Alim and Meghelli, forthcoming):

> I am a spiritual man so I have to speak to you from the Books (Bible and Qur'an). You may not think that I am too hip, but, when you hear from the Books who you are, why you are called, and, what your mission is that you have just begun to see, then, you will know that the Prophets of Allah (God) who saw all the way to the judgement and to the end of the present world, had to have seen hip-hop. You will not find the words "hip-hop" necessarily in the Bible or in the Qur'an, but, you are there in a very big way . . . In the countries where governments do not like western music or western civilization, people are sneaking around listening to the word and moving to the beat of the hip-hop generation. If in the beginning was the Word and the Word was with God and the Word was God, then, God here means Force and Power. The Word has Force. The Word has Power; Force and Power to move men to think new thoughts and to do new things.
>
> (Minister Louis Farrakhan 2001)

What I have attempted to do in this chapter is to demonstrate the creativity and complexity of language use in contemporary Black American expressive culture, particularly HHNL, language use in the HHNSC, and the Hip Hop cultural modes of discourse. In the next chapter, we take a more in-depth look at one particular aspect of HHNL, the Rapper's ability to styleshift and forge connections with the audience through language. Chapter 6 also takes a more in-depth look at an aspect of HHNL, that of Hip Hop poetics.

Chapter 5

Spittin the Code of the Streets

The strategic construction of a street-conscious identity

When Hip Hop artist Guru rapped about Black street speech—what he called "the code of the streets"—he did so with outright defiance to a standard language ideology that stifles those without access to formal education. His rhymes, as it has been said of all Rap lyrics, constituted more than just a resistance discourse; they created a context where issues of identity and in-group solidarity took center-stage (Spady *et al.* 1991). Guru fiercely rapped that he was never afraid to "let loose his speech," because his "brothas" knew that he *spit* ("rapped") the code of the streets. In this proclamation—as with the lyrics of many socially conscious Hip Hop artists (Smitherman 2006)—we witness Guru's attempt to resist the dominant culture with words—but he ain't gon do it alone. He and his *brothas* are rappin in a code of communication that reflects both the ideational and material aspects of what has come to be known as Hip Hop Culture. As we just read in the previous chapter, *spittin* ("speakin, rhymin") the code of the streets is essential to the notion of a Hip Hop Nation (HHN).

Stylistic variation in Black Language

The "variationist paradigm" focuses on the statistical analysis and comparison of the distribution and relative frequencies of linguistic variables. Sociolinguistic researchers have outlined three major domains of linguistic variation: linguistic, social, and stylistic (Labov 1972a, Bell 1984, Rickford and McNair-Knox 1994). Much attention has been given to interspeaker variation ("social" factors include class, age, social networks) and systematic variation within a system ("linguistic" factors include phonology, morphology, syntax). In addition, sociolinguists are beginning to pay attention to the way an individual speaker's speech varies across situations ("stylistic" factors include race, familiarity, setting, topic; see Eckert and Rickford 2001) and have discovered that some speakers, as we saw with Sunnyside's Bilal in Chapter 3, exhibit a remarkable range of styleshifting.

Early studies of BL (Labov *et al.* 1968, Wolfram 1969, Fasold 1972) utilized the quantitative methodology of variation theory to present the systematicity of BL, that is, to prove statistically that BL was rule-governed in nature and not a "random" set of "errors" based on "White English." These studies also demonstrated the relationship between linguistic variables and social class: BL features tended to appear more frequently in the speech of working-class Black Americans.

The development of a sociolinguistic theory of stylistic variation begins with Labov's (1966, 1972b) isolation of contextual styles, a unidimensional approach focusing on "attention paid to speech" as the main factor influencing speaker style. While Labov's analysis has been criticized for being unidimensional, it is useful here as an introduction to the early work on stylistic variation. Labov was working in a time period when most linguists ignored stylistic variation. Furthermore, they considered the techniques of linguistics inadequate to handle stylistic variation, although they knew it was occurring. Labov's aim was to develop a methodology sufficient to measure the extent of regularity in stylistic variation.

Labov studied five linguistic variables as they appeared in five different contextual styles:

Context A: casual speech
Context B: the interview situation (careful speech)
Context C: reading style
Context D: word lists
Context D':   minimal pairs (i.e. words that have a single differentiating element, e.g., "singer" and "finger")

These contexts are listed in order of increasing formality, with "casual speech" being the least formal and "minimal pairs" being the most formal. The (in)formality of the context is based on the amount of attention paid to speech. Labov believed that speakers paid little or no attention to their own speech when engaged in casual speech, and increasingly more attention to speech as they moved down the list. His studies revealed that, indeed, most speakers used more "nonstandard" or stigmatized forms in their casual speech, and that these forms decreased in the same person's speech as they engaged in the more formal situations. Importantly, Labov's isolation of contextual styles demonstrated that stylistic variation is context-based and follows a certain amount of regularity. However, Labov was aware that the results he obtained might have been artifacts of the procedure, and several scholars have since built upon his unidimensional approach to variation.

Building upon the work of Labov, Baugh's (1979, 1983) study of what he labeled "Black street speech" was a quantitative variation study of language in *situational* contexts. Baugh, a member of the Black American Speech Community, witnessed in his childhood what he would later come to describe as the "chameleon" quality of Black speakers. He was describing the ability to shift through a range of speech styles—as he often saw his mother do on the telephone. (He was able to discern the race of the speaker to whom his mother was talking by "analyzing" her speech style.) Thus, rather than controlling for the language content and context of the linguistic interview, Baugh's research led him straight "to the people" in all types of social circumstances. He was attempting to tackle the daunting task of obtaining the casual speech of his informants in various settings. Word lists and minimal pairs were abandoned for "ethnosensitive" interviews in an attempt to describe the informant's speech in various social contexts. Baugh recognized this work as tedious, from an analytical point of view, but felt that it was "the responsibility of black scholars to establish the standards for this kind of research" (1983: 25).

In establishing the standards, Baugh developed a grid for the analysis of speech in four different situational contexts (see Figure 5.1). Two key factors came into play: whether or not the speakers were familiar with each other, and whether or not the speakers were members of the Black street culture. Baugh outlined the four types of speech events:

Familiar (Frequent Contact)	Unfamiliar (Occasional Contact)	
TYPE 1 Familiar Exchange	TYPE 2 Intracommunity Contact	Members of Black street culture
TYPE 3 Intercommunity Exchange	TYPE 4 Outsider Contact	Outsiders to Black street culture

Figure 5.1 Baugh's speech event subdivisions

TYPE 1: Depicts speech events that have familiar participants, all of whom are natives of the Black vernacular culture. They also share long-term relationships, which tend to be close-knit and self-supporting.

TYPE 2: Represents speech events where participants are not well acquainted but are members of the Black vernacular culture.

TYPE 3: Indicates speech events where participants are well acquainted but Black street speech is not shared; solidarity may or may not exist between any two or more individuals.

TYPE 4: Corresponds to speech events where participants are not familiar nor is Black street speech common to all.

Baugh had originally expected race to be the major factor in influencing the styleshifting of Black Americans, but his results were far more complicated than that. For example, he noted that the frequency of contact between individuals (familiarity) also played a key role.

Rickford and McNair-Knox (1994) built upon Baugh's work on styleshifting in the Black American community. They examined two interviews with the same 18-year-old Black American female informant, one done by a 41-year-old Black American woman with whom the informant was familiar, and the other by a 25-year-old White American woman with whom she was unfamiliar. They also discovered that race and familiarity were important variables (although they could not distinguish between the two since the variables were conflated).

Conscious stylistic variation

The present study, while drawing upon variationist methodology, explores variation in BL with the additional perspective of linguistic anthropology, which views language as cultural practice and as a tool for constructing one's identity. This chapter challenges sociolinguists (particularly scholars of BL) to go beyond the mere quantifying of linguistic variables and to problematize the perceived passivity of linguistic variation and change. Speaker agency, the conscious and strategic use of language, as others have argued (see Rampton 1999), must be considered when discussing these processes. At the same time, linguistic anthropologists are urged to embrace quantitative analysis, which would add tremendously to their already rich descriptions. The complexity of the Black American linguistic situation demands a multidisciplinary approach.

In the remainder of this chapter, I will present an analysis of the conscious stylistic variation in the language of Black American Hip Hop artists. Recognizing the high degree of linguistic creativity present in the HHN, this research demonstrates how Black American youth (like the youngens in them Sunnyside streets in Chapter 3) possess extraordinary linguistic capabilities that make high school English classes seem *hella* boring. Specifically, this chapter focuses on Hip Hop artists' strategic construction of a street-conscious identity through language. By consciously varying their language use, these Rappers are forging a linguistic-cultural connection with the streets (meaning both members of the Black street culture and the sets of values, morals, and cultural aesthetics that govern life in the streets—peep the Geto Boys' "G-Code," *The Foundation*).

This study presents an analysis of two artists' lyrics *and* conversational speech (or as close to natural conversation as one can achieve). The natural conversation data comes from interviews conducted by the author, as well as those found in a Hip Hop publication that utilizies the interview format exclusively. Although this research is interesting on comparative grounds alone, it also raises some important questions: How much do we know about the conscious control of grammatical features in language use? If there is conscious control of certain features, how does this control serve the speaker? These questions address the strategic nature of language use and tell us about the personal investment speakers have in the construction of their linguistic identities.

The sociocultural context of Hip Hop

Sociolinguists have always been interested in analyzing language and language use within varying contexts. Given sociolinguistics' healthy respect for vernacular languages, and given the richly varied and diverse speech acts and communicative practices of the HHN, language use in this community can provide a rich source of data for sociolinguistic studies.

My research on Hip Hop Nation Language (HHNL) has examined language use within this community in the sociocultural context of the streets. As a member of the Black History Museum research team in Philadelphia, we have conducted hundreds of tape-recorded ethnographic interviews with Hip Hop artists from around the world (Spady and Eure 1991, Spady et al. 1995, Spady et al. 1999, Spady et al. forthcoming). Our goals were manifold. Among them, we set out to investigate the cultural and aesthetic values that govern the Hip Hop World, and to examine the linguistic-cultural practices of this diverse community. In the volumes that have resulted from this study, particularly Spady et al. (1999), we have documented that the street is the site, soul, sound, and center of the Hip Hop Culture-World.

The street, as you recall from the previous chapter, is the locus of the linguistic-cultural activity known as Hip Hop. Hip Hop Culture not only began in the streets of Black America, but the streets continue to be a driving force in contemporary Hip Hop Culture. Legendary Hip Hop producer, Marley Marl, explains what it means to be "street-conscious" in a Hip Hop-saturated world:

> I got to stay true to my people, you know what I'm saying? I stay true to Hip Hop. I be in the streets, you know what I'm saying? So, I see my youth. I got to stay true to my people. I got to make music for them, because if I don't, ain't nobody else going to. So, you know, I know that the music I make and the connection I have with my youth, is that yo, that's what adults need to do. They need to have that connection with the youth and keep the strong connection because they're the future.
>
> (Spady et al. 1999: 27)

Like Guru's lyrics in the introduction to this chapter, Marley Marl expresses a tremendous sense of community and identification with "his people," and he knows that in order to "stay true to his people," he must make both a physical and cultural connection ("I be in the streets, you know what I'm saying?").

As Rapper Scarface explained in Chapter 4, one of the unique uses of language in this community, rappin, is as a culturally specific "code of communication" that allows the various Hip Hop communities that comprise the HHN to stay in contact:

> It's a code of communication, too . . . Because we can understand each other when we're rappin. You know, if I'm saying, [in a nasal, mocking voice] "Well, my friend, I saw this guy who shot this other guy and . . ." I break that shit down for you and you say, "Goddamn, man! Them muthafuckas is goin crazy out where this dude's from." You know what I'm saying? It's just totally different. It's just a code of communication to me. I'm lettin my partner know what's goin on. And anything White America can't control they call "gangsters." *Shit!* I get real.
>
> (Spady *et al.* 1999: xix)

These comments from Marley Marl and Scarface are both indicative and representative of the importance attached to *stayin street* (being physically and culturally connected to the HHN within the broader Black American Street Culture).

Analysis of linguistic features in Hip Hop Nation Language

Several scholars have argued that the syntax of HHNL—language used by the Hip Hop Nation Speech Community—is essentially the same as that of BL (Remes 1991, Smitherman 1997, 2000, Yasin 1999, Rickford and Rickford 2000, Morgan 2001). There is a general tendency in linguistics, as well as among the general public, however, to claim that slang is the most noteworthy feature of language use within the HHN, and thus little attention is paid to syntax. Edwards (1999) reports that Hip Hop artists do not employ the central grammatical features of BL in their lyrics, although they do display some tokens. His main conclusions are:

1   Slang is the main aspect of language that Hip Hop artists use to "connect" with Black Americans;
2   Hip Hop artists employ standard English grammar in an attempt to appeal to Whites.

Edwards conducted a preliminary study in which he used forty-one songs from eight artists, an average of five songs per artist. This amounts to approximately fifteen minutes of speech data per artist. Edwards contends that there is a "virtual absence" of central BL features in Hip Hop artists' lyrics—features such as perfect/completive *done* (which emphasizes the completed nature of an action, e.g. *I done been through it all*), future completive *be done* (which operates like a future perfect, e.g. *By the time he get home, she be done ate the whole damn cake!*), distributive or invariant *be* (which refers to the habitual nature of an action, e.g *Y'all be rappin to every girl you see*), and aspectual *steady* (which indicates intense actions that occur continuously, e.g. *She be steady typin on that computer*). These particular BL grammatical features, however, appear relatively infrequently in the corpus of Black American speech. Therefore, we should expect them to be used less frequently relative to other features in Hip Hop lyrics. Further, to say that such features, especially invariant *be*, are absent from Hip Hop lyrics is most likely a function of the narrow corpus and not the general rule.

Smitherman (1997) provides several examples of BL features as they appear in Hip Hop lyrics. In discussing the communicative practices of the HHN, Smitherman cites five common features of Black American syntax and two common features of Black American phonology, respectively:

1   Habitual *be*—indicates actions that are continuing or ongoing. Example: "He *be* gettin on my nerves."
2   Copula absence—absence of *is* and *are* in some present tense forms. Example: "We tryin to get all this paper, cousin."
3   Stressed *been*—denotes the remote past. Example: "I *been* had that Jay-Z album" (meaning I had it a long time ago, and I still have it).
4   *Gon*—indicates the future tense. Example: "You better watch him cause he *gon* take credit for the work that you did."
5   *They* for possessive. Example: "*They* schools can't teach us nuthin noway."
6   Postvocalic *-r*—Mother becomes "Mutha" (the *r* after the vowel is absent).
7   *Ank* and *ang*, for "Ink" and "ing." Example: "I'ma get me some dr*ank*" and "You wouldn't understand; it's a Black th*ang*" (dr*ank* = drink, and th*ang* = thing).

Smitherman's observations can readily be confirmed. Beyond Smitherman's analysis, I argue that one can find every feature of BL represented in Hip Hop lyrics (see Rickford (1999) for a "checklist" of BL features). Hip Hop artists employ the wide body of features that make up BL. This leads to other, perhaps more important, questions. These features may very well appear in Hip Hop lyrics, but with what frequency do they occur? Are these rare, isolated incidents, or do they represent a specific language pattern? Do the patterns of these features in Hip Hop lyrics differ from the patterns found in naturally occurring speech? And, if so, what does that mean? In an attempt to answer these questions, I have analyzed the linguistic variability of copula absence in the lyrics *and* speech of two Hip Hop artists—Eve and Juvenile (artists described shortly).

Copula absence, as seen in the Smitherman example 2 above, refers to the absence of *is* and *are* in some present tense forms. In simple terms, the copula is the linking verb that connects the subject of a sentence with its predicate. In BL, a speaker can produce sentences like *He is the leader* (full form), *He's the leader* (contracted form) and *He the leader* (absent form), all of which have the same meaning. The BL copula cannot be absent in some present tense forms. This sample from a Black Minister's speech is illustrative: "The Black Man on the rise, and the White Man, he runnin scared now, because we wide awake today and he know we not just gon lay down and accept things as they are." While the copula can be absent before prepositional phrases (*on the rise*), progressive verbs (*he runnin scared*), adjectives (*we wide awake*), and negatives (*we not just gon lay down*), it cannot be absent when it is in sentence-final position (*as they are*). The copula also cannot be absent in the first person singular form. A sentence such as *I the boss* is ungrammatical in BL; the present tense form must be *Uhm the boss*, *I'm the boss* or *I am the boss*.

Rickford *et al.* (1991) refer to the BL copula as the language variety's "showcase variable." This pattern is one of the most extensively studied sociolinguistic variables, so much so that a linguist once made this joke at a conference, "Let the copula *be!*" (Only funny to linguists, you know what I'm saying?) The BL copula is important for several reasons. First, it is one of the features that gives BL its distinctiveness, setting it apart from other varieties of American English. Second, the BL copula has been used to support the fact that BL is diverging (growing further away) from other varieties of American English. And third, the BL copula plays a crucial role in heated debates about the historical reconstruction of BL. The feature has been analyzed extensively to draw support for the creole origins of BL (Bailey 1965, Baugh 1979, 1980, Alleyne 1980, Holm 1984, Rickford 1998). I will return to this point in the discussion of methodology.

Methodological considerations

In obtaining data for analysis, I transcribed one full-length CD by each artist: Eve's *Let There Be Eve . . . Ruff Ryder's First Lady* (1999) and Juvenile's *Tha G-Code* (1999). In addition, I transcribed interviews with these artists, who were chosen because of the availability of their speech data. I was careful to make sure that I had nearly equal amounts of speech data and lyrical data for each artist. I transcribed about one hour of speech from each artist's interview to match the approximate length of their CD recordings. Eve's interview data were compiled from two sources: from an interview from a volume on Hip Hop Culture, *Street Conscious Rap* (Spady *et al.* 1999), and from a recent interview in Philadelphia. Juvenile's speech data were also obtained from two sources: from an interview I conducted and from an interview by Black Dog Bone and associates in *Murder Dog*, a Hip Hop magazine that specializes in the interview format. The interviewers interact regularly with the HHN and can be considered members of the Hip Hop Nation Speech Community, as well as the larger Black American Speech Community. The data were organized into four groups: Juvenile interview, Juvenile lyrics, Eve interview, and Eve lyrics.

As is well known in linguistics (although not widely reported in linguistic studies) there is more than one way to calculate copula variability. Rickford *et al.* (1991) provide an in-depth look at the varying methods of calculation and their underlying theoretical assumptions. The different formulae exist due to differing hypotheses about the nature of the BL copula. Some linguists believe that the copula is an underlying form in BL, while others believe that it is not. One the one hand, Anglicists (linguists who assert the English origin of BL) believe that the copula, as in older dialects of British English, was always present in BL (*He is the teacher*), and that speakers contract it (*He's the teacher*) and then delete it to its zero form (*He the teacher*). On the other hand, Africanists/Creolists (linguists who assert the African language(s) origin of BL) believe that the copula has not always been present in BL, and that it was inserted into BL as some Black Americans gained contact with speakers of American English varieties in which the copula must always be present. In this case, the process is ordered in reverse: *He the teacher → He's the teacher → He is the teacher*. Thus, as this line of argument goes, the BL copula, resembling creole language varieties, was initially absent then inserted as Black American speakers acquired the contracted and full forms. (See Romaine 1982 for insightful argumentation on this issue.) Several linguists have shown convincingly that patterns of BL copula variation connect BL to creole language varieties.

This study analyzes synchronic data (data in the present time) and does not attempt to make any diachronic (historical) claims. When viewing synchronic data, there need not be a discussion of "deletion before contraction" or "contraction before deletion." What is important to the synchronic analysis of the data is whether or not the copula, in a given utterance, is in the full, contracted or absent form. This is not to say that the diachronic analysis is unimportant; it is just beyond the purview of this study. Whether an Anglicist or a Creolist (and whether subscribing to the strong or weak interpretations of these positions), the linguistic researcher must recognize that his/her choice of formulae (if working within the variationist paradigm) essentially aligns him or her with a historical position. I have chosen formulae that are in line with the considerable evidence supporting the creole origins hypothesis, and can be used for both synchronic and diachronic analyses. This is precisely why we are speaking of copula *absence* rather than *deletion*.

Analysis of the data

In order to provide a clear picture of what and how copula forms were counted in the data analyzed here and to exemplify the type of copula absence found in BL, an excerpt from the data is given below. It is taken from my interview with Juvenile (Alim 2000). In this exceprt, sentences containing copula patterns are highlighted: full forms are underlined, contracted forms are italicized, and absent forms are in bold. We are focusing only on present tense copula forms—specifically *is* and *are*—because in the past tense the copula is always present in BL. It is also present in first person singular contractions as well as in *it's*, *that's*, and *what's*.

Following Rickford *et al.*'s (1991) notational schema, the examples that I included in the quantitative analysis are labeled [C] for "counts" and the ones that I excluded are labeled [DC] for "don't counts." As stated above, I analyzed copula variation in the speech *and* lyrics of both Hip Hop artists, using the same analytical procedure.

```
 1  A:  Do you remember the first rap record you heard at that time or that
 2      you bought at that time?
 3  J:  You know, I wasn't allowed to have that.
 4  A:  Oh, yeah?
 5  J:  Yeah. Couldn't bring that in the house!
 6  A:  [Laughter] Who didn't allow that in the house?
 7  J:  My moms, man. My mama didn't want me to rap. Uh-uh. She all
 8      with it now [C]. She's down with it now [C]. Because, you know, it
 9      wasn't a big thing when I was young. She was like, "You better think
10      of something else!" Back then it was like a one to a million in my
11      chance of becoming a star. And I wanted to be a star.
12  A:  So she was concerned about you.
13  J:  She wanted me to make sure that I was straight, and that I didn't
14      spend all my time worrying about rap music and forgettin about what I
15      got to do.
16  A:  What do you think brought her change about?
17  J:  Because it opened up to where you could make it out a career. You
18      know, when I was young, a lot of cats would make a song, and they
19      ain't make a record since then, you know what I'm [DC] saying? Now
20      you got it to where artists is [C] goin out there makin money like
21      football players and baseball players, you know what I'm [DC] saying?
22      [Laughter]. She [C] widdit! I ain't [DC] doin nuthin. I ain't [DC]
23      causing no harm to nobody. I'm [DC] livin. She [C] widdit, you know
24      what I'm [DC] saying? I ain't [DC] cuttin off nobody arms or nuthin to
25      get it; I'm [DC] just doin my thing. Believe me.
26  A:  What do you like the best about being with Cash Money?
27  J:  It's [DC] family, man. We [C] family. We're [C] still livin, man.
28      Everything [C] the same. Ain't nuthin changed since I got here. We
29      [C] still doin the same thangs. We [C] paperchasin, cousin. We [C]
30      tryin to get all the money, cousin.
31  A:  How important is that to have family around you?
32  J:  If you don't work, you don't eat, man. That's [DC] the importance.
33      It's [DC] real important to have them around me. Because with them
34      along with me, I'm [DC] workin. That mean a lot, you know what I'm
35      [DC] saying? That's [DC] less amount of work. As long as it's [DC]
36      with the family, it's [DC] all gravy. We get a lot accomplished when
37      we're [C] together, and we're [C] always together. Just family.
```

If we examine only a portion of this transcript, lines 19–30, there are numerous examples to illustrate the process of counting the various copula forms. The only full form in this section occurs in line 20 (*Now you got it to where artists is goin out there makin money like football players and baseball players, you know what I'm saying?*). This is an example of a "count" full form, despite the fact that *are* is rendered as *is*. The absent form occurs seven times in these lines: Twice in lines 22 and 23 (**She widdit** [with it]), and five times in lines 27–30 (**We family; Everything the same; We still doing the same thangs; We paperchasin, cousin; We tryin to get all the money, cousin**). The contracted form occurs ten times in lines 19–30. It is important to note that there is only one case that can be counted out of the ten contracted examples. The one example in line 19 (I'm saying) and the four examples in lines 21–25 (I'm living; I'm just doing my thing; and the two cases of I'm saying) are "don't counts" because, as stated above, the BL copula is *never* absent in the first person singular. Therefore, those forms are excluded from the analysis. The use of *ain't* in lines 22 and 24 are also "don't counts" because the BL copula is never absent in this negative form. The first form in line 26 (It's family, man) is also a "don't count" case. As mentioned earlier, the BL copula is rarely absent in cases of "it's," "what's" and "that's" (see lines 32–36 for numerous examples of this "don't count" case). Thus, all those forms are also excluded from the analysis. The only "count" case in this excerpt of the transcript (lines 19–30) occurs in line 27 (*We're still living, man*) because, in this environment, the BL copula can appear in the full, contracted or absent form. Again, the lyrical data were analyzed using the same procedure.

Before proceeding, a brief biographical sketch of each artist might be helpful. Eve, as a former member of the Ruff Ryders, is a Rapper who represents Philadelphia. She grew up in the Mill Creek Housing Projects in West Philadelphia and moved to Germantown and other areas in recent years. As a young girl of 9 years old, Eve recalls hearing and enjoying the "gangsta" Rap of NWA, one of the most hardcore West Coast Rap groups in the history of Hip Hop. She made a name for herself as a young teen on the Philly talent show circuit, and she was known as the female Rapper who would "bust" into any "cipher"—a highly competitive rhyme circle of Rappers (see Chapter 4). As she put it one time:

> I'm used to being in ciphers. And I'm a female that will break in a cipher. I don't care if it's fifty guys in the cipher! I'm going to break in the cipher! Guys tend to look at you like, "Oh, you rap?" And I'm very feminine. I dress very feminine. So, it's like guys look at you, "You rap like this?" you know what I'm saying? It's like, "What are you rappin about?" And the thing is, I *love* for people to underestimate me. Especially guys, I live for them to laugh and snicker. Because as soon as I open my mouth, they're like, "What?! Where did you get that from? Who wrote that for you?" And I'm like, "I write all my own rhymes."
>
> (Spady *et al.* 1999: 486–498)

Eve—the self-described "pitbull in a skirt"—explains that, in high school, she used to be rappin in ciphers "all the time!", even to the point where she was knockin creole-speakers out the cipher in they own language.

> I was just known for battlin in the lunch room. I was doing Reggae. I did Reggae! I was battlin Jamaicans. They was like, "*How* is this American doin this?!" I sounded real good . . . Like, "This girl right here will bust any guy!" . . . [We rapped in the] lunchroom, outside, after school, in the neighborhood, around the school, in the bathroom . . . [Laughter].

While Eve's songs cover a broad range of topics (from self-esteem to domestic violence), she often discusses her many trials and tribulations "growin up in the hood." At the same time, she does not lament her upbringing. In fact, she proudly proclaims that she was raised both by her family *and* the streets.

Juvenile, as a former member of the Hot Boy$ and the Cash Money Million-aires, is a Rapper who represents New Orleans. Like Eve, he made a name for himself as a local Rapper and began his career as a teenager. As we saw in the conversational discourse above, wasn't nuthin Juvenile mother could say or do to stop that boy from rappin! Juvenile mentions the name of his projects (referred to as "The Nolia") in nearly every one of his songs. In an interview, he describes what it was like growin up in The Nolia:

> We had our goods and our bads, you know. I remember seeing a lot of poverty, you know what I'm saying? They had a few people out the projects that were livin good, you know what I'm saying? But like I say, they got people with God in they life and people with the devil in they life *inside* of Magnolia. They got good people and bad people. It's on you to make the decision on where you gon stand at. If you gon be with them, or you gon stand alone, you know. My own thing to do is stand alone and mind my business.
>
> (Alim 2000, unpublished interview)

Juvenile's attachment to the Magnolia Projects is evident from his music videos. When asked why he decided to film one of his music videos in the projects, he explained: "I owed that to myself, man . . . And I wanted it to be known how people live up there in the projects, you know what I'm saying? People ain't never really seen or been through our projects, you know what I'm saying?" (Juvenile and other rappers from New Orleans exposed the racism of neglect long before Hurricane Katrina brought that issue into the national spotlight in 2005.)

Both Eve and Juvenile claim to be "from the streets" and tell tales of street life in their lyrics. As they gain international acclaim, both artists claim to "stay attached to the streets." They maintain their ties to their local communities, and celebrate their upbringing in the Black community, even as they continue to sell millions of records and their social networks continue to expand beyond "the hood." As Eve can now be heard rappin, "It's all good now, we out the hood now."

In Table 5.1, data from Juvenile interviews are juxtaposed with data from his lyrics. Similarly, Eve's interview data are juxtaposed with data from her lyrics. The data are displayed this way for comparative purposes. The separation of *is* and *are* allows for additional points of comparison. The reader is reminded that what is being compared is the frequency of copula absence between the artists' interview speech and the artists' lyrics.

We see an increase in the frequency of absence—for all three columns and for both artists—when moving from the interview data to the lyrical data. For Juvenile, *is* absence increases from 55 to 68.75 percent. *Are* absence increases from 57.58 to 78.85 percent. *Combined* (both *is* and *are*) absence increases from 56.6 to 75 percent. For Eve, *is* absence increases from 3.39 to 28 percent. *Are* absence increases from 12 to 87.23 percent. *Combined* (both *is* and *are*) absence increases from 5.95 to 56.7 percent. So, it is clear that both of these artists display the absent form more frequently in their lyrical data than in their interview speech data.

Strategic construction of a street-conscious identity

In this study, I examined copula variation in two different language contexts: informal interviews and Hip Hop lyrics. The informal interviews were conducted in a conversational manner, but with several goals in mind: to arrive at a better understanding of Juvenile and Eve as artists, rappers, and, most of all, human beings. Some of the topics covered in the interviews included the writing process, the recording process, Hip Hop as an art form, early Hip Hop experiences, school experiences, hometown experiences, and relationships with family and friends. The interviews most closely related to the concept of "casual speech" in Labov's Context A. The lyrics do not fit any of Labov's contexts, but they do benefit from Baugh's social contexts in terms of familiarity and Black street culture membership. As we just read, both artists "got love for the streets." Eve proudly raps on her album that the "Philly streets, they raisin her right!" And Juvenile has developed the concept of *Tha G-Code*, something not unlike what sociologist Elijah Anderson has recognized as "The

Table 5.1 Rate of copula absence (%)

	Interviews			Lyrics		
	is	are	combined	is	are	combined
Juvenile	55.00	57.58	56.60	68.75	78.87	75.00
Eve	3.39	12.00	5.95	28.00	87.23	56.70

Code of the Street." In an interview, Juvenile accounted for his success: "I stay down to earth and I stay attached to the streets" (Alim 2000).

Juvenile and Eve are not unlike many of their Hip Hop contemporaries. As we have seen time and again in this book, street-consciousness is a key value for members of the HHN. From the perspective of Baugh's social contexts, when we examine Hip Hop lyrics, we must ask ourselves: Who is the intended audience? In other words, who are the "interlocutors" in this Hip Hop "conversation"? Certainly, both Eve and Juvenile have sold hundreds of thousands of records to White consumers; however, their target audience (as with Hip Hop in general) remains largely Black. It is important to note that not only are the artists directing their lyrics to people of African descent, but they are directing their lyrics to members of the Black American Street Culture in particular. Thus, according to Baugh's speech event grid, the most appropriate context would fall somewhere in between Type 1 (familiar participants, all of whom are natives of the Black vernacular culture) and Type 2 (participants who are not well acquainted but are members of the Black vernacular culture). Type 2 is not entirely fitting for this situation because there may not even be "occasional contact." Although the familiarity may vary, membership in Black Street Culture is important. Familiarity in this sense refers to group experience (sharing cultural norms, values, aesthetics, and experiences), rather than to the frequency of contact between individuals (as Baugh described it).

I am not only suggesting that the artists target members of the Black American Street Culture as their audience, but I am further suggesting that they modify and vary their speech accordingly. Baugh's study demonstrated that Black Americans, like many other groups, vary their speech on the basis of the social interactant. Baugh was concerned with naturally occurring everyday speech. In examining Hip Hop lyrics, we cannot assume that they are comparable to naturally occurring everyday speech, and as the data illustrate, there are some distinct differences. For the most part, Hip Hop lyrics are not as spontaneous as free flowing speech (although some artists come pretty damn close!). Lyrics are sometimes written, rehearsed, performed, and recorded several times before they appear on CD. Hip Hop artists, in general, pay a great amount of attention to their speech. This is key. Labov witnessed that the variation in speech depended largely on the attention paid to speech. In his study, the more attention the speakers paid to their speech, the more "standard" their speech became. However, in the case of Hip Hop lyrics, the data suggest that the more attention the artists pay to their speech (comparing interviews to lyrics) the more "nonstandard" their speech becomes—as indicated by the increase in the frequency of copula absence.

This raises fundamental questions about the conscious control of phonological and grammatical features in speech. Labov was convinced that, at least with low-level phonological variation (for example, consonant cluster reduction when *last* is realized as *lass*, or *test* as *tess*, etc.), variation was independent of conscious control. Baugh, on the other hand, suggested that although street speakers may not necessarily understand the variable nature of speech, they are conscious that changes are taking place. For example, in his examination of the variable forestressing of bisyllabic words (as in *PO-lice* for "police" and *DE-troit* for "Detroit"), Baugh discovered that the feature was sensitive to speaking contexts. He concluded that it is possible that adults have elevated this aspect of dialect difference to the level of (comparatively) conscious manipulation. Such data, of course, point to the refined communicative competence of adult street speakers. Although neither Labov nor Baugh discusses the conscious control of grammatical forms, I am proposing that Hip Hop artists are indeed in conscious control of their copula variability.

Cultural consciousness and Black Language

Thus far, we have discussed the conscious control of variables in cognitive terms. However, consciousness can also be viewed in cultural/ideological terms, that is, Black consciousness may include awareness of a distinct Black identity, culture, and language. Two theories of stylistic variation are important here—Bell's (1984) *audience and referee design* and LePage and Tabpiret-Keller's (1985) *acts of identity*. Bell, like others before him, states that a speaker's style depends primarily on the speaker's audience. Although claiming not to do so, Bell's audience design essentially views stylistic variation as a passive phenomenon. Not until he discusses referee design do we see some sense of agency given to the speaker. Interestingly enough, the speaker is given the most agency when responding to an audience that is not present, as is the case in mass communication. This has direct bearing on this study because the Hip Hop artists are responding to an audience that is not immediately present. The members of the Black American Street Culture, to whom the artists are directing their lyrics, are not physically present, yet they are in conversation.

LePage and Tabouret-Keller's framework gives the speaker a greater sense of agency by claiming that speakers can modify their language to match the language of a group with which they wish to identify if, and only if:

1   they can identify the desirable group;
2   they have both adequate access to that group, and the ability to analyze their behavior, i.e. their speech patterns;
3   they have a strong enough motivation to "join" the group, and this motivation is either reinforced or rejected by the group;
4   they have the ability to modify our own behavior.

Consider the situation where Hip Hop artists are producing lyrics for the Black American Street Culture:

1   they have identified the desirable group;

2   they have had and still have adequate access to this group;
3   they have a strong motivation to join the group as "street credibility" is key to a Rapper's success in Hip Hop Culture;
4   they have the ability to modify their own behavior, as this study has demonstrated.

Hip Hop artists assert their linguistic acts of identity in order to "represent" the streets. This may be viewed as a conscious, linguistic maneuver to connect with the streets as a space of culture, creativity, cognition, and consciousness. If we view Hip Hop artists as social interactants communicating with members of the Black American Street Culture, copula variation appears to be conscious— street-conscious (both cognitive and cultural). Hip Hop artists, by the very nature of their circumstances, are ultraconscious of their speech. As members of the HHN, they exist in a cultural space where extraordinary attention is paid to speech. Speech is consciously varied toward the informal end of the continuum in order to maintain street credibility. "The streets," as rapper Method Man says, "is where you get your stripes at" (Spady *et al.* 1999: 67).

The overwhelming majority of Hip Hop artists in the US, as Black Americans, are subjected to the "double consciousness" that Dubois spoke of in the early 1900s, and to what Smitherman (1977) calls a "linguistic push-pull." In discussing linguistic adjustment, Baugh (1983: 121) states: "The issue is even more complicated for street speakers because of the question of group loyalty from within and because of social and economic pressures from without the vernacular black community." The case of Hip Hop artists is complicated by the fact that both pressures operate in the same direction. That is, both group loyalty from within the Black community (speaking BL to connect with their intended audience) and economic pressures from without (speaking BL to maintain street credibility in order to continue selling records and *earn a living* in a highly competitive capitalistic economy) favor speaking BL.

Since Hip Hop artists are members of the larger Black American Speech Community, street-conscious copula variation raises questions about the conscious control of copula variation within the broader Black American community. As we have seen in studies by White linguists (Dillard 1972, Labov 1972a, Bailey 1987), Black American adults are sometimes perceived not to be representative speakers of the vernacular. Could it be that adults do not display features like copula absence and habitual *be* (when in the presence of Whites) because they possess a refined communicative competence and a heightened sense of the stigmatized forms in their speech, as perceived by White speakers of English? And, if so, couldn't this refined communicative competence allow these same forms to be used regularly as a sign of solidarity (among other things) within the Black American Speech Community? (Baugh 1999, Smitherman 2000).

Can this conscious use of BL patterns (in Hip Hop, and the broader Black American Speech Community) help to maintain and impact the development of the unique language of Black Americans? As several scholars have noted, BL persists in a society that readily recognizes its linguistic prejudice. Furthermore, despite the belief by many (whether true or not) that mastery of "standard English" will lead to greater economic opportunity, BL beats on. To paraphrase P. Diddy and the Bad Boy Family, one thing is for certain, BL ain't goin nowhere—it ain't goin nowhere—and it can't be stopped now!

Final thoughts

What I have described in this chapter is *street-conscious copula variation*—the conscious variation of copula absence in order for the artist to "stay street," or to stay connected to the streets. More research is needed regarding the strategic use of language to construct identity in the Black American community. The role of identity, ideology, and consciousness (both cognitive and cultural) in the processes of linguistic variation and change needs to be further explored. Not only will this research shed light on the nature of these linguistic processes, but it will also provide greater insight about, as Rapper DMX says, *who we be*. If the goal of language scholars is to ultimately uncover what it means to be human, to gain insight into humanity and the complex relationships between language, life, and liberation, we must consider the use of language to not only construct our *worlds* but also to construct our very *beings*. To paraphrase Rapper Mos Def, linguistics is our hammer—let's bang the world into shape and let it fall—HUH!

Chapter 6

"Every syllable of mine is an umbilical cord through time"
Toward an analytical schema of Hip Hop poetics

(Example 1)
Every syllable of mine is an umbilical cord through time
For the sick typical niggaz who choose to pick pitiful rhymes—to spit
Shit, it's more dimes to git
More higher levels of spirituality to reach
And I'm tryin to win.

(Pharoahe Monch)

In recent years, scholars have begun to examine the artistic complexity of Hip Hop Culture, to deconstruct its aesthetics, and to develop means of analyzing this increasingly popular literary and linguistic form. This chapter is designed to explicate aspects of Hip Hop poetics by focusing on sound/lyrical production (commonly known as "rappin"). I have chosen Pharoahe Monch's CD, *Internal Affairs*, because it provides a uniquely diverse body of contemporary poetic expression as creative as it is complex.

I have come to view Hip Hop lyrics/poetics as literature—something like what Rapper Ice-T once called "Power Poetry" or a "Hi-tech Combat Literature" (Spady *et al.* 1999: 114). I am aware that Hip Hop poetics, like Hip Hop Culture in general, is a phenomenon that remains highly misunderstood and marginalized by those who do not, or cannot, grasp the linguistic-cultural aesthetics, traditions, and ideologies that both govern and mediate this culture-nation-world (Smitherman 1997, Morgan 2001). In Chapter 4, I described HHNL as the synergistic combination of speech, music, and literature, what Yancy (1991) referred to as "*musical literature* (or rhythmic-praxis discourse)." Henderson (1973), analyzing the poetry of the Black Arts Movement in the 1960s and 1970s, asserted that it is most distinctly Black when it derives its form from Black speech and Black music. So, HHNL is simultaneously the spoken, poetic, lyrical, and musical expression of the HHN. The complexity of Hip Hop poetics is not lost upon many rhymers. Pharoahe Monch explained earlier how he sees the relationship between "Rap" and "poetry":

I mean, poetry is a awesome art form in itself. I dabble in it before I write some of the songs that I do. I try to be poetic with some of the songs. Hip Hop is based upon a mixture of that, but more writing musically. Points and timing, you know. So is poetry. But on a level where it's based upon the music, you have to be more rhythmatically connected with your listener and crowd, in terms of rhythm, you know. And *how* are you riding that beat. You know, you could do the same thing with poetry without any music at all, you know what I'm saying? Get a response rhythmatically. So, I'm not disrespecting that. I'm just saying, Hip Hop, it's about where you are on that fourth bar, where you are on that first bar.

Importantly, this chapter is not one that simply states that "Hip Hop is poetry," in an attempt to legitimize Hip Hop lyrical production. While many scholars emphatically claim that Hip Hop *is* poetry—and it is—Hip Hop Headz are sayin, "Don't just limit us by sayin what we do is just poetry." What Pharoahe's and other Rappers' comments reveal is that Hip Hop is similar, but different, to most poetry in that there are multiple layers of complexity required in order to "get a response rhythmatically."

By excavating the rhymes found on Pharoahe Monch's *Internal Affairs*, along with other Hip Hop lyrics, I wish to reveal both the complexity and creativity of Hip Hop lyrical production. This innovative form of verbal art requires an equally innovative analytical schema to deconstruct its aesthetic, and this chapter takes the first step in constructing that analytical schema. Before I present the poetic analysis, however, we need to take a look at the relationship between the Black Arts Movement and the Hip Hop Cultural Movement. The next several sections of this chapter take us straight into a conversational cipher between Hip Hop artists and Black Arts Movement poets. Peep game as we get poetic widdit . . .

The Black Arts Movement and the Hip Hop Cultural Movement

What is the language that bonds/binds Sista Sonia Sanchez with Miss Trina? What elements of aesthetic value link William A. Thigpen (Thig Life) and Tupac A. Shakur (Thug Life)? Were you there when Fresno Brother Marvin X rocked the crowd like Fresno's hometown Brother Planet Asia? What existential elements exist in the philosophical *Twisted Tales* of North Philly's Larry Neal and West Philly's Schoolly D? What are the communicative practices that allow Chi-Town Brothers Haki Madhubuti and Common to express everyday life experiences with the uncanniness of a sixth sense? What are the core values of Amiri Baraka and Chuck D that enable them to speak the truth—or *be* the truth (like my man Beanie Sigel say)? Liberated Black Poets with a Blues Streak of Hip Hop Wisdom.

It is clear that the set of questions we are asking requires one to take a deep, long look at the last half-century of Black Art. In our discussions with Sista Sonia Sanchez, her vision is not only deep, but *deeply* deep. Y'all know what I'm talkin bout. Sista Sonia Sanchez, one of the founding mothers of what is known as the Black Arts Movement, discusses the multiple issues that arise from the above questions with crystal clarity—even as she remains an active member of the creative processes that gave rise to these questions in the first place.

How shall we begin to examine the relationship between the Black Arts Movement and the Hip Hop Cultural Movement, and by extension, all other Black creative movements? In describing this familiar and familial relationship, the language that one uses is of utmost importance. Do we speak of parallels? Do we speak of similarities? Amiri Baraka, one of the pioneering poets of the Black Arts Movement, provides a personal/collective narrative that speaks to the dimensions of a Black Arts Continuum:

> In the Black Arts Movement in the 60's, when we went Uptown to Harlem in the Black Arts Repertory School, we said we wanted to do three things. We wanted to create an art or a poetry that was Black American, let's say, as Black American as Bessie Smith or Duke Ellington. We wanted to create an art that was *mass*-oriented, that would come out of the universities, that would get into the street, that would reach our people, you know. And I'm sure the rap thang today is directly comin out of the whole 60's poetry movement. And the third thing we wanted to do was create an art that was revolutionary.
>
> (Gross 1986)

Sista Sonia, in concentric conversation with Brotha Baraka, strikes a similar chord:

> Well, you know I really don't call it *similarities*. What I do, is I say the Hip Hop Movement came *out of* the Black Arts Movement. And it was a natural progression, just as in the way we really came out of the Harlem Renaissance period, you know. The Depression and the War, and then, here we came! The Civil Rights Movement. And then there was a lull again. And then the country *took* everything that it could away from these young men and women in school. But you know the most important thing about us is that we are so inventive, my brotha. We *invent* stuff. I mean, the first time I heard it [Hip Hop], I said to my children—and I have to give praise to them, really. Because I heard it, you know, and I said, "What is that music?!" And they told me it was a turntable. And I thought, "Oh my goodness!" I said, "They take away the instruments, and we make our own music." I mean, that is amazing . . .
>
> (Unpublished interview with Alim 2000)

Sista Sonia is speakin on a *continuum* of Black Arts. Through her remarks about Hip Hop one sees that the creative Black Arts Movements are all intricately tied to—and are reflections of—the social, economic, and political circumstances Black people must face in North America. Developing the courage and creativity to speak up and out became a means of survival in the wilderness. Who shall speak the truth, and at what cost?

Sonia, Chuck D, and Beanie Sigel: We be the truth

Reminiscing on the first time she ever heard Hip Hop music, Sista Sonia takes it back to the Old School: "This was a long time ago, right. That was a loooong time ago. See, when I heard it from my children, it was like Chuck D and it was like the brothas comin out of the Bronx. And that was some *amazing* stuff, you know. I mean, it was like . . . Yeah! You heard that, and you said, 'Woooooh!' And then I said, out loud, 'They gon get in trouble!' [Laughter] Because that's what we did. That's what we did . . . We got in trouble because we told the truth. And I knew they were gonna get in trouble. Once you tell the truth about this country, about what's goin on, you get in trouble. And especially Chuck D, you know . . ." (Unpublished interview with Alim 1999.)

Shortly after rockin a sold-out crowd in San Francisco's Maritime Hall, Chuck D enters the cipher. We join the conversation as Chuck reflects on his poetic influences: "Of course, the Last Poets. My uncle played the Last Poets. The Last Poets were very influential in the beginning of rap. And, of course, Gil Scott Heron. So, they definitely put it down. Later on I found out about the Watts Prophets. But as far as poetry is concerned, I mean, comin up in the late Sixties and early Seventies it was like you could hear a def poet up the block . . . Sonia Sanchez. My mother played her a lot. My moms just played a bunch of stuff from Sonia Sanchez."

Sista Sonia smiles broadly as she says: "Oh, wonderful, wonderful. Yes, I mean, and that's what I'm saying. We are an extension of each other. Or we are a continuation of each other. We continue the tradition and we bring an innovation to it each time." Chuck's comments are particularly revealing. Def poets up the block were the prime creators, maintainers, and preservers of the African Oral Tradition. Writing in, of, and about that oral tradition, Geneva Smitherman captures its essence:

> Rap music is rooted in the Black Oral Tradition of tonal semantics, narrativizing, signification/signifyin, the Dozens/playin the Dozens, Africanized syntax, and other communicative practices. The Oral Tradition itself is rooted in the surviving African tradition of "Nommo" and the power of the word in human life . . . As African America's "griot," the rapper must be lyrically/linguistically fluent; he or she is expected to testify, to speak the truth, to come wit it in no uncertain terms.
>
> (Smitherman 2000)

It's no wonder that Chuck D and Public Enemy (and a nation of millions) bust onto the scene droppin that Nation-conscious wisdom. One of the primary ideological/spiritual/political/cultural forces behind the poetics of the Black Arts Movement and the Hip Hop Movement is, as we read in Chapter 2, the Nation of Islam. Many Muslim poets in the 1960s and 1970s (including Baraka, Sanchez, Alhamisi, Marvin X, Rahman, Spriggs, Toure, Iman, Neal, Dumas, and others), under the training of the Honorable Elijah Muhammad, spilled poetry to the people for the purpose or raising consciousness. All over the United Streets of America (as Lil' Wayne be sayin) heads gathered from the Bay Area to the Harlem Area to hear the poets speak the truth. Can you imagine Sista Sonia spittin in the streetz of "the town," Oakland, California?

> ima talken bout THE NATION OF ISLAM
>   this poem is about a Messenger
>   about his blk/truth
>   thumpen like drums . . .
> ima talken about Minister Farrakhan
>   singen his songs of black unity
>   about a Blk/nation already here
>   ripenen our minds
> till our bodies grow like a thousand red rubies
>   and our bodies be full of Elijah
>   and our bodies be full of Elijah
>   and our bodies be full of Elijah

Chuck D and many others were listening. Public Enemy's *A Nation of Millions* reads like a fresh copy of Elijah Muhammad's *Message to the Blackman in America*. Chuck D explains in *Nation Conscious Rap*:

> Minister Farrakhan is the link, and the reason that we all understand that we do have this one thing in common, and this mission to be self sufficient in America or in the rest of the world and learn how to deal with it the same way that they're dealing with us. My whole reason is I try to bring the youth into a level where they'll be interested to even begin to get into what the Minister's been speaking and the teachings of Elijah Muhammad, and the reason for self sufficiency in America, and the curiosity to learn more about themselves.
>
> (Spady and Eure 1991)

This generation of young Hip Hop headz not only raps *about* the truth, but they possess a deep understanding that their very presence and condition here in America speaks volumes of truth. Muslim Rapper Beanie Sigel spits it with that arsenic flow: "Every time I step in the booth, I speak the truth/ Y'all know what I'm bringin to you, I bring the truth/ Muthafuckas know who I be/ I be the truth, what I speak shall set you free!"

Sista Sonia Sanchez spittin in the streetz

Sista Sonia is a Sun Woman for all Seasons, reading her poetry to a Sun People with Rhyme and Reasons. Who can forget that hot day in June when she stepped *up* into the 1999 Hip Hop Week Cipher and tore it *down*?! Thirteenth and Chestnut. On the Philly streetz, right outside Robin's Bookstore. Da Fat Cat Clique, Parry P, Zxulu and Da Family, Supreem Da Regulata and hundreds of Hip Hop headz formed an ultimate cipher. DJ Sparkles and Kid Swift cuttin it up. As the sparkling record cuts, "Damn, she that chick! D-D-D-Damn she that chick!" Amidst so much hiphopological activity, I can remember the silence loud and clear. Sista Sonia was about to take the mic and enter the cipher, the hyperactivated, communal Hip Hop lyrical testing and stomping grounds of verbal mastery.

Sonia was quietly observing the activities before she emerged: "Well, I heard everyone before I got up in that circle. And, initially, I stood and watched it. And I watched not only the energy, but I watched the respect that people had for each other. And then I watched the young Brothas and Sistas, you know, rappin. And this Sista coming up saying, 'It's my turn now! Let me go ahead and do this,' whatever. And it reminded me a great deal of when we also got up on the stages. I was one of the first poets who got up on the stage with a lot of men. And you had to hold your own. You could not go up and go [making a weak attempt] . . . You had to hold your own. And so when I see those young Sistas holding their own, you know, I smiiile."

That day Sonia led the Family in an extremely emotional call and response session as she read a poem for the Late Great Tupac Amaru Shakur. After runnin down some 2Pac lines, she reads:

and he says: all eyez on me
and we say: kai fi African (come here African)
all eyez on ya from the beginning of time
from the beginning of time
resist.
resist.
resist.
[Holding the mic way up above her head] Can you say it?
[The crowd responds] "Resist! Resist! Resist!"
Can you do it?
[Again the crowd responds] "Resist! Resist! Resist!"

Sonia describes her reaction: "Well, it was not an alien circle. It was like, as I said, I belong there. Just as we open up our circle to the young Brothas and Sistas. When I read, I bring the young people with me." Flashbacking to the days of poetin in the streetz of the Bay Area where a young Tupac once roamed, she adds: "We used to go out a lot in California. We used to go out with Ed

Bullins and Baraka and Marvin X and Sarah Fabio. We used to go out and do our poetry and our plays in the streets of Oakland. In Oakland. And, you know, we'd go out and we'd beat the drum, whatever, and bring people outside. And they'd bring their little chairs out . . . [And they would come?] Oh, they would come!"

Q2Q—Conversatin with Queens

Queen 2 Queen. We join Queen Sonia at the IAAAM 2000 Conference in Philadelphia where she has just finished a reading of her brand new poem for Queen Latifah, who was also in attendance. As Sonia reflects on the poem, she gives us an insight on the purpose and function of her relationship with this next generation of poets (whom she affectionately refers to as the Hip Hop People): "I was trying to give her lead as to what her voice really is, you see what I'm saying? And what I was trying to do also is to ask the question: 'Did you come from the East or from the West?' You know, I mean, I tried to take it someplace else. Because I think that's a question that we all have not answered just yet. To me, I always want to take the rappers, the Hip Hop People, someplace else . . ."

Sonia continues the narrative with love: "I said, 'Did you come from the East or from the West?' That's a question she's got to answer in her music, you know. 'Do not answer. Make no sound.' Now, of course, you know she's going to make a sound, you know. But for the moment, I wanted her to listen, okay. 'I know you were there when the winds were born.' And, you know, what I'm trying to say is when she went back and called herself Queen Latifah, she was brought back to the beginning, to the Ancient. So, I tried to make it a poem that said to Queen, 'I recognize your search for the Ancient. I recognize your search for the old.' I knew a lot of people wouldn't get it, and I don't know . . . I hope she got it. I think she did. She said she really did like it. But the point is that whether people get it or not, it's that you put it out into the universe, you know. *Somebody* is going to get what I'm saying."

Oh, we get what you sayin, Sista Sonia. We can both get it and get *widdit*!

Blue Black Magic Woman navigatin that Black Star line all the way home

"That's a beautiful brother. That's a beautiful, beautiful brother. I'm very proud of Brother Talib and Mos Def. I'm very proud of all of the young Brothas and Sistas who are very, what I call, very righteous and who understand the role of the poet." Sista Sonia shows much love to Talib Kweli and the Mighty Mos Def—young poets of the new day. What is the role of the poet today? Sonia: "Well, the role of the poet is to come and tell the truth. And the role of the poet is to *learn* a craft, and be willing to extend that craft beyond, what I say, easy, ordinary things." And you see that in Mos and Talib? "Oh, yeah, Mos Def! You listen to that album, you know, and you see . . . First of all, I like what he says. I like *how* he says it."

Linking Mos Def and Talib Kweli (Black Star) to rhyme legend Rakim Allah and the broad community of Hip Hop artists, she adds: "Well, I think they're part of that younger group comin up, that they have a history and a herstory with them. They have information. And they got it from their parents, right. And in the music also, too, with the fusion of different kinds of music that you feel in there. They're not afraid to jump into jazz, you know. They're not afraid to jump into rock and R&B. I mean, they do it, they mix it, whatever. And I think that's what's so good about them. I know Talib is doing the remake of 'Four Women,' Nina's [Simone's] song, you know. They're not afraid to dip back into some of the old, and bring it back and reinterpret it, and make it their own. Make it their period, their time, you see. And they walk with it. But above all, I guess what I like about them very much is how, similar to like Rakim, how they use the words like poetry."

As many critics struggle with defining Rap and poetry, Sonia once again lays it down. "Well, rap *is* poetry. You know, there's no separation. Some people *want* it separated, because some people want to say rap is not poetry, that it's not *official* poetry. 'It's just some young kids up there rhymin.' But what you see, especially with Rakim and with Def and Talib, and Lauryn, of course, is that they've taken it out of that very simple beat, you know, where you expect it. Sometimes there's that forced rhyme, you know what I mean? And that forced beat. And they've taken it out sometimes and they slow it down, you know what I mean? And you hear something else happening. You hear the old masters in their voices, you see, and I think they're not afraid to do it. That's what I like about it."

Rollin in that Black SUV with the speakers bumpin "Ms. Fat Booty," Mos Def enters the conversation: "Well, I mean, Hip Hop is poetry. All Hip Hop is poetry. It rhymes. It's the difference between technically qualifying as poetry and being poetic. Not everything that's poetry is poetic, but all Hip Hop is poetry. Anything that rhymes is poetry, but it takes something else to be poetic." Now, what is that "something else?" What does it take to be *poetic*? Listening to Mos describe what it means to be a dope MC tells it all: "It's a sense of personal investment. Temperature. Like, Biggie *really* believed it in his heart. Pac was like . . . It's the passion. It's the sincerity, man, you know what I'm saying? That pushes a lot of MCs forward. Of course, there's a lot of other technical facilities like flow, delivery, something that makes you distinctive. Slick Rick is one of the greatest MCs ever born because he has so many different facilities that he would use. Style. Vocal texture. The way he even would record. Like, he was doing call and response with himself! He would leave four bars open, and then do another character, you understand what I'm saying? So, I mean, the facilities of Slick Rick portray very few MCs. That's part of the reason Redman is so good, because he's like a hardcore version of Slick Rick. Like, he's funny. He uses a lot of the same recording technique where he leaves four bars open.

He assumes characters. He's witty. He has a very *inventive* use of language
. . . Sort of the way like Black Thought sorta like bends his words. Just to have
a unique way of saying things, you know. Doing things with the language that
draws relationships that not everybody might draw. Just, I mean, being as
creative as you can with the language." (Alim interview with Mos Def 1999.)

Personal investment. Temperature. Heat/Heart. Passion. Sincerity. Flow.
Delivery. Distinctiveness. Style. Vocal texture. Humor. Inventive use of language.
Unique phrasing. Creativity. Mos Def's love for this Hip Hop thang is only truly
told by that glimmer in his eye as he speaks passionately about the aesthetic
qualities which he values most in an MC.

Black Nation Language and Hip Hop Nation Language

When Mos Def speaks of being as "creative as you can with the language,"
what language is he talking about? It's the language of the "most recent chapter
of Black American folklore," as the Rickfords would say (Rickford and Rickford
2000). It's Hip Hop Nation Language (HHNL), the youngest child in the African
Family of Black Nation Languages. This HHNL is a language that lives and
breathes, moves and grooves, creeps (but never sleeps) in the Black communities of the United States Ghetto (as Onyx would say). In actuality, HHNL is
inextricably linked to the Language of Black America "from the hood to the
Amen corner."

Sista Sonia provides a poetic example of how Black Nation Language has
rescued the word/world. Paraphrasing James Baldwin, Sonia begins: "America
has nothing goin for it in terms of language. They're not British. They don't speak
British, you know, like the English, whatever. They speak this American
language which is corny. I mean, it is corny. And that's why the dictionary has
expanded so, because we have contributed in such a fashion to the language
. . . What we've done, is that we have co-opted this language and said, 'It don't
sound good' [and jokingly she adds, 'I know I teach English!'] 'It don't sound
good unless we put *our* input into it.' And we've made it *live*. We've given this
language life, a life that is *unbelievable*, you know. I can't imagine this American
language without our input. And without the Latino input. And what it does is
that it makes it breathe. It gives it life. It gives it color. It gives it a sense of what
is really goin on in the world."

Connecting Black Nation Language to Gospel music and Hip Hop, Sonia
continues: "I mean, like the Gospel, you hear the Gospel, you know. I mean,
the argument was, Blacks (Africans in this country) really didn't come up with
these Gospel songs. We got into this big argument where they took what was
in the Church . . . Well, they sure like hell took it! And made something of it!
Changed the language. Changed the beat. Reworked it. And threw it back out.
And it gave it life. Whatever. You know, you ever go to some of the churches?
They stand there and they sing these things [making a boring face] and you

look up and you go, 'Woah, where am I?!' you know. Whatever. You go to a Black church, you know, and the same song, and they sing it *out* there, you know! And that's what you do. I think what we have done, as African people, is that we have given this Earth life. We have given *words* life. What many of the young rappers are doing is that they have taken these words out. They rescued the words, you know what I'm saying, and they brought them out and said, 'Now, I'm going to turn it around. I'm going to emphasize this a little bit more. I'm going to slow it down. Especially that part, I'm going to slow it down. I'm going to go *right between the beat*! I'm going to play the silences,' you know. So, sometimes you listen to Mos Def and I hear the silences. And I go [nodding her head with the *feelin* and understanding] 'Yeah, yeah.' [Smiling] And that's what we did. That's how I know that these are our children. He's our child. Because, you see, what you heard from us on the stage, is that you heard the silences. The imagery. The beat and the silences, you know what I'm saying? And that's why people would say, 'Uh-huh!' They would say, 'Uh-huh!'" Always affirming and reaffirming. Sista Sonia has indeed given words life.

San Francisco's ultimate Hip Hop soulja from the Filthy Moe, JT the Bigga Figga (Brother Joseph Muhammad), joins the concentric conversation. Using a uniquely familiar street-orientated narrative style, Brother JT extends the Black Nation Language Thang all the way back to the days of Captain John Hawkins: "The Black Language is constructed of—alright, let me take it all the way back to the slave days and use something that's physical. The slaves, all the slave masters gave our people straight chittlins and greens and filled with stuff that they wasn't eating, but we made it into a delicacy. Same thing with the language. It's the *exact* same formula. How our people can take the worst, can take our bad condition, and be able to turn it into something that we can benefit off of. Just like the drums. They didn't want the slaves playing drums because we was talkin through the drums. 'What the hell is my slaves doin?! Oh, no, take them drums!' You feel me? So, that's kinda like goin on now with the rap thang, the rap culture." (Interview with Alim 2000.)

Brother JT and Sista Sonia on the same vibe. Speakin on and in that Black Nation Language. Talkin about rescuing the word from the grave. Linguistic gravediggaz comin to raise the verbally dead. They are both members of what Kalamu ya Salaam recently called, "The Live Poets Society." Both *live* and *a-live*.

They some baaaddDDD sistas in 3D

Sista Sonia sees and hears the Black Nation Language all throughout the rhymes of these forward-looking Hip Hop artist poets: "Oh, well it permeates the whole thing! I mean, what I know Chuck D did, is he took the spirit of our language in the Sixties and he took the aggressive part, you know. The part that said 'Fight the Power,' you know. We said the same thing. Whatever, et cetera. You see people, like even the Booty People, you know what I mean?

They gon say, [and she quotes from rapper Trina of Miami] 'I'm the baaaddest bitch.' So, we said, 'We a baaaddDDD people.' But they've taken it and they've stretched out the baaaddDDD just like we did, but except it's a bad bitch, you know what I mean? So, we said 'We a baaaddDDD people.' Well, you know, I will say this. Every now and then I would stand up on the stage and I would say, 'That muuthaaaa . . .' you know, and I would stop! [Laughter] So, that's why I say I don't get mad when I hear that. I understand it. What I do get mad at, however, is when women allow themselves to be marginalized, you see. And they really don't see themselves through their own eyes, you see. And as a consequence then, well, that's the only real hold up that I see, you know, when you allow yourself to be marginalized."

The references to Miami's Miss Trina almost call for her to answer. Exuding confidence and one helluva baaaddDDD attitude, Trina is concerned about one thing and one thing only—doin her thang! And it ain't all that easy being a female in the Rap game, as Eve, Latifah, and Rah Digga will all testify. So, is there any functionality to using the word "Bitch" to describe yourself? What does it mean to Trina to be "The Baddest Bitch," which is the title of one of her albums? "It's actually a great feeling. A great thing. That's a strong word to use so you got to be ready to stand up to it. I'm just doin my thing. People respect me for what I am and for who I am. Therefore I feel like there ain't nuthin that I can't accomplish. Nothing that I can't endure. That is why I use that title . . . Actually, it is a term of empowerment as far as women are concerned because most women seem to have a tendency to have low self-esteem. To me, I feel that whatever situation that we be in, always hold your head up." (Unpublished interview with James G. Spady 2000.)

Speaking on the worldwide impact of her album, Miss Trina continues: "I felt like it would have a very strong impact because Bitch is a strong word. If you gon use the word Bitch you've got to represent to the fullest. I just wanted to make sure that when I stepped out with it that it captured the ears of the people that were actually listening to what I was trying to say and to make sure that when it blew up (I had some feeling that it was going to blow up) I wanted to make sure that it was known that I am defending women. I'm lettin you know you can do whatever you wanna do. [As far as 'bitch' is concerned] I reversed that to let you know, 'Yeah, Ok, if you gonna say bitch, just say, "Miss Bitch." Please call me Miss or whatever. Don't just say Bitch like you're saying any other bitch.' I like to stand out. I'm very dominant. I'm very controlling. So, I'm always gonna be on top of my game. So, therefore, bitch doesn't offend me at all. That's why I can use it so brazenly and so strongly . . . BAMMMM! It's in your face. That's that and it doesn't even matter how you feel about it."

Marginalization or empowerment? No matter how you feel about this question, the importance of this Sonia–Trina dialogue is that it allows for community discussion about the role of language in our world. Whether you a "Brotha" or a "Sista," a "Bitch" or a "Nigga," the conversational cipher is always open . . .

Sonia's message to the Hip Hop Nation: Planting seeds

What is the role of a word sorcerer? In the African Oral Tradition we wreckognize that words have a certain kind of concrete, if not magical, power. Recognizing the incredible impact and influence that Hip Hop Culture is xzibiting across the globe, and the fact that Hip Hop voices now reach oppressed peoples from South Philly to South Africa and back, Sista Sonia speaks on the transformative power of language. "The great thing about language, to me, is that it changes, and it's always dangerous . . . in the hands of people who understand language. People always say that poetry can be nice or it can be the kind of thing that people like to hear. But it also can talk about change." In the background, if you listen close, Afu-Ra and Rza are rhyming, "We get you open with the dangerous language!"

Sonia's final message to the Hip Hop Nation shows that she got nuthin but love for all of the Hip Hop People. You can hear and feel the urgency of a Mother in her voice: "I love you. I love what you do. I know that you're all evolving. One of the most important things I can say is to study. Study this history, this herstory. Go back and listen to Duke Ellington symphonies, you know what I mean? Go back and listen to the people. Go back and read the poetry of the Black Arts Movement, you know. Read the poetry of a Bob Kaufman and just see how seditious we all are. And we were seditious not because we cursed. We were seditious because of how we would plant seeds, you know. And it's time for the rappers to become subtle and plant the seeds."

> The life that we lead, travel at high speed
> Circulate worldwide rap degreez
> Travel on the breeze/ to every shore
> Populate the planet with rhymes galore
> *I'm plantin' seeds* . . .
> It's no coincidence that we came
> Through the radio to penetrate your brain
> To leave a stain of the Most High's intent
> We recognize that we all heaven sent.

Comin straight outta the ATL experience and reppin Berkeley is the Hip Hop group known as Zion I. Zion touched on some of the very same issues that Sonia mentioned in her message: "I'm a poet. I write poetry . . . This cat Don Lee (Haki Madhubuti), yeah, he off tha hook, man! I mean, I just got hip to him like last year and I was trippin like, 'Damn, this cat was *ill*!' Just the way he would just capture words and put this ill-ass-Black-funk-ghetto up in it! But he had a crazy intellect, you know what I'm saying? So, when he expressed his shit, it sound like real street corner, but he was lookin at it like, 'This shit ain't cool,' you know what I'm saying? But it was so fresh that it was like Black folks was widdit, what he was sayin, you know what I'm saying? It was street-oriented, his style, you know what I'm saying? Like he was talkin about African tikis and ultraviolet-hip-triple-cool-Black, you know what I'm saying? He was one of the first cats that set off a lot of the Last Poets. He's like their inspiration. All of them, Last Poets is dope. Gwendolyn Brooks is off tha hook!" (Unpublished interview with Alim 2000.)

Zion's comments on Black Poetry represent what Dara Cook (2000) has written about as an intergenerational poetic exchange between Black poets of the 1960s and 1970s and the new millennium Hip Hop poets. Even as Sonia urges us on, many Hip Hop artists are indeed in tune with the Black Arts Movements. Zion continues to speak on the importance of creating art that will have the power to change things [A change gon come!]: "Besides just the happiness that comes from creating, I think that our willingness to accept responsibility for the ideas that we propagate brings us in line wit others in the past who have found it important to build wit the art that they create. They say that art imitates life . . . but, with all this hyped up media influence, we've seen how life has begun to imitate art as well. In that case, art has become our chance to influence the future in a direction that we see it fit to move in. Word."

It is not by chance that Zion's thought ends on the word "Word." Being influenced by Rastafarianism and Sufi Islam, Zion knows the principle of Word-Sound Power: "It's a principle that basically says that the words we use, and how we say them, impacts the world around us. It's founded on the theory that vibration is like the building block for all things. So, when one speaks, the entire universe is effected . . . no matter how minutely. Hence, it is best to cast a vibration that is uplifting to the universe in order that when the echo returns to sender, the self can be uplifted as well."

Zion's understanding of the transformative nature of language travels lightyears beyond the verbally dead. And like Sonia, you can hear that sense of urgency and concern in the Brotha's voice. That's why the insert on their critically acclaimed album, *Mind Over Matter*, reads: "We dedicate this album to the children of the Planet Earth. The world is in your hands, make of it what you will." That's real talk . . . *word*.

Pharoahe Monch and the analysis of Hip Hop poetics

In this section, and for the remainder of this chapter, we focus more closely on the work of Pharoahe Monch as we turn our attention to the task of developing an analytical schema of Hip Hop poetics. Pharoahe Monch is one of the most prominent and respected Hip Hop artists within the global Hip Hop community, yet, he remains largely unknown to the general public. He is but one example of the talent that lies just beyond the reach of the limelight of popular programs like MTV's TRL (Total Request Live). Pharoahe Monch is one-half of the dope-ass Hip Hop duo, Organized Konfusion (with his partner Prince Poetry). They recorded three critically acclaimed albums together: *Organized Konfusion* (1991), *Stress: The Extinction Agenda* (1994), and *The Equinox* (1997). Like the artists who receive a great deal of mass exposure, Pharoahe takes his art and his writing very seriously. Always takin it to the next level. In a recent conversation with Pharoahe, he explained his brand of Hip Hop and how it relates to other art forms: "I'm talking about *any* artist who takes grave integrity to their painting, their ink drawings, their charcoal paintings, their jazz music, their poetry, you know. For some people it comes easier. For some people, they sit down, and it's really from the heart . . . In these artists [including Pharoahe Monch], you have people who take their craft seriously." (Alim 2000, unpublished interview.)

Internal Affairs is Pharoahe Monch's first solo release after his nearly decade-long career as one-half of Organized Konfusion. For his first solo album, Pharoahe gives listeners an in-depth look into his life, hopes, dreams, philosophies, multiple personalities, and personal dilemmas as he flips *madd styles and skillz*. Let's go ahead and examine the Hip Hop poetics of this skilled lyricist/street linguist comin up outta Southside Queens.

As we've seen throughout this book, Pharoahe operates in a Hip Hop saturated environment where there is stiff competition among lyricists to devise unique ways of communicating thoughts, emotions, and everyday realities. Succinct statements with multiple meanings are highly valued. In introducing his album on "Intro," Pharoahe flexes one of the most remarkable aspects of his rhyming—his ability to squeeze an incredible amount of syllables into a short amount of time. Leading us into the rhyme below, Pharoahe launches a polysyllabic attack and hits us with:

(Example 2)

1	Cuz she's feelin the flow best believe I'm drillin the hole	14
2	[Singing] Heads hi-igh, kill 'em wit the low	07
3	Revealin, chillin, fillin up positioned to be killin the show	17
4	Stop illin I'm top billing plus I'm grillin the dough	13
5	For a couple of million or so I'll be willin to blow	16
6	Pharoahe look up in the air and a million niggaz are feelin 'em on the low	21

Example (2) (88 syllables) is loaded with assonance and various rhyme forms. Pharoahe is engaging in what I call *multirhyming*, the poetic equivalent to multitasking. We have a string of quadruple rhymes throughout the verse. Check it:

feel	in	the	flow
drill	in	the	hole
kill	in	the	show

grill	in	the	dough
will	in	to	blow
feeling	'em on	the	low

The pattern of this series of quadruple rhymes consists of four positions (phonetically): [ɪl . . . ɪn . . . də . . . o]. We notice in Line 2 that Pharoahe mixes things up a bit and borrows a line from a famous dancehall song. He not only borrows the line, but he borrows the exact intonation as well. When we get to Line 3, we are overwhelmed by numerous examples of assonance (discussed later in greater detail). Pharoahe repeatedly hits us with the [ɪ] sound, and in addition, continues the [ɪl] sound found in the quadruple rhyme. Pharoahe spits eleven [ɪ] syllables in Line 3 alone and continues the assonance with: feelin, million, and niggaz. We have a string of the [ɪl] sound combination with (orthographically): fillin/ billieve/ drillin/ kill/ rivillin/ chillin/ fillin/ killin/ illin/ billin/ grillin/ mill/ willin/ mill/ fillin/. In addition we have an internal rhyme (explained later) in Line 1 with "feelin the flow" and "drillin the hole." And consequently, in the middle of all of this verbal intricacy, the meaning is communicated quite profoundly.

Line 6 then leads us back to Example (1) at the beginning of this chapter. Pharoahe further displays his multirhyming skillz, where rhymes/rhyme tactics are imbedded within rhymes/rhyme tactics. He continues the [ɪ] sound assonance and engages in several new rhymes. Reread the lines and it becomes clear that "syllable" rhymes with the last three syllables of "umbilical" and with "typical" and "pitiful." Imbedded within that rhyme series is the additional two-word rhyme of "sick typical" and "pick pitiful." Furthermore, another rhyme combination is "rhymes to spit" and "dimes to git."

Before we excavate the rhyme tactics of Hip Hop lyricists, it is important to note that even now, approximately three decades after Hip Hop's birth, these skilled lyricists/poets/rhymers/street linguists remain almost entirely unexamined. Is it not time (shoot, it *been* time) to explore the high level of verbal virtuosity displayed by Black America's street linguists on some serious next millennium Rap ishhh? F-f-f-f-f-f-f-f-f-follow me for now . . .

Rhyme tactics

Pharoahe's acrobatic rhyme tactics are just one way he displays his verbal gymnastics. In poetry, whatever the form, three main types of full rhyme are recognized: masculine, feminine, and triple. A masculine rhyme simply refers to a one-syllable rhyme, such as: **sink/pink**, de**feat/eat**, and **sleep/creep**. Feminine rhymes are rhymes that involve two syllables, with the first syllable of the rhyme being the accented one: **drilling/grilling**, repa**ration/nation**, and **quiet/riot**. Triple rhymes, as the name suggests, are rhymes that consist of three syllables. The stress is on the antepenultimate syllable: **daringly/glaringly**, **steadily/readily**, and au**dacity/te**nacity.

Masculine, feminine, and triple rhymes can be found throughout Hip Hop lyrics. In addition, Hip Hop artists employ quadruple, quintuple, and even sextuple rhymes. On the album *Internal Affairs*, one finds several examples of this polysyllabic rhyming. Take this verse:

(Ex.3) 1 Get ate like cannibalism and sliced **surgical**
        2 In any *extremity* y'all get *infinity* **vertical**
        3 Every line to word of mine will be verbally placed to **murder you**
        4 The master, flippin **convertible** flows **irreversible**
        5 Unobtainable to the brain it's unexplainable what the **verse'll do**
        6 Pharoahe's the sperm your mind is the egg I'm **burstin through**
        7 Y'all <u>heard of me</u>, I pack macs and crack <u>vertebraes</u>
        8 Leave niggaz with <u>third degree</u> burns and back <u>surgery</u>
        9 Mics, guns, knives, pick, *declare which object*, flip
      10 I love niggaz on the run like ***the Blair Witch Project***

In this verse, the **bold** words represent triple rhymes that follow this phonetic pattern: [ɜr . . . ə . . . u]. The <u>underlined</u> words represent another set of triple rhymes that follow the phonetic pattern [ɔr . . . ə . . . ey]. Pharoahe stretches the pronunciation of every word in that rhyme sequence to rhyme with "vertebraes," so that "heard of me" sounds like "heard of may," and so on. This changing of pronunciation is deliberate, unlike the previous rhyme, and serves as an example of the primacy of sound over orthography in Hip Hop poetics. Pharoahe is using poetic license in order to achieve a near perfect match. The *italicized* words represent a quadruple rhyme that is near perfect. The ***italicized bold*** words represent a perfect quintuple rhyme that follows the phonetic pattern [də . . . er . . . hwɪtʃ . . . a . . . jɛkt]. The full complexity of this verse will be explored in a later section.

Busta Rhymes, whom Pharoahe admires for his lyrical word games and for his incredible work ethic, appears alongside Pharoahe on a song appropriately titled "The Next Shit." Busta rhymes **credible** with **schedule, federals**, and **pedestal**, creating a triple rhyme (and double internal rhyme) that follows the phonetic pattern [ɛ . . . ə . . . l]. Note that Busta pronounces "schedule" in such a way as to make it fit into the perfect triple rhyme match. Brick City's Redman joins Pharoahe, Busta, Method Man, Shabaam Sadeeq, and Lady Luck on the "Simon Says Remix," and adds his own series of triple rhymes with **barrel up, Arab bus**, and **karat cut** that follows the phonetic pattern [ær . . . ə . . . ʌ].

In "Behind Closed Doors," Pharoahe strikes again with a series of "off tha wall" triple rhymes:

(Ex. 4) 1 Cut off his hands and send his girl multiple finger **sandwiches**
        2 If she **manages** to do **damages**, put her in **bandages**
        3 The **amateurs—bananas** is the u**nanimous** way we choose to live **scandalous**

4 Even with doorknobs you couldn't **handle this**
5 Pharoahe's the host, the audience, and the muthafuckin **panelist**

The phonetic pattern here is [æ... nasal (either n or m)... ə... ɪs]. This series of ten triple rhymes occurring in only five lines is so highly compacted as to suggest that Pharoahe's main purpose was to create this incredible rhyme string. However, the five lines fit meaningfully into the first and last part of this verse (not shown) in which Pharoahe gains verbal advantage over other rappers by claiming that he is a "high evolutionary rebel" in the Rap game.

Pharoahe's verses are loaded with examples of quadruple rhyme, as we noted above. On "The Next Shit," with Busta Rhymes, both MC's drop some quadruple rhymes and quintuple rhymes. Busta Rhymes spills a perfect quadruple rhyme in the midst of a four feminine rhyme series. The perfect quadruple rhyme (**hibernation** and **hyper nation**) is enhanced by the presence of the additional feminine rhymes (**moderation** and **situation**). The phonetic pattern follows [hay... bilabial (either b or p)... ɜrneyʃɪn].

In his verse on the same song, Pharoahe analogizes his flow with a baseball player's game as he drops a near perfect quintuple rhyme:

(Ex. 5) 1 The **last batter ta hit, blast shattered ya hip**
         2 Smash any splitter or fastball, **that'll be it**

The quintuple rhyme follows the phonetic pattern [æst... ædə... ɪ]. Following right behind the quintuple rhyme pair is "that'll be it," which rhymes with the last four syllables of the rhyme pair.

Pharoahe kicks several other quadruple rhymes on his album. The next two come from "Rape," and the "Simon Says Remix," respectively:

back	to	tha	case
slap	in	tha	face
crack	in	a	safe
hap	pens	ta	base
spec	tac	u	lar
ver	nac	u	lar
mir	ac	u	lous
im	mac	u	late

While the last set is not perfect, the rhymes still show Pharoahe's creativity with matching four syllable words. Two sets of perfect quadruple rhymes from "Behind Closed Doors" follow:

(Ex. 6) 1 *How I made it* you **salivated** over my **calibrated**
         2 Raps that **validated** my ghetto cre<u>dibility</u>

3 *Still I be* packin <u>agilities</u> unseen
4 Forreal—a my killin <u>abilities</u> unclean <u>facilities</u>

In these four lines we have two sets of quadruple rhymes:

sal	i	vat	ed
cal	i	brat	ed
val	i	dat	ed

Note that Line 1 begins with the phrase "How I made it." While this is not a perfect four-syllable rhyme match with the others, it serves to prepare us for what lies ahead. The next set of quadruple rhymes follows:

a	gil	i	ties
a	bil	i	ties
fa	cil	i	ties

As with the phrase "How I made it," this quadruple rhyme begins with "Still I be," which prepares us for the upcoming quadruple set by rhyming with the last three syllables (see the section on *bridge rhyming*).

Prince Poetry, Pharoahe's partner from Organized Konfusion, gets in on the action and spits a perfect quadruple rhyme in, "God Send."

(Ex. 7) 1 Stray bullets continue **shatterin dreams, batterin spleens**
            2 I'm **gatherin schemes** had only cream just as <u>bad as a fiend</u>

shat	ter	in	dreams
bat	ter	in	spleens
gat	her	in	schemes

In addition to this near perfect set of quadruple rhymes, Prince Poetry rhymes two additional four-syllable phrases, but this time only the first and last syllable rhymes with the quadruple rhyme set.

In "Simon Says," Pharoahe perfects a quintuple rhyme by reducing "you" to [yə]:

(Ex. 8) 1 You all up in the Range, then your shit's **inebriated**
            2 Phased from your original plan, **ya deviated**
            3 I **alleviated** the pain with a long term goal . . .

in	e	bri	at	ed
ya	de	vi	at	ed
al	le	vi	at	ed

Rapping alongside Pharoahe on "The Truth," Common writes a remarkable set of three sextuple rhymes which exhibit parallelism in the first two instances:

(Ex. 9) 1 See the truth in **the thighs of a stripper, the eyes of my nigga**
         2 If it's only one, **then why should it differ**?

The phonetic pattern here is [ə . . . ay . . . ʌ . . . ə . . . i . . . ə]. The last phrase does not fit the sextuplet perfectly because it does not continue the parallelism witnessed in the first two rhymes. Nonetheless, this is an impressive display of polysyllabic rhyming.

Compound internal rhymes and chain rhymes

Some of the rhymes we have seen above are end rhymes, simply meaning that they are positioned at the end of a line. End rhymes, if used cleverly, can be quite complex. In this example, Pharoahe's end rhymes are all feminine rhymes that follow the phonetic pattern of [i . . . əm]:

(Ex. 10) 1 [Yo, where you at?] Uptown let me **see 'em**
          2 Notorious for the six-fives and the **BM's**
          3 Heads give you beef, you put 'em in the mauso**leum**
          4 And the shit don't start jumpin til after 12 **PM**
          5 Ungh, ignorant minds, I **free 'em**
          6 If you tired of the same old everyday you will a**gree I'm**
          7 The most obligated . . .

Whether the end rhyme consists of a verb + pronoun, a two-letter abbreviation, the last two syllables of a four-syllable word, or the last syllable of a verb + a pronoun contraction, the end result is always the same: [i . . . əm]

Internal rhyme is often used to add a level of complexity to the typical end rhyme. A simple internal rhyme may sound like this: "I spit rap **poetics** like energy **kinetic**/ Can't keep up with the flow cuz it's madd **frenetic**." While there are three rhymes, the internal rhyme is between **poetics** and **kinetic**, since **poetics** falls in the middle of the line. Pharoahe often creates an astonishing effect by using a series of internal rhymes. For example, we return to Example (3) (labeled 11 below), but this time we will only focus on the use of internal rhyme:

(Ex. 11) 1 Get ate <u>like</u> cannibalism and <u>sliced</u> surgical
          2 In any <u>extremity</u> y'all get <u>infinity</u> vertical
          3 Every <u>line</u> to word of <u>mine</u> will be *verbally* placed to murder you
          4 The master, flippin <u>convertible</u> flows <u>irreversible</u>
          5 <u>Unobtainable</u> to the <u>brain</u> it's <u>unexplainable</u> what the verse'll do
          6 Pharoahe's the sperm your minds the eggs I'm burstin through
          7 Y'all <u>heard of me</u>, I *pack macs* and *crack* <u>vertebraes</u>

8 Leave niggaz in <u>third degree</u> burns and *back* <u>surgery</u>
9 Mics, guns, knives, <u>pick</u>, declare which object, <u>flip</u>
10 Have niggaz on the run like the Blair Witch Project

We see a diverse and effective usage of internal rhyme in these ten lines. Pharoahe uses the typical internal rhyme, in which the rhymes are positioned in the middle and the end of the line (such as Lines 4, 8, and 9). He also uses a type of internal rhyme in which none of the rhymes fall in the end position (such as Lines 1, 2, 3, 5). Line 5, for example, ends in "verse'll do," which rhymes with "irreversible" in Line 4. However, Pharoahe places three rhymes in between those end rhymes with "unobtainable," "brain," and "unexplainable."

In addition to these two types of internal rhyme, he also utilizes what I call *compound internal rhyme* (CIR) (such as line 7). A compound internal rhyme can be described as a poetic construction where an internal rhyme is imbedded within another internal rhyme. The internal rhyme on the outer edge is the *primary internal rhyme* (PIR) and the internal rhyme on the inner edge is the *secondary internal rhyme* (SIR). In Line 7 of Example (11) reads, "Y'all <u>heard of me</u>, I *pack macs* and *crack* <u>vertebraes</u>." The PIR is with <u>heard of me</u> and <u>vertebraes</u>, while the SIR is with *pack*, *macs*, and *crack*. The complexity of Pharoahe's internal rhyme tactics can be overwhelming, especially when one looks at Line 8 in conjunction with Line 7. Pharoahe continues the rhyme with the phrase "back surgery," which is a quadruple rhyme with "crack vertebraes." Further, in Line 3 he places the word "**ver**bally" in perfect position to accentuate the /ver/ sound in the rhymes of **ver**tical, con**ver**tible, irre**ver**sible, and **ver**se'll do.

In this next verse, Pharoahe provides another example of *CIR*:

(Ex. 12) 1 Yo, I stick around like hockey, now what the *puck*
2 **Cooler than fuck**, <u>maneuver</u> like <u>Van**couver** Canucks</u>

This CIR is so intertwined that the separation between the PIR and the SIR is almost indiscernible. However, a closer listen reveals that **Cooler than fuck** plays a dual role. Not only does "fuck" rhyme with the previous "puck," but the entire phrase is a quadruple rhyme with **couver Canucks**. This quadruple rhyme serves as the PIR, while <u>maneuver</u> rhymes with <u>Vancouver</u> as the SIR.

Another illuminating example of Pharoahe's internal rhyme abilities can be seen in Example (4). The phonetic pattern follows [æ . . . nasal (either n or m) . . . ə . . . ɪs]. The abundance of rhyming words that are strung together in these two lines almost obliterates the distinction between internal rhyme and end rhyme. In cases like this, the rhyme becomes what I call a *chain rhyme*—where the rhymes need not fall in either the middle or the end positions, but can be placed anywhere (continuously) in the line.

Alliteration and assonance

Pharoahe enhances his intricate rhyme schemes by exploiting two fairly commonly known poetic techniques—alliteration and assonance. It is Pharoahe's decision to use these techniques with precision, making surgical incisions like a verbal physician. In fact, the use of these two techniques is often what makes a listener be like, "Yo, that sound ill right there!" In other words, these techniques are sought in poetry to create euphony—a harmonic, *dope*-sounding musical effect. This effect is highlighted by the proximity of the words/sounds and by the timing and flow of the sound patterns.

When these two techniques are used in a witty way they can sneak into your subconscious without you even realizing what just happened. At the same time, though, the techniques can also be used in a "in yo face" type of way as a means of displaying one's verbal ingenuity. Alliteration is a technique that Pharoahe adopted early on before he was signed as a member of Organized Konfusion (the alliterative verse on their demo tape actually helped to clinch their record deal). On his solo debut, *Internal Affairs*, he returns to this technique almost as a way of signifying a new beginning as a solo artist.

In this next verse, we follow Pharoahe as he flexes his phonetic skillz fiercely on a fly freestyle flow:

(Ex. 13)   1   **F-f-f-f-f-f-f-f-f**-follow me **f**or now
         2   **F**or no **f**ormidable **f**ights I've been **f**ormed to **f**orget
         3   **F**or **Ph**aroahe **f**ucks **f**amiliar **f**oes **f**irst
         4   Be**f**o **f**ondling **f**emale MC's **f**iercely
         5   **F**ocus on the **f**act that **f**acts can be **f**abricated to **f**orm lies
         6   My **ph**onetics alone **f**orces **f**eeble MC's into de**f**ense on the **f**ly
         7   **F**eel me, **f**orreal-a

In Line 1, Pharoahe gives us fair warning for what's about to fall upon us by forming the first syllable in a stuttering format. "F-f-f-f-f-f-f-f-f-follow me for now," he begins, as he takes the listener on an alliterative ride. Alliteration is normally used in word pairs, such as "**w**ord **w**arrior" or "**h**ip-**h**op **h**ead," and is often a subtle technique. Yet, Pharoahe's complex and creative use of alliteration here is performed "in yo face" style.

This "in yo face" style of alliteration has been used by the more creative Hip Hop poets and provides for a poetic effect that keeps the listener dangling off of the MC's every word. Rapper Gift of Gab from California's Blackalicious provides one of the more memorable examples of this alliterative style on "A2G." He rhymes seven stanzas, starting each stanza with a single sound. For example:

(Ex. 14)   1   We're going to learn to hear words with the vowel **A** sound . . .
            Listen with c**a**re

2   I be the analog arsonist aimin at your arteries
3   All-seeing abstract, analyze everything
4   Adding on, absolutely abolishing
5   Average amateurs' arsenal, just astonishing . . .
6   I be the big bad body rock in Bombay to Boulevard bully BACK
7   Batter bring a bomb to the battlefield
8   Bloody black beats bringing bottoms of boom
9   Basically build barriers, bewilder buffoons

The rhymer continues with this alliterative rhyme technique until he reaches the letter /g/, where he begins to play on his name, "Gift of Gab." Other rhymers, like Saigon and Kool G Rap, get real street widdit and warn all other MCs that they "ain't gotta shit on y'all niggas; we P on y'all bitch-ass niggas!" The clever use of the letter P throughout this hardcore lyrical storm has made Hip Hop Headz worldwide rewind the track to get a closer listen. Saigon, as if predicting this, raps, "I pause for you people to peep the letter P, poetically putting the paragraphs so perfectly."

   Aside from alliteration, Hip Hop headz are skilled users of assonance as well. We witnessed an example of Pharoahe's use of assonance with the [ɪ] sound earlier. In the next verse, Pharoahe hops from the rhyme sounds of [i followed by a nasal], [[ay] followed by a nasal], alliteration with /f/ and /m/, and various internal rhymes.

(Ex. 15)   1   My exterior serene with the potential of a killin machine
            2   Ex-marine you drag queen, we tag team
            3   Queens finest the alliance defiant we bag fiends
            4   The fuck you lookin in my *face* fo nigga?
            5   I *mace* *m*ics and then lace the bass with figgas

The interplay of assonance, alliteration, internal and end rhymes in this verse constitute a *multirhyme matrix* while making the poet's point perfectly clear. Pharoahe challenges MC's to "bring it on if you think you can hang."

   Pharoahe's album is laced with assonantal and alliterative gems. In many instances the assonantal rhymes are loaded with humor:

(Ex. 16)   1   "Hell'll be froze over when I celebrate celibacy, case closed"—
               Pharoahe Monch
            2   "Shabaam Sadeeq, injure your fleet into delete/ Y'all crabs are
               weak, frail like a fiend's physique/ I stay on the street, stay on the
               beat, stay with the heat/"—Shabaam Sadeeq
            3   "Like when British civil servants pass secrets to the Soviets"—Busta
               Rhymes
            4   "Never you devils, my level's that of a high evolutionary rebel"—
               Pharoahe Monch

5 "Then I'm gonna let it hang, and sit it on/ the desk of any redneck record exec"—Pharoahe Monch
6 "Every line to word of mine was like a rhyme I wouldn't lie I swear"—Pharoahe Monch

Back-to-back chain rhymes and mosaic rhymes

As we have seen thus far, Pharoahe employs various types of rhymes and rhyme styles in his Hip Hop poetry. Earlier we saw an example of a **chain rhyme**, where the distinction between internal and end rhymes is nearly obliterated due to the frequency and positioning of the rhymes in the multiple rhyme sequence. Another type of chain rhyme used by Pharoahe is what I call the **back-to-back chain rhyme**. In this type of chain rhyme, he strings several perfect rhymes together consecutively. For example, in "Simon Says," the chorus contains the lines:

(Ex. 17) 1 New York **City gritty committee pity** the fool that
         2 Act **shitty** in the midst of the calm the **witty**

The **bold** words represent the six rhymes in these two lines. The back-to-back chain rhyme consists of four links: "City gritty committee pity."
   In another example, Pharoahe creatively uses three links to make perfect rhymes out of seemingly "unrhymable" words:

(Ex. 18) 1 I **scatter data that'll** hammer niggaz . . .

When Pharoahe fires this line in his rapid spit-fire flow: scatter → scatta, data → datta, and that'll → thatta, forming a perfect back-to-back chain rhyme effect.
   In the previous example we also see what has been called a *mosaic rhyme*. A mosaic rhyme is "a feminine or triple rhyme in which at least one element is composed of more than one word" (Steele 1999: 24). Mosaic rhymes are highly complex in that they allow the poet to vary the parts of speech with which he chooses to rhyme. Steele continues: "Since rhymes please most when the words included make unexpected yet persuasive connections between ideas, objects, and qualities, good rhymers often match different grammatical categories—nouns with verbs, verbs with adjectives, adverbs with nouns, and so forth." Although not using this same technical language, recall Kurupt's vivid description of how he constructs a perfect rhyme in Chapter 4.
   Pharoahe, and other Hip Hop rhymers, take mosaic rhyming to "da next level" by putting together some of the most unlikely rhyme candidates. Pharoahe exemplifies this technique in Lines 3, 4 and 5 of Example (4) and the phrase "man'll miss." This series of perfect triple rhymes follows the phonetic pattern [æ . . . nasal (either n or m) . . . əl . . . ɪs]. This mosaic rhyme catches the listener off-guard because the rhymes consist of four different parts of speech: (1) an

adjective (**scandalous**), (2) a verb + pronoun (**handle this**), (3) a noun (**panelist**), and (4) a noun + contraction + verb (**man'll miss**).

In another surprising mosaic rhyme combination, Pharoahe pieces together a triple rhyme set that follows this phonetic pattern: [a . . . stop . . . ɪ . . . ɪl]

(Ex. 19) 1 Truth had me up against the ropes and semiconscious with no **boxing skills**
2 Fear of it makes hair on my neck grow like Min**oxodil**
3 Watchin the **clock is ill** when faced with the truth
4 Parallels observing, amateur video tapes of
5 Twenty-one top notch NYPD **cops git ill**
6 Fill they minds **not to kill**, still son, never revealed
7 True feelings, we speakin on the truth right now in itself is healing

The noun phrase **boxing skills** rhymes with the last three syllables of the word Min**oxodil** which rhymes with these three word phrases—**clock is ill**, **cops git ill**, and **not to kill**.

Two more examples of Pharoahe's use of mosaic rhymes follow:

(Ex. 20) 1 The master, flippin con**vertible** flows irre**versible**
2 Unobtainable to the brain it's unexplainable what the **verse'll do**
3 Pharoahe's the sperm your mind's the egg I'm **burstin through**

In the following example, he rhymes three separate words with one four-syllable word:

(Ex. 21) 1 I told you I'd **hurt the music**
2 Travelin back . . . before Christ was **persecuted**

Next level poetry: The bridge rhyming technique

Taking a closer look at Pharoahe's Hip Hop poetics, the lyricists and the dope MC's know "from the git" that he doin some serious next level poetry ishhh in his music. A prime example of this next level poetry is what I call the *bridge rhyming technique*, which is widely used in Hip Hop poetics. In musical terms, a bridge is a transitional passage that connects two subjects or movements. The important point here is that the bridge is *transitional*, allowing two seemingly disparate or distant objects/movements to coalesce into one.

Pharoahe and his crew of Hip Hop collaborators use this bridge rhyming technique to form a continuous highway of rhymes that connects two seemingly "unrhymable" words/verses. This technique is used in a variety of ways. In a verse by Shaolin's Method Man, he attacks his critics and answers a weak "diss record" which was made by another rapper who shall remain nameless. The end rhymes are: **have one, blast sun, fast one, passion, fashion, clashin**. At first glance, these do not appear to be rhymes, but the bridge in this verse is **flashin**, which is inserted before the fourth rhyme (**passion**). Flashin allows for the smooth transition between rhymes 1–3 and rhymes 4–6. In rhymes 1–3, the phonetic pattern is [æ . . . ʌn] and ends with the near perfect rhyme, **blast sun** and **fast one**. **Passion** also rhymes with this pattern. The use of **flashin** in this line allows the rhyme to continue with **fashion**, and **clashin**, which follow the pattern [æ . . . ɪn]. The smooth transition, when done skillfully, is noticeable only on a subconscious level. For instance, when hearing these six lines the listener will know that the rhymes sound "on point." However, if the average person were to read the rhyme (probably focusing on the end rhymes), **have one** and **clashin** would never be expected to function as end rhymes in the same verse. It is the *bridge* that makes this possible.

Returning to Talib Kweli's verse on "The Truth" (p. 86), we notice an intricate use of bridge rhyme:

(Ex. 22) 1 The way you speak is lighter than a <u>pamphlet</u>
          2 Cuz the truth gives the words the weight of a <u>planet</u> <u>goddammit</u>
          3 I <u>ran wit</u> what God <u>planted</u> [**in my heart**] and I under<u>stand</u> it
          4 To be to **bring the light to the dark, breathe some life in this art**

In the first three lines, we have six rhymes with the pattern [æ . . . ɪt]. The bridge is built in Line 3 when Talib, amidst the [æ . . . ɪt] rhymes, drops the phrase [**in my heart**]. This phrase acts as a bridge to set up the next sextuple rhyme and to complete the thought. This bridge rhyming technique is incredibly complex and, in this case, the effect works so much on the subconscious level that the transition flows like water.

Pharoahe takes the subtlety of this technique even further in this next verse:

(Ex. 23) 1 How I made it you <u>salivated</u> over my <u>calibrated</u>
          2 Raps that <u>validated</u> my ghetto [**credibility**]
          3 Still I be packin <u>agilities</u> unseen
          4 Forreal-a my killin <u>abilities</u> unclean <u>facilities</u>
          5 For more than [**military**] tactics <u>obscene</u>, <u>extreme</u> confidential
          6 My exterior <u>serene</u> with the potential of a killin <u>machine</u>

In these five lines we see two bridges built on assonance alone. That is, the foundation of the bridges stands on the fact that key sounds contained within them are present in previous lines. This makes the transition between very different rhymes far less bumpy and allows for a smooth ride.

The word [**credibility**] is full of sounds that occur in the previous rhymes (like /d/ and /b/ and the repetition of the [ɪ] sound). This places [**credibility**] in a connective position that binds Lines 1 and 2 with the rest of the verse. The rhymes immediately following [**credibility**] rhyme with the last three syllables of the bridge. In Line 4, the second bridge is built by the use of the word [**military**]. This bridge contains a crucial sequence of sounds that are found in the previous rhymes—**ilit** (as we see in credi**bility**, agi**lities**, a**bilities**, and faci**lities**). The precise positioning of this bridge allows it to serve as the connective tissue that links the line to the remainder of the verse.

Perhaps the most widely used type of bridge is one that places a rhyme in the first part of the line, when it is expected to be an end rhyme. This method allows the poet to switch direction and still stay on course. For example:

(Ex. 24)   1   Some might even say this song is <u>sexist-es</u>
          2   Cuz I asked the girls to rub on their <u>breast-eses</u>
          3   Whether you ridin the train or in <u>Lexus-es</u>
          4   This is for either or Rollies or <u>Timex-eses</u>
          5   Wicked like [**Exorcist**], this is the *joint*
          6   If you holdin up the wall, then you missin the *point*

The rhymes begin following the pattern: [ɛ . . . ks . . . ɪs . . . ɪs] (substitute /s/ for /x/ in Line 2). Pharoahe uses [**Exorcist**] here, which follows the same pattern, to switch directions entirely and lead us into the chorus.

Pharoahe's ability to strategically place these bridges is remarkable. This bridge rhyming technique gives the Hip Hop poet's lyrics a melodic, musical quality. The voice is played as an instrument and the musical bridge analogy is fully realized. The arrangement of these lyrical bridges not only holds the verse together, but also allows the poet to be far more creative and expand beyond the standard rhyme format. This new rhyming innovation demands further study.

Wordplay, metaphor, and narrativity

In the last example of the bridge rhyming technique, Pharoahe is also exhibiting humorous wordplay. Notice how he forces the rhymes in that sequence to match "breast-eses," which is how some Black Americans pronounce words with the final cluster /st/. (You might hear something like "tesses" instead of "tests," or "artisses" instead of "artists"). This particular word, "breast-eses," has been a popular source of Hip Hop humor ever since the Wayans brother used it on the once popular television comedy show, "In Living Color." There are numerous verses where Pharoahe plays with words, and he even dedicates an entire song to wordplay, "Official."

Pharoahe often employs the metaphor in his work, or as many Hip Hoppers say, "word-pictures." As he did with wordplay, he dedicated an entire song to the metaphor entitled "Rape," which is a song about a Rapper who's tired of the "million MC's who ain't sayin nuthin" (as Pharoahe borrows a line from legendary Philly Rapper Schoolly D). In the story, Pharoahe sneakily stalks the beat while it plays on, oblivious to his presence. The metaphor is fully realized when one places his rhymes in the broader, in-group, evaluative discourse among Hip Hop headz. Hip Hop headz often criticize wack ("unskilled") MC's for "raping" Hip Hop, that is, writing rhymes that fall beneath the aesthetic "standard" for the sole purpose of *gittin paid*, while forsaking the culture.

In "Rape," Pharoahe's rhymes unfold in story format. Undoubtedly his narrativity is at its peak when he engages in personal reflection. Personal narrativizing is a technique many Hip Hop artists use to draw the listener closer into their wor(l)ds and their way of seeing the wor(l)d (Smitherman 1977: 112). Some examples that stand out in most Hip Hop heads' minds right now are Raekwon's verse on "C.R.E.A.M," Tupac's "Dear Mama," Jay-Z's "You Must Love Me," Dr. Dre's "The Message," and Ghostface Killah's "All That I Got Is You."

In "God Send," Pharoahe uses several techniques to narrate a story about the murder of his friend, Donovan, including flashback (when he recounts the days Donovan used to ball on the courts), role play (when he performs the dialogue between Donovan and his mother), suspense (right before the shooting), imagery (the description of Donovan's fluttering eyes and bloody mouth), simile and wordplay ("they wet him like Reggae Sunsplash"), and voice inflection (in his heartfelt search for an answer, "Whyyyyyyy, whyyyyyyy???"). The literary techniques employed by Pharoahe are too numerous to discuss in this chapter, and are the subject of future research.

On some serious next millennium Rap ishhh: Watch out!

> The next millennium rap now everybody listen
> Condition yourself to be knocked outta commission
> Watch out! Cuz this is a new world transmission
> Permission to shine now our time to glisten
> > The next shit!
> > The next shit!
> > Th-th-th-the next shit!

Like Busta and Pharoahe rhyme on this chorus, now is the time for Hip Hop poetics to glisten. Ridin on the shouldas of Black Arts Movement souljas, Hip Hop poets be bringin that next, next, other, new, different ishhh that's revitalizing poetry as we know it. Like Busta rhymes on his verse: "Yo, Busta Rhymes, the imperial lyrical, ya heard?/ Kill like a one syllable word!" Not only will Busta slay MC's with a simple one-syllable word, but "kill," in fact, *is* a one-syllable word. And Pharoahe joins in: "Didn't figure the ridiculous flow would hit vigorously/ Triggerin a rigorous amount of energy!"

Whether stringing together multiple polysyllabic rhymes, or endless assonance and alliteration, or creating compound internal rhymes, or back-to-back chain rhymes, or multiple mosaic rhymes, or building bridge rhymes, Hip Hop poets/MC's offer a vast body of poetic and linguistic data. We have only begun to explore the intricate ways that Hip Hop headz like Common "be forever puttin words together"—we are simply scratching the surface. There are numerous other factors that remain unexplored. Although we mentioned the *parallelisms* at work in Hip Hop poetics, the full complexity has not been revealed. For instance, when Snoop Dogg rhymes on "Bitch Please II," with Xzibit, Dr. Dre, and Eminem, what's goin on here? Now, you would have to listen to this yourself to see how Snoop measures the syllables to "ride the beat", but the parallelism in timing and phrasing is striking. The rise and fall of Snoop's voice between the first and second half of his lines match perfectly and this enhances the rhyme tremendously. In fact, it's the main feature here. Snoop often extends the theme of parallelism by picking up the pace and firing off a string of triple rhymes with the same three-word phrasing.

Eminem, "the great American white hope" (as Snoop jokingly calls him), and Fabolous are experts at this technique of parallel phrasing. Check Eminem out on his album *Marshall Mathers*, where his use of parallel intonation and timing is nearly overwhelming. He often splits his lines into two segments, with each segment containing numerous syllables and ending in polysyllablic rhymes. He can be heard spittin *octuple rhymes*, I guess one would call them, that follow a clear phonetic pattern. The aural effect of this parallel phrasing is amazing. Fabolous is perhaps one of the most advanced users of parallel phrasing. His verse on "Trade It All," found on the *Barbershop* soundtrack, contains a string of *fifteen* sextuple rhymes! These two artists' use of parallelism and polysyllabic rhyming constitutes a future study in itself.

But, still, there are various other factors that have to be taken into account such as flow, delivery, vocal texture, range, timing, style, and other Hip Hop aesthetic elements (recall Mos Def's description of a dope MC earlier in this chapter). Take this example from Biggie (the Notorious B.I.G.) where the notorious one boasts about his sexual prowess by rhyming **spec—tacular** with **neck to yo back then ya**. The spectacular aspect of this rhyme is how Biggie times it. The pause in **spec—tacular** is done in such a way as to match the phrase **neck to yo back then ya**. It's easier to see when it's laid out like this:

(Ex. 25)	spec	—	tac	u	lar
	neck	to yo	back	then	ya

By adjusting his timing, Biggie is using *ghost syllables* to make his rhyme complete. Manipulation of the *flow* constitutes an area for future investigation. For a preliminary, yet illuminating, analysis, see Wood (1999).

One quick listen to the new album by Blackalicious or *any* of Aceyalone's albums lets us know that we got a ways to go. Hip Hop headz are moooovin FAST and time travelin at hi speeds. And Pharoahe and his crew *definitely* on some serious next level poetry type ishhh, and the next millennium rap is some next level poetry. No doubt! I ask again: Is it not time (shoot, it *been* time) to explore the high level of verbal virtuosity displayed by Black America's street linguists on some serious next millennium rap ishhh? Can the scholarly world keep up with these highly skilled street linguists? Or, like my man Pharoahe say, will it condition itself to be knocked outta commission? I don't know about y'all, but this sounds like a job for the newly formed Hip Hop Linguistics . . . Watch out! We on some next shit!

Chapter 7

"I'm Pharoahe when I'm on stage; I'm Troy when I'm home in Queens"

An interview with Pharoahe Monch

San Francisco, California
June 30, 2000

P = Pharoahe Monch
A = Alim

A: What's the importance of the Spitkicker Tour for Hip Hop, and for you, personally?

P: I mean, for Hip Hop, it brings about like minds and a like mentality on stage, which is something that me and Mos was talkin about years ago in terms of trying to bring a balance to the tours and what's goin on with the radio. And what I mean by that balance is, you know, you watch the video channels and you get *smacked* with a certain brand of Hip Hop. But it's other forms and, I mean, it's deeper forms. In these artists, you have people who take their craft seriously. And I thought I had incredible integrity until I got together with these like minds and went in the studio with De La Soul. I seen the type of integrity they put into their work. And what me and Mos was just talkin about at the time—this was like a couple years ago at the height of a bunch of bullshit that was goin on—we was like, "You know what? It's not about hatin or bringin down other music." Because without humorous music, or dance music, or fun music, or hardcore music, it's no variety. And that's what Hip Hop is based on. But we believe in a fairness. And in Black music, and in Hip Hop music, it needs to be a balance. Because a human, and common sense, should just be able to have a choice. A choice to be deep and choose. A choice to choose this brand of art or a time to be silly. It's time for all of that. But our brand doesn't get put out there, and we was just like, "Let's bring it to the people."

A: Now when you say "our brand," how would you define or how would you characterize that?

P: Yeah, I'm talkin about *any* artist who takes grave integrity to their painting, their ink drawings, their charcoal paintings, their jazz music, their poetry, you know. For some people it comes easier. For some people, they sit down, and it's really from the heart. And, I mean, you can listen to these artists and tell when they're havin fun, and tell when they're serious. And, I mean, we have fun. We're serious. We're assholes. We're political . . .

A: [Laughter]

P: You know what I'm saying? We're activists. Everybody, even on this tour, is a different brand. You know, Common is bringin the soul. Kweli is bringin the Black nationalism, the culture. De La is bringin the fun, and the good music. I'm tryin to bring a little bit of *all* of that stuff. And it's good for me. And to answer your second question, I'm just so inspired, you know, just watching how the people are reacting to Talib and Common and De La. And it's what's inspiring me to go back and record my new album, which is what I feel this is all about. 360 Degreez of Inspiration. You hear my album, you're like, "Okay." Friendly competition, you know. "When I put my shit out, I'ma let the people know!" And that's healthy for Hip Hop because it keeps it elevating on a lyrical level and a music level. I mean, you got to come with some *shit* now to come better than the Common album. You got to come with some *shit* now to come better than the De La album. Talib's lettin me hear his new album, I'm like, [Eyes Buggin] "Yo, man!"

A: He hit you off early with it?

P: Yeah, I gotta go *back*!

A: How important is it to have that group to internally check and elevate yourself like that?

P: It's dope. And, I mean, we did a song for Lyricist Lounge where me and Common and Black Thought were just, you know, freestylin on it, rappin, some written, some off the top. And we were just sayin how—Black Thought was sayin how straight up and down he picked up the Pharoahe Monch album, enjoys it, listens to it. But then he's like, "Fuck *that*!"

A: [Laughter]

P: You know?! "When my album come, I'm comin better than that!" You know what I'm saying? And I expect him to elevate. And I expect him to inspire me when he drops his shit. That's what art is about, you know. On a jazz level, Hip Hop is so reminiscent of those cats who kept buildin off each other with harmonies and melodies and, you know, you could see the progression. And that's what Hip Hop needs to get back to, the progression. And it's hard, I won't lie, because the people are not well-educated. The new listeners are just brainwashed and they might not easily recognize . . .

A: What leads to that brainwashing, you think?

P: What leads to it is the fact that there's not a balance, you know, or enough integrity. And it doesn't take a lot to brainwash someone or make those type of songs that are for the radio. But, again, what's beautiful now is you have a Mos Def goin gold. You have a Roots goin platinum. And that's some education for your ass, right there! Because, you know, you pick up the Roots album because of the single you heard on the radio with Erykah Badu [and Eve]. You put that CD on, you gon get *blasted* with well-arranged music and you're goin to get an education—whether you know it or not. And that's very important, you know what I'm saying? It's very important, because all things are mathematical. All things have a right and wrong. And your approach to life should be calculated. Your approach to life should be long term, you know what I'm saying? And the music that you put out, you know, we try to calculate it and arrange it. It's a beautiful manifestation that's almost God-like. You get a thought. It comes to fruition. You're like, "I wonder if people gonna view the same manifestation the way I did when I conceived it?" You put it out. They see the beauty in it, and they respond back to you. And that's the 360 of it all. Mission accomplished, you know. With *life*, what I found out that is much deeper than music is a 360 in itself, where you materialize from a spiritual world to a physical manifestation. Common sense tells you that you have to return back to that spiritual world. We all do. We all will not remain in this existence. So, your time spent here, although it may seem long, is limited. Your time spent here actually should be dedicated to what's going to happen after you perish. But the brainwash is to keep people from seeing life in that manner, and to keep people clawin at each other, and keep people from arranging the shit properly. And praying, and basically, just treatin people like you wanna be treated. And the confusion in that is, you know, if you keep people from knowin about God, then they exist on a freestyle level just goin about, and they're not well-educated. I mean, those arrangements are placed there for us, whether you're Jewish, Muslim, Christian. It's basic arrangements there for you to follow and you could avoid a lot of bullshit if you follow those arrangements. And that's how I liken life to music, you know what I'm saying? And we need to get back to that. And the brainwashing of it all is to clutter people with the bullshit that doesn't allow them to stay on the path, you know what I'm saying? And I'm not sayin that Hip Hop is the be-all-end-all answer and the cure, and the answer for people. But if you follow the history and you study, you will see the *likeness*, and therefore, you can draw metaphors from that, you know what I'm saying? That's how I embrace music, you know, especially Hip Hop. Every Hip Hop song is almost quotable to this day. Me and my crew, we almost carry on conversations with Hip Hop lyrics, you know what I'm saying?

A: [Laughter] That's deep! Now when did you get this sense of spirituality? Because on the album it comes through really strong, you know what I mean? That's something you can feel. When did that come about for you?

P: I think the Word is innate. It's just in my nature, man.

A: What do you mean by that?

P: It's just something that I evolved into. It's actually a struggle that I'm goin through right now, like we expressed on the last Organized album, *The Equinox*, which is expressing a medium between the light and the dark side. And people who know the Truth, but they don't go a hundred percent with the Truth. They're still caught up in these earthly things. And it's not a easy thing, you know. I know a lot of righteous people in music and in life, that's a struggle, because we're all human. And to me, you know, it's a side of the music industry that's God-like that I enjoy because I get goose bumps when I bring my thoughts to fruition, you know. It's like a perfect plan almost if you say, "What if you was to make this song that would make people listen to it over and over again because the ending is the beginning and the beginning is the ending?" You get that concept, and you work on it, and you do it. And a kid comes up to you and he says, "Yo, I listened to that song twenty times in a row!" That's a beautiful thing, you know what I'm saying? And on that side it's joyous. On the other side, you have the façade. You have the afterparties and a lot of things that you get into doin when you relinquish yourself to your career. And I don't know if it's right for me and how I feel spiritually, yet. I think that's one of the major things that's held me back as a artist . . .

A: What do you mean held you back? How could that hold you back?

P: Because I haven't fully committed myself, I don't think, to being a artist because of some of the things I believe spiritually. I'm not talkin about lyrically cursin, you know, it's just that I feel that I'm Pharoahe when I'm on stage; I'm Troy when I'm home in Queens. I feel that if I cut Troy off . . . And I've always tried to hold on to Troy because Troy keeps me grounded. If I cut Troy off and go full-fledged Pharoahe, I believe I can make it in the industry. But I'm afraid to do that, you know, because people don't see you for who you are, you know what I'm saying? And little things like that which I see a lot of artists don't struggle with. They like, they want the limelight. They want that a hundred percent, and you got to be like that to win in this industry. And I've never been that way where I'm like hungry, hungry, hungry for it all, you know what I'm saying? I'm just like, "Let me get my props from my peers. Let them congratulate me as a artist. Let the people feel me. Still let me be able to go see *Shaft* and chill . . ."

A: [Laughter]

P: [Laughter] You know what I'm saying?! So, on that note, I think it's something in me that still kinda hold back. But this tour, and being around a lot of hungry artists, is allowing me to push forward and work towards, you know, trying to "blow." And I still don't know if that's the right thing for me. If God wants that for me . . . I know God wants me to be in the industry. But I don't know . . . My Trojan Horse plan deep inside is to, if I was to blow, and I believe I will. Because this next album is going to be *incredible*. Just a Trojan Horse in terms of, if you make it to a certain status like some of the top artists are today, you know . . . And I shouldn't reveal it, but I can reveal it anyway, because people gon find out eventually. I want to turn around and about face and switch it to a total 100 percent positive thing, where I just drop the whole industry thing and use your ability as a artist and people that are feelin you right now, to go out there and just try and

flip it. I know it changes when you bring it that way, and people run from
that message. But that's what's in me, you know what I'm saying?

A: Why do you think people run from that message, and what makes you so
ready to take it again right now at this stage?

P: I don't think you can deny what's in you, but for so long, you know what I'm
saying? Again, you know, I know what's right. I can't put that full-fledged
on my album because that's not me. I would be frontin and it would hurt
me to front to people. Because I watch porn. I fuckin, you know, I have my
drink now and then, you know what I'm saying? I'm not a angel. So, I think
it's artistic of me to make a song about this porn tape I was watchin and
let people get that side of me, too, and not front like I'm Reverend such-
and-such, you know what I'm saying? But in the end, you know, my goal is
to reach a certain status—and not preach to kids—but just have a conversation like I'm havin to you *right now*. And I know you can't reach everybody,
but people had this conversation with me when I was younger, and it stuck.
The music that my parents and my family had me listen to . . .

A: Do you remember what you would listen to?

P: Anything I grew up in. Gospel. Coltraine. Hendrix. Zeppelin. And it allowed
me to leave my radius, my one block radius, even though I was still there.
I knew through Coltraine that music was colors and how pretty Africa was.
And it gave me ambition to be like, "I gotta see Africa!" If he feels Africa
like this, *with no words,* I have to see Africa.

A: Damn! Have you been?

P: I haven't been, yet. But I been to Japan, Italy, all over the world. I got to get
to Africa. I'm just saying, you know, those things, I remember those things.
And people might not even remember those things. Things that inspire me,
I hold *deeply*. You know, like I was telling Talib. It could be a conversation,
and I'll take that with me, and I'll utilize that for songs. And I utilize that for
strength, you know what I'm saying? I get my butterflies before I go on stage.
I look back to those inspiring moments, you know.

A: When did you first get a knowledge of Islam, because I can hear it in some
of the lyrics and the music?

P: I mean, Islam is a natural thing. I just think we're uneducated. And I'm not
talkin even from a religious standpoint. I'm just talkin about with me, let
me keep that on me. My brothers, who are Islamic, they tell me that I have
natural tendencies of how I eat, how I feel, how I perceive, and the energy
that I give and the way that I think. You know, for me, right now, to take
that on—and I take on things so heavily—I would like to not be in the industry
when I take that on, you know. So, it's like . . .

A: But you have conversations with your brothers about this.

P: Yeah, we do all the time. And, you know, it's different philosophies. One of
the best philosophies is you can't wait until you're perfect to become a
perfect Muslim, because no one is a perfect Muslim. You jump into it and
you strive towards that. And . . .

A: That's probably what they try to tell you, too, right?

P: Yeah. But, you know, for me, I know my heart. And to front on your heart is to front on God. And I believe that God will let me know, you know what I'm saying? It's something that I want real bad, because I felt that hand touch me. I felt it through music, you know what I'm saying? And I would like to be in a position where a lot of weight is lifted off your shoulders, and I think that's what that brings to you. When you rid yourself of anxieties . . .

A: Do you feel a weight or anxieties at all, man?

P: Oh, definitely! I have *madd* anxieties.

A: Get outta here?!

P: People around me be like, "Yo, man! Why you stressin?!"

A: [Laughter] Right.

P: I mean, my best friends, we kick it and it's like therapy for me, you know what I'm saying? I could feel [takin a huge, deep breath] like monkeys jumpin off my back! When I just kick it, you know what I'm saying? And one thing that religion teaches you, is that if you have Faith, that rids you of a lot of anxieties. You live for now. God said, not for yesterday and not for tomorrow. Things will be provided. So, that alone takes a lot of pressure off you. But me in the industry, I'm stressin the next show. I'm stressin that my DJ was off key. You know . . .

A: I know that before the show things were kinda hectic today. [Laughter]

P: Yeah, and I'm like, "Yo, you know, we gotta get things ready." And I'm like the key figure. I'm tryin to get everybody in the mode to where they take care of their own thing and then I have less to worry about.

A: Without you askin, right.

P: Right.

A: Pharoahe, people talk about you and the rest of the artists on this tour as dope MC's. "Y'all tight MC's." What, to you, in your opinion, are two or three or four qualities of a dope MC, or a tight MC?

P: For me, I like to hear concepts. I like to hear rhythm. And I like to hear what I call the inflection in someone's voice that could give you goose bumps. Me and a friend of mine who produced my last album, Lee Stone, we were talkin about how certain lyrics, certain songs have given us goose bumps, and what makes that happen, what gives you goose bumps. An inspiring speech or a certain moment in a sporting event, a lot of different things can give you goose bumps. But just tappin into that, mathematically, those things and always tryin to strive for them. And lyrically, we was talkin about the projection in someone's voice and the content of what they're saying. And truth is another thing that gives me goose bumps. When I hear somebody say something that's so true, it's like, "Wow, that's beautiful," you know what I'm saying? So, you know, it's a lot of things that make up a tight MC. You gotta have flow, you know. You gotta have flow, and I think that's something that just comes natural.

A: What exactly do you mean by that, by flow?

P: I mean, how the person rides the beat, you know. Some MC's ride the beat soulfully 100 percent like Slum Village, and they're funky with it. Some MC's go against the grain of the beat, but they're so on point and you understand what they're doing, you know. I appreciate all of that in a MC, you know. And I think the diversity of that on this tour is what, as a fan, I would just be in the audience like, "This is dope!" Talib is like one of the illest. And then you got Pharoahe comin on and it's like, "Okay, he takin you back with a little Old School style, a little New School shit." And then you got Common who's like the funkiest soul brotha in Hip Hop right now . . .

A: [Laughter] Why do you say that, man?

P: It's just, yo, ever since I've known Common, you know, *all* of his albums have had the soul ingredient. This is not a pitch for soul music; this is just naturally him. He couldn't help it, it would just come out. Me and my crew, when we was on tour with him years ago, we'd always say he got some old man in him, you know.

A: Yeah! He got a old man in him because it comes out like that. Now for Talib, what does he bring to it?

P: Talib brings to the table something that has changed Hip Hop single-handedly. And what he's brought to the table is that senseless babbling on the microphone is not tolerated no more!

A: [Laughter]

P: Everything he says has relevance! You know what I'm saying? And there's room for me to be like, be be be be be bcbop dc dc-dc-dccc, you know. There's room for that. But what Talib brings to the table, if you listen to his albums and you a MC and you listen to his lyrics, it kinda makes you be like, "Yo, let me bring some relevance to what I'm saying," you know what I'm saying? And he points that out in the Manifesto. And it's such a true thing because we're gifted to be selected to be doin this. *Millions* of people hear what we say, regardless of how many records we sell. And I think that's like a blessing and it's very important, you know what I'm saying? If you make a song like "Simon says get the fuck up!" in the projection of the song, people will know the purpose of the song. They'll know that it's not malicious. They know it has a purpose, even though it's one of my lighter songs. The character in that song is hosting the club and he's flabbergasted and he gets to the point where he's like, "I don't know *what* to do?" "Girls rub on your titties!"

A: "Yeah, I said it."

P: Then he's like, "Yeah, that's what I said!" [Laughter] That's the character in that song. And "Rape" is another character. All of these songs have some type of relevance to them, you know what I'm saying?

A: Now you see yourself goin through different characters?

P: Every song is a film, you know what I'm saying? Every song I write is a different film. Some are short. Some are feature. The character that I play on the song "Rape," which has been kinda controversial . . . And, I mean, I know it's a touchy subject, but I seen *Pulp Fiction* and I seen people walk out of that movie. And I sat there and I thought, this is great to me because it was so repulsive to them that they couldn't stand it and it's their choice to leave. We have the freedom to create that way. The first week I heard mixed reactions. It was one of my favorite movies. In creating that song, I wanted to do something that was repulsive, and I wanted to become that character. I denounce rapists, but in this film it's about a rapist. I'm workin on scripts. I would have liked to do a film that way even though people might have walked out, some people might have got the artistry behind it. And I can't let that stop my artistry. So, you know, I try to become that serial killer, serial rapist who's obsessed with nude photographs of the beat. And it's a Hip Hop metaphor. And he's stalkin the beat. And he feels that the way that other MC's have relationships with the beat is not fitting. So, he's gonna rape that beat. He's gonna fuck that beat. And he thinks in his mind that when he fucks the beat that Hip Hop is gonna be like [looking up as if surprised] . . . It's totally a ego trip song. Because when I fuck the beat, nobody can fuck it like me!

A: Now the writing process itself, how do the songs come about from the beginning?

P: With the last album, I just let things flow a lot more freely than in the past with the Organized albums. I would get a beat that I would feel and I would freestyle the chorus, or I would freestyle some of the lyrics and just feel it out. In the past, I would take a separate amount of time to write with the music, separate from the music. And this time I tried to go more from a vibe, you know. Like "Simon Says," that song made me say "Get the fuck up!" That song made me think, "You need to be direct with the audience right now and not give them an opportunity. You need to tell them what to do."

A: When the thought entered your mind for that song, what was the next step?

P: No, I just was in my room. I finished the beat. I pumped it up. I just stood with my head in the speaker freestylin, "Get the fuck up!" At first I was like, "Put your hands up . . ." But I was like, "Whatever, that's fuckin corny." "Get the fuck up" is hardcore. It's vulgar. This character is, you know, I was singin it with like an Italian accent [Puttin on his Italian accent] "Get the fuck up!" That's the character I wanted to be on there. That type of Italian guy who's talkin to somebody like, "Get the fuck out my house," you know.

A: [Laughter] The relationship between Rap and poetry, what do you see as the relationship between the two?

P: I mean, poetry is a awesome art form in itself. I dabble in it before I write some of the songs that I do. I try to be poetic with some of the songs. Hip Hop is based upon a mixture of that, but more writing musically. Points and timing, you know. So is poetry. But on a level where it's based upon the music, you have to be more rhythmatically connected with your listener and crowd, in terms of rhythm, you know. And *how* are you ridin that beat. You know, you could do the same thing with poetry without any music at all, you know what I'm saying? Get a response rhythmatically. So, I'm not disrespecting that. I'm just sayin, Hip Hop, it's about where you are on that fourth bar, where you are on that first bar.

A: Right, there's more timing to it.

P: Yeah.

A: Now comin up in Queens, did you hear any of the poetry?

P: I didn't get up on the Last Poets until later. I was late with poetry, you know. I never read it. I thought it was mushy . . .

A: [Laughter] Right . . .

P: But it's nice pieces out there. I been to a couple of shows. This girl Latasha Diggs, she's pretty dope. We speak. She reads me some of her pieces. And actually, with poetry, you can get fifty times more abstract, you know. And it opens my mind up, when I hear readings, to concepts. And I was there one time . . . The reason why I separated the two is because I was losin myself in poetry and the mixture between Hip Hop. And I think for those who are deep-minded, they were into it. But you need to be on record labels that's gonna get that to that deep-minded audience. And if the radio is fast food, you know. You get up in the morning, you go to McDonald's. You don't got time to cook the grits. Fast food is needed. You go to the drive through. And radio music sometimes is like drive through music. If you come with the too deepness, it's like, "What are you doing?! I don't have time for this!"

A: You think that hampers certain artists sometimes?

P: Definitely. I mean, you have to get yourself, your deepness across in a arrangement that makes it digestible, you know. I was watchin Sting on "Storytellers." And this was one of the greatest lessons I've learned in the last five years. He was like, "These songs are hits of mine," and [Pharoahe starts singing Sting] . . . These songs are arranged in a certain way mathematically, four bars to this, to this . . . If you wait too long to give them the chorus, meanings are lost. This is a mathematical fact. And you could be abstract—and I thought he was talkin to me when he said it—you could put all the shit in your verse if you want, but it has to be mathematically correct. So, let's say there's twelve bars, there's twenty-four bars. You can get in that verse and be talkin about how saliva contains the chemicals for the cure for AIDS. And if you mix, blah-bla-blah-blah-bla-blah—cool. If you get to your chorus and the arrangement of the music is in a certain way and the chorus is in a certain way . . . And your chorus is "A-I-D-S-save the world-A-I-D-S!" Mathematically, arrangement-wise, you can make these songs work, you know what I'm saying? Even though they're deep topics.

A: How did you sharpen your MC skills or your rhymin skills comin up?

P: Well, my partner, number one, Prince Poetry and OC from Diggin in the Crates and all that, they helped sharpen me up. And like what I'm goin through now, with just the company I keep. It's not like we spittin at each other like we used to do. I mean, everyday it was like, "Oh, you wrote some shit? I'ma write some shit!" It was like, "Doo-do-doo-do-doo-brrrrrrrrrr!" And you're like, "Okay, muthafucka, check this out!" Now it's more industry because you're hearing finished songs and what have you. But it's the same thing. So that's what helped me sharpen my skills, tryin to do one up on my partner.

A: Now were there rhyme ciphas or anything like that that you used to get into?

P: Yeah between us. We rarely got into anything outside the click. We always was like . . . I always was so big-headed I was like, "I don't want nobody stealin my shit!"

A: [Laughter]

P: And you won't hear it till it comes out, you know!

A: Right, right. What's the importance of those inter-click ciphas, and the importance of the cipha in Hip Hop in general?

P: I mean, it's just that, it's exciting. You know, when I was in the studio, Common and Talib did a song on my album called "The Truth." They came to the studio, man, I was like in tears. That's how much I look up to them.

A: Dag!

P: And Talib tells me, "I was listening to Organized Konfusion when I was such-and-such and such-and such. Y'all inspired me, and your new record is inspiring me. I like this song on your album," and it's vice versa. But I know for a fact that Talib, in the early stages that he's in, is one of the best to spit on the mic. Common the same thing. To have these people in the same room, I was very passionate about that, because I'm passionate about music and jazz. And I think about, "Damn! Miles was in the same room with Coltraine and they was composing songs together," you know what I'm saying? Damn! And these cats in the same room with me?! We might not be on the same stature, but in my little mind, that's what I liken it to. And I'm like, "I'm about to go in there *next* and do my rhyme . . ."

A: What was that like doin that song, because that's one of the deepest ones? How did that day progress from start to finish, do you remember?

P: I mean, I had the music. Was talkin to Common and was like, "I gotta have you on the album in this type of song," because he's definitely tight at writing some meaningful shit. He came in, and he wrote his rhyme in the studio! That's how good he is. Talib had some stuff written. He finished it up in the studio. And it was like that and I was like, "Yo, man, this is crazy!" you know what I'm saying? It's a blessing for me to work with those cats.

A: Did you have your stuff already written, too?

P: My rhyme is like three years old.

A: When you rhyme about "The Truth," each one brings his own understanding.

P: Exactly.

A: Did y'all discuss that?

P: Yeah, I told them, you know, "The truth is what it is to you," you know what I'm saying? Even though there's only *one* truth, we perceive it how we perceive it. I'm not gon try to make you feel my truth. I wanted that variation. For me, I was strugglin with the truth in the beginning . . .

A: "Truth had me up against the ropes . . ."

P: "Truth had me up against the ropes . . ." Beatin me up, because I didn't want to believe what the truth was. I couldn't look in the mirror, you know.

A: Some of your collaborations are almost like it was just picked specifically for the beat or for the song. How do you choose who you want on there?

P: I mean, that's something that comes natural for me. I don't think it's hard for a lot of artists to do that. I mean, if I make a certain music, or I get a certain type of music that's soulful, I'ma be like, "Damn, Cee-lo would be perfect on this." And, I mean, with "The Next Shit," da-da-dan-da-da-dan type beat. It's only one person for that song! [Laughter]

A: [Laughter] Busta tore that up!

P: Since I had a variation of music, which I think people like about me, and I think hurts me, too. Because people want an artist they can grab on to. By havin so many different dimensions, I don't think I'm easy to grab on to as if I was just a "titty man." I would be more accessible. But you hear "The Light" on the next single and you see me and I'm like, you know, "Hydrogen to Oxygen," and they're like, "Who are you, the titty man or what?!"

A: [Laughter]

P: But that's how I wanted to come with that album just to let people know different dimensions. Because it was my *Internal Affairs*, and that's how I am as a person. You know, I did that "Next Shit" beat and was like, "I gotta get Busta."

A: What was that like recording with Busta in the studio? What was that like?

P: Whenever I get down on the industry, or whenever I get to a low, I just think of that day . . .

A: Damn, you serious?!

P: With Busta in the studio. And I just be like, "You better get up! You better do that interview!" Because he's a 100 percent non-stop. He's "Go!" twenty-four hours a day! I think it might be thirty minutes to a hour—or one time in the time that I've known him, and I've known him for a long time—when I see him do like this [Pharoahe sits quietly as if he is resting or taking a break] . . .

A: That's all he needs.

P: That's all he needs. And he's just ready to go again.

A: What is it about his style that attracts you?

P: Busta is *beyond* incredible. Every time he spits, he tries to elevate. He battles hisself. You listen to his album, I mean, it's shit lyrically, rhythmatically on his new album—on *all* his albums—that I'm just like, "There's no need to even try and do that." [Laughter] And that's why he's the fuckin man, you know what I'm saying? That's why I respect Busta. He's not afraid to experiment, you know. None of these songs that he's *ever* put out has been, you know, old Diana Ross loops or fuckin Teddy Pendergrass, you know. He uses himself, and for that, he's one of the all-time greats *ever* in music history, not even in fuckin Hip Hop.

A: He's amazing, man! Did you ever see his live show?

P: Yeah, yeah.

A: That's incredible, right? Yep, that's that energy right there.

P: Yep.

A: You know, you came off the stage tonight and you were just pooped, man! Exhausted. I mean, you left it all out there on the stage . . .

P: [Laughter]

A: What makes a good stage show for you?

P: I leave it out there every night, man! I don't save nuthin. And, I mean, I'm asthmatic and I have to pace myself, you know what I'm saying? And some of the old stuff I'm doin—because I've been doin this for quite some time now—you know a lot of the young kids is like, "Alright, we wit you, but what the fuck are you doin?" [Laughter]

A: [Laughter] But you do it anyway!

P: But I do it anyway because they need to be educated. They need to hear it anyway. And when I get to the new shit . . . I mean, from the new generation, they've only heard two songs from me radio-wise, which is "Simon Says" and "The Light." And I'm just really buildin up that career solo-wise, you know what I'm saying? And I'm tryin to get on a level where Common is at, De La is at, and even Talib. Because Talib, he has a Black Star which is very recent and these fans today is like, "What else, what else?" [Snapping his fingers] "That was good, what else you got?" That's why I'm eager to get off this tour and work on some new stuff because before you know it it's gon be some guy named Harrow Honch and shit!

A: [Laughter] With a record!

P: And kids is gonna think he's cool.

A: That's a fast-paced world right now. I want to ask you about the re-mix for "Simon Says," that's some *tight* artists on there. How did they all end up gettin on there? Redman, Method Man, Shabaam, Lady Luck, Busta again . . .

P: Me and Mos was workin on our albums at the same time. And I was listenin to his stuff, his direction and workin on my stuff, my direction. And I came across the "Simon Says" shit, did a demo, brought it to the label. The label was like, "Yeaaah, this shit is hot!" And I hit my manager off with copies. And I was like, "Yo, I'ma play this for Mos and see what he thinks." Because some people at the label was like, "I don't know about this chorus and shit." And I was like, "I want to get Mos opinion." I played it for him and he was like, "Yo! This shit is craaazy! This shit is crazy!" And he was workin on a song with Busta at the time. It's called "Do It Now." And I kept tryin to come to the studio to catch Busta to ask him to be on "The Next Shit" also.

Busta didn't show up, Busta didn't show up. So the third time I was like, "I'm not even goin." Busta shows up! And Mos, they finished. Busta was like, "I gotta break out, gotta go to another session." And Mos was like, "Yo, before you go, I gotta play you this Pharoahe shit." And he played it for Busta, and they said Busta was *knockin* shit over!

A: [Laughter] Damn!

P: Got on top of the table in the studio! Was like, [doin a Busta voice] "What the fuck?!" He called me the next day. I hadn't spoke to him in years. He was like, "Yo, this is Busta. That shit is *crazy*, man!"

A: "That shit is crazy!" I can hear him say it. [Laughter]

P: [Laughter] And he was like, "Yo, we gotta hook up." I was like, "Yeah, I want you to do this song with me." He was like, "No problem." So we get to the studio to do "Next Shit," and he's just like playin "Simon" over and over. He was listenin to it. I was like, "Cool, cool." So then, he was really feelin it. He was like—it wasn't even mastered. I'm gonna take this shit to the radio, let Flex hear it, see what Flex think about it. And, yo, big up to Funkmaster Flex and Busta. Flex played the shit that night like eight times without it being mastered. I was like, "Woah!"

A: That shit was hot, though!

P: But to get to your question. Once that song came out, *all* the MC's was like, "Yo! What's up with the re-mix?!"

A: Oh, get outta here!

P: Redman was like, "Yo, *I* wanna be on that re-mix!" You know what I'm saying? Busta was like, "Yo, if you do that, you gotta put me on there." So, we had Red and Busta and I was out in LA and they was recording. And Red called me from the studio and was like, "Somebody wanna speak to you." He put Meth on the phone . . .

A: Ohhhh!

P: He was like, "Yo, I can get down with this?" "What am I gon tell you, no and shit?!" [Laughter] I was like, "Yo, whatever." It was supposed to be like a short song, and Meth spit like thirty-six bars on the shit! After a while I was like . . .

A: How did Shabaam and Lady Luck end up on there?

P: Shabaam's my man, you know what I'm saying, from the label. I was like, "Yo, he gon bring that vibe to it that the song has, that we need on it." Lady Luck is up and coming, you know, she's out of that camp with Red and them. And, you know, she got down on it.

A: Let me ask you a couple of final questions. How do you see yourself when the history goes down, when the history is written, what are they gonna think about Pharoahe Monch?

P: When it's all said and done, I just want people to say that he tried to do it from different dimensions. I'll tell you what *I* like about Pharoahe on some out of body experience shit. The reason I rate Pharoahe up there is because he coulda stuck with one style. He could stick with the style that he did with

"Simon Says," or "Hypnotical Gases," goin back to the first album, or "Stress." But he chooses to move around and not stay in the same area, tryin to come with something a little different. I think that's real risqué for a artist to do, so I give him props on that level. Because, you know, I think if I woulda stayed with a certain style, it woulda been easy for people to grasp. But I like to change my voice on different songs that I do. I like to change my flow on different songs that I do, and my approach to doin songs. That's one of the main reasons why I like Pharoahe as an MC. Aside from the fact that a lot of the shit that he do is just *tight*! [Laughter]

A: [Laughter] Besides that fact!

References

Abd al Malik. 2004. *Qu'Allah Benisse La France*. Paris: Albin Michel.

Abrahams, Roger. 1964. *Deep Down in the Jungle: Negro Narrative Folklore from the Streets of Philadelphia*. Chicago: Aldine Publishing Co.

Abrahams, Roger. 1970. Rapping and capping: Black Talk as art. In John Swzed (ed.), *In Black America*. New York: Basic Books.

Abrahams, Roger. 1976. *Talking Black*. Rowley, Massachusetts: Newbury House.

Ahearn, Charlie. 1991. The Five Percent Solution. *Spin* 6(11) (February): 54–57, 76.

Ahmed, Akbar S. and Hastings Donnan (eds) 1994. *Islam, Globalization and Postmodernity*. London: Routledge.

Alim, H. Samy. 1999. The Roots Rock Memorial Auditorium. *Intermission*. Stanford University.

Alim, H. Samy. 2000. 360 Degreez of Black Art comin at you: Sista Sonia Sanchez and the dimensions of a Black Arts continuum. In James G. Spady (ed.), *360 Degreez of Sonia Sanchez: Hip Hop, Narrativity, Iquawe and Public Spaces of Being*. Special issue of *Bma: The Sonia Sanchez Literary Review*, 6(1), Fall.

Alim, H. Samy. 2001a. THREE-X-BLACK: Mos Def, Mr. Nigga (Nigga, Nigga) and Big Black Africa X-amine Hip Hop's cultural consciousness. In H. Samy Alim (ed.), *Hip Hop Culture: Language, Literature, Literacy and the Lives of Black Youth*. Special issue of the *Black Arts Quarterly*. Stanford, CA: Committee on Black Performing Arts, Stanford University, 4–8.

Alim, H. Samy (ed.). 2001b. *Hip Hop Culture: Language, Literature, Literacy and the Lives of Black Youth*. Special issue of the *Black Arts Quarterly*. Stanford, CA: Committee on Black Performing Arts, Stanford University.

Alim, H. Samy. 2001c. "I be the truth": Divergence, recreolization, and the "new" equative copula in African American Language. Paper presented at NWAV 30, Raleigh, North Carolina, October.

Alim, H. Samy. 2002. Street-conscious copula variation in the Hip Hop Nation. *American Speech* 77(3), 288–304.

Alim, H. Samy. 2003. On some serious next millennium rap ishhh: Pharoahe Monch, Hip Hop poetics, and the internal rhymes of Internal Affairs. *Journal of English Linguistics* 31(1), 60–84.

Alim, H. Samy. 2004a. *You know my steez: An ethnographic and sociolinguistic study of a Black American speech community*. Durham, NC: Duke University Press.

Alim, H. Samy. 2004b. Hip Hop Nation Language. In Edward Finegan and John Rickford (eds), *Language in the USA: Perspectives for the 21st Century*. Cambridge: Cambridge University Press.

Alim, H. Samy. 2005. Exploring the transglobal Hip Hop *umma*. In miriam cooke and Bruce Lawrence (eds), *Muslim Networks: From Hajj to Hip Hop*. Chapel Hill, NC: UNC Press.

Alim, H. Samy and Alastair Pennycook (eds). In press. *Global Hip Hop Culture, youth identities, and the politics of language education*. Special issue of *Journal of Language, Identity, and Education*.

Allen, Harry. 1991. Righteous indignation: Rappers talk about the strength of Hip-Hop and Islam. *The Source* 48 (March/April): 48–53.

Alleyne, Mervyn. 1980. *Comparative Afro-American*. Ann Arbor: Karoma.

Anderson, Elijah. 1999. *Code of the Street: Decency, Violence, and the Moral Life of the Inner City*. New York: W.W. Norton & Company.

Anderson, Monica. 1994. *Black English Vernacular (From "Ain't" to "Yo Mama": the Words Politically Correct Americans Should Know)*. Highland City, Florida: Rainbow Books.

Asante, Molefi. 1990. African elements in African American English. In J. Holloway (ed.), *Africanisms in American Culture*. Bloomington, Indiana: Indiana University Press, 19–33.

Bahloul, Maher. 1993. The copula in modern standard Arabic. In Mushira Eid and Clive Holes (eds), *Perspectives on Arabic Linguistics V: Papers from the fifth annual symposium on Arabic linguistics*. Amsterdam, The Netherlands: John Benjamins, 209–229.

Bailey, Beryl. 1965. Toward a new perspective in Negro English dialectology. *American Speech* 40, 171–177.

Bailey, Beryl. 1969. Language and communicative styles of Afro-American children in the United States. *The Florida FL Reporter, Spring/Summer, Special Anthology Issue: Linguistic-Cultural Differences and American Education* 46: 153.

Bailey, Guy. 1987. Are Black and White vernaculars diverging?" In Ralph Fasold *et al.* (eds), *American Speech* 62.

Ball, Arnetha. 1995. Text design patterns in the writing of urban African-American students: Teaching to the strengths of students in multicultural settings. *Urban Education* 30(3).

Baugh, John. 1979. Linguistic style-shifting in Black English. PhD dissertation, University of Pennsylvania.

Baugh, John. 1980. A reexamination of the Black English copula. In William Labov (ed.), *Locating Language in Space and Time*. New York: Academic Press, 83–106.

Baugh, John. 1983. *Black Street Speech: Its History, Structure, and Survival*. Austin, Texas: University of Texas Press.

Baugh, John. 1991. The politicization of changing terms of self-reference among American slave descendants. *American Speech* 66(2): 133–146.

Baugh, John. 1999. *Out of the Mouths of Slaves: African American Language and Educational Malpractice*. Austin: University of Texas Press.

Baugh, John. 2000. *Beyond Ebonics: Racial Pride and Linguistic Prejudice*. London: Oxford.

Baugh, John. 2003. Linguistic profiling. In S. Makoni, G. Smitherman, F. Ball and A. Spears (eds), *Black Linguistics: Language, Politics and Society in Africa and the Americas*. London: Routledge.

Baugh, John and Geneva Smitherman. In press. Linguistic emancipation in global perspective. In H. Samy Alim and John Baugh (eds), *Black Language, Education, and Social Change*. New York: Teachers College Press.

Beanie Sigel. 2000. Unpublished interview with James G. Spady. Philadelphia.

Bell, Allan. 1984. Language style as audience design. *Language in Society* 13: 145–204.

Bell, Allan. 1991. Audience accommodation in the mass media. In Howard Giles, Justine Coupland, and Nikolas Coupland (eds), *Contexts of Accommodation: Developments in Applied Linguistics.* Cambridge: Cambridge University Press, 69–102.

Bell, Allan. 2001. Back in style: Reworking audience design. In Penelope Eckert and John Rickford (eds), *Style and Sociolinguistic Variation.* Cambridge: Cambridge University Press, 139–169.

Bertrand, Marianne and Sendhil Mullainathan. 2004. Are Emily and Brendan more employable than Lakisha and Jamal? A field experiment on labor market discrimination. *American Economic Review* 94(4): 991–1013.

Bickerton, Derek. 1975. *Dynamics of a Creole System.* Cambridge: Cambridge University Press.

Braithwaite, Fred (Fab Five Freddy). 1992. *Fresh Fly Flavor: Words and Phrases of the Hip-Hop Generation.* Stamford, CT: Longmeadow Press.

Braithwaite, Fred. 1995. *Hip Hop Slang: English–Deutsch.* Frankfurt am Main: Eichborn.

Brathwaite, Kamau. 1984. *History of the Voice: The Development of Nation Language in Anglophone Caribbean Poetry.* London: New Beacon Books.

Brown, H. Rap. 1972. Street talk. In Thomas Kochman (ed.), *Rappin' and Stylin' Out: Communication in Urban Black America.* Urbana, IL: University of Illinois Press, 205–207.

Bucholtz, Mary. 2003. Language and gender. In Ed Finegan and John Rickford (eds), *Language in the USA.* Cambridge: Cambridge University Press.

Calloway, Cab. 1944. *Hepster's Dictionary: Language of Jive.* Republished as an appendix to Calloway's autobiography, *Of Minnie the Moocher & Me.* 1976. New York: Thomas Y. Crowell.

Chang, Jeff. 2005. *Can't stop won't stop: A history of the Hip Hop generation.* New York: St. Martin's Press.

Chuck D. 1999. Interview with H. Samy Alim, San Francisco. November.

Cook, Dara. 2000. The aesthetics of rap. *Black Issues Book Review.* March–April.

Cook, David. 2005. *Understanding Jihad.* California: University of California Press.

cooke, miriam and Bruce Lawrence (eds) 2005. *Muslim Networks: From Hajj to Hip Hop.* Chapel Hill, NC: UNC Press.

Cutler, Cecelia. 1999. Yorkville Crossing: White teens, Hip Hop and African American English. *Journal of Sociolinguistics* 3/4: 428–442.

Daniel, Jack and Geneva Smitherman. 1976. How I got over: Communication dynamics in the Black community. *Quarterly Journal of Speech* 62, February.

DeBose, Charles. 2005. *The Sociology of African American Language: A Language Planning Perspective.* New York: Palgrave Macmillan.

DeBose, Charles and Nicholas Faraclas. 1993. An Africanist approach to the linguistic study of Black English: Getting to the roots of the tense-aspect-modality and copula systems in Afro-American. In S. Mufwene (ed), *Africanisms in Afro-American Language Varieties.* Athens, GA: University of Georgia Press, 364–387.

Decker, Jeffrey Louis. 1993. The state of Rap: Time and place in Hip Hop Nationalism. *Social Text* 34: 53–84.

Dillard, Joseph. 1972. *Black English.* New York: Random House.

Dillard, J. L. 1977. *Lexicon of Black English.* New York: Seabury.

DJ Hi-Tek. 2000. Unpublished interview with the author.

Duranti, Alessandro. 1997. *Linguistic Anthropology*. New York: Cambridge University Press.

Duranti, Alessandro. 2004. *A Companion to Linguistic Anthropology*. Malden, MA: Blackwell.

Dyson, Michael Eric. 1991. Performance, protest and prophesy in the culture of Hip Hop. *Black Sacred Music: A Journal of Theomusicology* 5(1), Spring.

Eades, Diana. 2005. Beyond difference and domination? Intercultural communicaton in legal contexts. In Scott Kiesling and Christina Bratt Paulston (eds), *Intercultural Discourse and Communication: The essential readings*. Malden, MA: Blackwell, 304–317.

Eckert, Penelope and John Rickford (eds). 2001. *Style and Linguistic Variation*. Cambridge: Cambridge University Press.

Edwards, Walter. 1999. The sociolinguistics of Rap lyrics. In Barbara Lalla *et al.* (eds), *Studies in Caribbean Language, Volume II*. University of West Indies Press.

El-Sabawi, Taleed. 2005. Palestinian conflict bounces to a new beat. *Angelingo* 2(2), Spring. University of Southern California (http://angelingo.usc.edu).

Eve. 1999. Unpublished interview with James G. Spady. Philadelphia.

Fairclough, Norman. 1989. *Language and Power*. London and New York: Longman.

Fanon, F. 1967. *The Wretched of the Earth*, trans. C. Farrington. Hammondsworth: Penguin.

Farrakhan, Louis. 1986. Self-improvement: The basis for community development. Speech delivered in Phoenix, Arizona on September 21.

Farrakhan, Louis. 2001. Hip Hop Summit: Accept the responsibility of leadership. *Final Call*, June 26.

Fasold, Ralph W. 1972. *Tense Marking in Black English: A Linguistic and Social Analysis*. Washington, DC: Center for Applied Linguistics.

Floyd-Thomas, Juan M. 2003 A jihad of words: The evolution of African American Islam and contemporary Hip-Hop. In Anthony B. Pinn, *The Religious and Spiritual Sensibilities of Rap Music*. New York: New York University Press, 49–72.

Folb, Edith. 1980. *Runnin' Down Some Lines: the Language and Culture of Black Teenagers*. Cambridge, MA: Harvard University Press.

Forman, Murray and Mark Anthony Neal (eds) 2004. *That's the Joint! The Hip-Hop Studies Reader*. New York, NY: Routledge.

Foucault, Michel. 1984. The order of discourse. In M. Shapiro (ed.), *Language and Politics*. Oxford: Basil Blackwell, 108–138.

Frankenberg, Ruth. 1993. *White Women, Race Matters: The Social Construction of Whiteness*. Minneapolis: University of Minnesota Press.

Gardell, Mattias. 1996. *In the Name of Elijah Muhammad: Louis Farrakhan and the Nation of Islam*. Durham, NC: Duke University Press.

Giddens, Anthony. 1984. *The Constitution of Society: Outline of the theory of structuration*. Cambridge: Polity Press.

Giles, Howard. 1973. Accent mobility: A model and some data. *Anthropological Linguisitics* 15: 87–105.

Giles, Howard and P. F. Powesland 1975. *Speech Style and Social Evaluation*. London: Academic Press.

Ginzburg, Ralph. 1962. *100 Years of Lynchings*. New York: Lancer Books.

Goffman, Erving. 1967. *Interaction Ritual: Essays in Face to Face Behavior*. Garden City, New York: Doubleday.

Grandmaster Flash. 1999. *The Vibe History of Hip Hop.* New York: Three Rivers Press.

Green, Lisa. 2004. African American English. In Edward Finegan and John Rickford (eds), *Language in the USA: Perspectives for the 21st Century*, Cambridge: Cambridge University Press.

Gross, Terry. 1986. Interview with Amiri Baraka. WHYY Radio Philadelphia. March 27.

Gumperz, John. 1982a. *Discourse Strategies.* Cambridge: Cambridge University Press.

Gumperz, John. 1982b. *Language and Social Identity.* Cambridge: Cambridge University Press.

Hager, Steven. 1984. *Hip Hop: The Illustrated History of Breakdancing, Rap Music and Graffiti.* New York: St. Martin's Press.

Henderson, Stephen. 1973. *Understanding the New Black Poetry: Black Speech and Black Music as Poetic References.* New York: William Morrow.

Hill, Jane. 1998. Language, race, and White public space. *American Anthropologist* 100(3), 680–689.

Hill, Jane. Forthcoming. *The Language of White Racism.*

Holloway, Joseph and W. Vass. 1997. *The African Heritage of American English.* Bloomington: University of Indiana Press.

Holm, John. 1984. Variability of the copula in Black English and its creole kin. *American Speech* 59: 291–309.

Hussein, Anwar A. 1995. The sociolinguistic patterns of native Arabic speakers: Implications for teaching Arabic as a foreign language. *Applied Language Learning* 6(1–2): 65–87.

Hymes, Dell. 1972. Models of interaction of language and social life. In John Gumperz and Dell Hymes (eds), *Directions in Sociolinguistics.* New York: Holt, Rinehart and Winston, 35–71.

Hymes, Dell. 1974. *Foundations in Sociolinguistics: an Ethnographic Approach.* Philadelphia: University of Pennsylvania Press.

Hymes, Dell. 1981. Foreword. In Charles A. Ferguson and Shirley B. Heath (eds), *Language in the U.S.A.* New York: Cambridge University Press.

Ibrahim, Awad. In press. "Hey, whassup homeboy?": Performativity, Hip Hop and the politics of identity. In H. Samy Alim and Alastair Pennycook (eds), *Global Hip Hop Culture, youth identities, and the politics of language education.* Special issue of *Journal of Language, Identity, and Education.*

Ibrahim, Awad, H. Samy Alim, and Alastair Pennycook. Forthcoming. *Global Hip Hop Culture, language, and youth identities.*

Jackson, Austin, Tony Michel, David Sheridan, and Bryan Stumpf. 2001. Making connections in the contact zones: towards a critical praxis of Rap Music and Hip Hop Culture. In H. Samy Alim (ed.) *Hip Hop Culture: Language, Literature, Literacy and the Lives of Black Youth.* Special issue of the *Black Arts Quarterly.* Stanford, CA: Committee on Black Performing Arts, Stanford University.

JT the Bigga Figga. 2000. Personal interview with H. Samy Alim, November.

Juvenile. 2000. Personal interview with H. Samy Alim.

Keyes, Cheryl. 1984. Verbal art performance in Rap Music: The conversation of the 80's. *Folklore Forum* 17(2), Fall: 143–152.

Keyes, Cheryl. 1991. *Rappin' to the Beat: Rap Music as Street Culture Among African Americans.* Unpublished doctoral dissertation. Indiana University.

Kochman, Thomas. 1969. "Rapping" in the Black Ghetto. *Trans-Action*, February, 26–34.

Kochman, Thomas. 1981. *Black and White Styles in Conflict*. Chicago: University of Chicago Press.

KRS-One. 2000. *The First Overstanding: Refinitions*. The Temple of Hip Hop Kulture.

Labov, William. 1966. *The Social Stratification of English in New York City*. Washington, DC: Center for Applied Linguistics.

Labov, William. 1969. Contraction, deletion, and inherent variability of the English copula. *Language* 45: 715–762.

Labov, William. 1972a. *Language in the Inner City: Studies in the Black English Vernacular*. Philadelphia: University of Pennsylvania Press.

Labov, William. 1972b. *Sociolinguistic Patterns*. Philadelphia: University of Pennsylvania Press.

Labov, William. 1982. Objectivity and commitment in linguistic science: The case for the Black English trial in Ann Arbor. *Language in Society* 11: 165–201.

Labov, William, Paul Cohen, Clarence Robins, and John Lewis. 1968. *A Study of the Non-standard English of Negro and Puerto Rican Speakers in New York City*. Report on Co-operative Research Project 3288. New York: Columbia University.

Lee, Carol. 1993. *Signifying as a Scaffold for Literary Interpretation: The pedagogical implications of an African American discourse genre*. Urbana, IL: NCTE.

Lee, Jooyoung. 2005. "You wanna battle?": Negotiating respect and local rules in the emcee cipher. Paper presented at The Lehman Conference on Hip-Hop: From Local to Global Practice, New York.

LeMoine, Noma. 1999. *English for Your Success: A Language Development Program for African American Children*. Maywood, NJ: The Peoples Publishing Group.

LePage, Robert. 1980. Projection, focusing, diffusion. *York Papers in Linguistics* 9: 9–31.

LePage, Robert and Andree Tabouret-Keller. 1985. *Acts of Identity: Creole-Based Approaches to Language and Ethnicity*. Cambridge: Cambridge University Press.

Lippi-Green, Rosina. 1997. *English with an Accent: Language, Ideology and Discrimination in the United States*. London and New York: Routledge.

Major, Clarence. 1970 (1994). *Juba to Jive: A Dictionary of African-American Slang*. New York and London: Penguin.

Makoni, Sinfree and Geneva Smitherman, Arnetha F. Ball, and Arthur K. Spears (eds). 2003. *Black Linguistics: Language, Society, and Politics in Africa and the Americas*. London and New York: Routledge.

Masari. 2001. Unpublished interview with H. Samy Alim. San Francisco.

Massey, Douglas and Nancy Denton. 1993. *American Apartheid: Segregation and the making of the underclass*. Cambridge, MA: Harvard University Press.

Meghelli, Samir. 2004. Returning to *The Source, En Diaspora*: Historicizing the emergence of the Hip Hop Cultural Movement in France. *Proud Flesh* (3).

Meghelli, Samir. 2005. Le cactus de Siberie: The Hip Hop Cultural Movement among the African diaspora in France. *Newsletter of the Institute of African Studies at Columbia University*. Spring, 8–11.

Mitchell, Tony (ed.). 2001. *Global Noise: Rap and Hip-Hop Outside the USA*. Middletown, CT: Wesleyan University Press.

Mitchell-Kernan, Claudia. 1971. *Language Behavior in a Black Urban Community*.

Monograph No. 2. Language Behavior Laboratory. University of California, Berkeley.

Mitchell-Kernan, Claudia. 1972. Signifying and marking: Two Afro-American speech acts. In John J. Gumperz and Dell Hymes (eds), *Directions in Sociolinguistics*. New York: Holt, Rinehart & Winston.

Miyakawa, Felicia M. 2005. *Five Percent Rap: God Hop's Music, Message, and Black Muslim Mission*. Bloomington, IN: Indiana University Press.

Morgan, Aswan. 1999. *Why They Say What Dey Be Sayin': an Examination of Hip-Hop Content and Language*. Paper submitted for LING 073, *Introduction to African American Vernacular English*. Stanford University.

Morgan, Marcyliena. 1991. Indirectness and interpretation in African American women's discourse. *Pragmatics* 1(4): 421–451.

Morgan, Marcyliena. 1994. The African American speech community: Reality and sociolinguistics. In Marcyliena Morgan (ed.), *Language and the Social Construction of Identity in Creole Situations*. Los Angeles: Center for Afro-American Studies, UCLA, 121–148.

Morgan, Marcyliena. 1996. Conversational signifying: Grammar and indirectness among African American women. In E. Ochs, E. Schegloff, and S. Thompson (eds), *Grammar and Interaction*. Cambridge: Cambridge University Press.

Morgan, Marcyliena. 1998. More than a mood or an attitude: Discourse and verbal genres in African-American culture. In S. Mufwene, J. Rickford, G. Bailey and J. Baugh (eds), *African American English: Structure, History, and Usage*. New York: Routledge, 251–281.

Morgan, Marcyliena. 2001. "Nuthin' but a G thang": Grammar and language ideology in Hip Hop identity. In Sonja Lanehart (ed.) *Sociocultural and Historical Contexts of African American Vernacular English*. Athens: University of Georgia Press.

Morgan, Marcyliena. 2002. *Language, Discourse and Power in African American Culture*. Cambridge: Cambridge University Press.

Mos Def. 2000. Personal interview with H. Samy Alim. October.

Morrison, Toni. 1981. Interview with Thomas LeClair in the *New Republic*. March 21: 25–29, cited in John Rickford and Russell Rickford. 2000. *Spoken Soul: The Story of Black English*. New York: John Wiley & Sons.

Nelson, Havelock and Michael Gonzales. 1991. *Bring the Noise: A Guide to Rap Music and Hip Hop Culture*. New York: Harmony Books.

Newman, Michael. 2001. "Not dogmatically/ It's all about me": Contested values in a high school Rap crew. *Taboo: A Journal of Culture and Education* 5(2): 51–68.

Norfleet, Dawn. 1997. Hip-hop culture in New York City: The role of verbal music performance in defining a community. PhD dissertation, Columbia University.

Olivo, Warren. 2001. Phat lines: Spelling conventions in Rap Music. *Written Language and Literacy* 4(1): 67–85.

Osumare, Halifu. 2001. Beat streets in the global hood: Connective marginalities of the Hip Hop globe. *Journal of American and Comparative Cultures* 24.

Osumare, Halifu. 2002. Troping Blackness in the Hip Hop global 'hood. In H. Samy Alim (ed.), *Black Culture's Global Impact*. Special issue of the *Black Arts Quarterly* 6(3), Stanford, CA: Stanford University, Committee on Black Performing Arts.

Page, Helan E. and Brooke Thomas. 1994. White public space and the construction of White privilege in U.S. Health Care: Fresh concepts and a new model of analysis. *Medical Anthropology Quarterly* 8: 109–116.

Perkins, William Eric. 1991. Nation of Islam ideology in the Rap of Public Enemy. *Black Sacred Music:* A Journal of Theomusiology 5(1): 41–50.

Perkins, William Eric (ed.). 1996. *Droppin' science: Critical essays on rap music and Hip Hop culture.* Philadelphia, PA: Temple University Press.

Perry, Imani. 2004. *Prophets of the Hood: Politics and poetics in hip hop.* Durham, NC: Duke University Press.

Perry, Theresa and Lisa Delpit (eds). 1998. *The Real Ebonics Debate.* Boston: Beacon Press.

Peters, Rudolph.1996. *Jihad in Classical and Modern Islam: A Reader.* Princeton: Markus Wiener Publishers.

Peterson, James. 1996. On artistry and scholarship in Hip-Hop Culture. Paper presented at Philly's Hip Hop Summit, May 10–12.

Peterson, James. 2001. Paper Presented at the University of Pennsylvania's conference on Islam and the Globalization of Hip Hop.

Pharoahe Monch. 2000. Unpublished interview with H. Samy Alim. San Francisco.

Piestrup, Ann McCormick. 1973. Black dialect interference and accommodation of reading instruction in first grade. University of California, Berkeley: Monographs of the Language Behavior Research Laboratory, 4.

Pinn, Anthony B. (ed.). 2003. *The Religious and Spiritual Sensibilities of Rap Music.* New York: New York University Press.

Potter, Russell. 1995. *Spectacular Vernaculars: Hip-Hop and the Politics of Postmodernism.* Albany: State University of New York Press.

Prevos, Andre J. M. 2001. Postcolonial popular music in France. In Tony Mitchell (ed.), *Global Noise: Rap and Hip-Hop Outside the USA.* Middletown, CT: Wesleyan University Press.

Rampton, Ben (ed.). 1999. *Styling the Other.* Special issue of *Journal of Sociolinguistics* 3(4) (November).

Redmond, Edmond. 1976. *Drumvoices: The Mission of Afro-American Poetry.* Garden City, New York: Anchor Press/Doubleday.

Remes, Pieter. 1991. Rapping: a sociolinguistic study of oral tradition in Black urban communities in the United States. *Journal of the Anthropological Society of Oxford* 22(2): 129–149.

Rickford, John. 1977. The question of prior Creolization in Black English. In Albert Valdman (ed.), *Pidgin and Creole Linguistics.* Bloomington: Indiana University Press, 190–221.

Rickford, John. 1998. The creole origins of African American Vernacular English: Evidence from copula absence. In S. Mufwene, J. Rickford, G. Bailey and J. Baugh (eds), *African American English: Structure, History and Use.* London and New York: Routledge, 154–200.

Rickford, John. 1999. *African American Vernacular English: Features and Use, Evolution, and Educational Implications.* Oxford: Blackwell.

Rickford, John and Faye McNair-Knox. 1994. Addressee- and topic-influenced style shift: A quantitative sociolinguistic study. In Douglas Biber and Edward Finegan (eds), *Sociolinguistic Perspectives on Register.* Oxford: Oxford University Press, 235–276.

Rickford, John and Angela Rickford. 1995. Dialect readers revisited. *Linguistics and Education* 7(2): 107–128.

Rickford, John and Russell Rickford. 2000. *Spoken Soul: The Story of Black English.* New York: John Wiley.

Rickford, John, Arnetha Ball, Renee Blake, Raina Jackson, and Nomi Martin. 1991. Rappin on the copula coffin: Theoretical and methodological issues in the analysis of copula variation in African American Vernacular English. *Language Variation and Change* 3: 103–132.

Rickford, John, Julie Sweetland, and Mary Hsu. 2000. Prosodic conditioning of the copula: A second opinion. Paper presented at NWAV 29, Michigan State University, October 7.

Romaine, Suzanne. 1982. *Socio-Historical Linguistics: Its Status and Methodology*. Cambridge and New York: Cambridge University Press.

Rose, Tricia. 1994. *Black Noise: Rap Music and Black Culture in Contemporary America*. Middletown, CT: Wesleyan University Press.

Salaam, Kalamu. 2000. The Live Poets Society. *Black Issues Book Review*. March–April.

Sanchez, Sonia. 1992. Ima talken bout the Nation of Islam. In *Sonia Sanchez: A Sun Woman for All Seasons Reads Her Poetry*. The Smithsonian Institution Folkways Cassette Series.

Sanchez, Sonia. 1990. For Tupac Amaru Shakur. *Like the Singing Coming Off the Drums: Love Poems*. Boston: Beacon Press.

Sanchez, Sonia. 2000. Interview with H. Samy Alim, Philadelphia, International Association of African American Musicians. June.

San Quinn. Personal interview with H. Samy Alim and James G. Spady, November 2000.

Sarkar, Mela and Dawn Allen. In press. Hybrid identities in Quebec Hip Hop: Language, territory, and ethnicity in the mix. In H. Samy Alim and Alastair Pennycook (eds), *Global Hip Hop Culture, youth identities, and the politics of language education*. Special issue of *Journal of Language, Identity, and Education*.

Saussure, F. de. 1960. *Course in General Linguistics*, ed. C. Bally and A. Sechehaye, trans. W. Baskin. London: Peter Owen.

Schiffman, Harold. 1996. *Linguistic Culture and Language Policy*. London and New York: Routledge.

Sells, Peter, John Rickford, and Thomas Wasow. 1996. Negative inversion in African American Vernacular English. *Natural Language and Linguistic Theory* 14(3): 591–627.

Sexton, Adam. 1995. *Rap on Rap: Straight-Up Talk on Hip-Hop Culture*. New York: Dell Publishing.

Sister Souljah. Statement available at http://www.theroc.org/roc-mag/textarch/roc09/roc09-07.htm.

Smith, Ernie. 1998. What is Black English? What is Ebonics? In Theresa Perry and Lisa Delpit (eds), *The Real Ebonics Debate*. Boston: Beacon Press.

Smitherman, Geneva. 1973. The power of the Rap: The Black idiom and the New Black Poetry. *Twentieth Century Literature: A Scholarly and Critical Journal* 19: 259–274.

Smitherman, Geneva. 1977 (1986). *Talkin and Testifyin: The Language of Black America*. Houghton Mifflin; reissued, with revisions, Detroit: Wayne State University Press.

Smitherman, Geneva. 1981. *Black English and the Education of Black Children and Youth: Proceedings of the National Invitational Symposium on the King Decision*. Detroit: Wayne State University, Center for Black Studies.

Smitherman, Geneva. 1991. "What is African to Me?": Language, ideology and *African American*. *American Speech* 66(2): 115–132.

Smitherman, Geneva. 1994 (2000). *Black Talk: Words and Phrases from the Hood to the Amen Corner*. Boston and New York: Houghton Mifflin.
Smitherman, Geneva. 1997. "The chain remain the same": Communicative practices in the Hip-Hop Nation. *Journal of Black Studies*, September.
Smitherman, Geneva. 2000. *Talkin That Talk: Language, Culture and Education in African America*. London and New York: Routledge.
Smitherman, Geneva. 2006. *Word from the Mother: Language and African Americans*. New York and London: Routledge.
Spady, James G. 1989. *Larry Neal: Liberated Black Philly Poet with a Blues Streak of Mellow Wisdom*. Black History Museum/Umum Loh Publishers.
Spady, James. 1993. "IMA PUT MY THING DOWN": Afro-American expressive culture and the Hip Hop community. *TYANABA: Revue de la Societe d'Anthropologie*. December.
Spady, James. 1994. Living in America where the brother got to get esoterica: The Philly Hip Hop Language and philosophy of Schooly D. *Fourth Dimension* 4(1): 26–27.
Spady, James G. 2000a. The centrality of Black Language in the discourse of Sonia Sanchez and Rap artists. In James Spady (ed.), *360 Degreez of Sonia Sanchez: Hip Hop, Narrativity, Iquawe and Public Spaces of Being*. Special issue of *Bma: The Sonia Sanchez Literary Review* 6.1, Fall.
Spady, James G. (ed.). 2000b. *360 Degreez of Sonia Sanchez: Hip Hop, Narrativity, Iquawe and Public Spaces of Being*. Special issue of *Bma: The Sonia Sanchez Literary Review* 6.1, Fall.
Spady, James G. 2001. Kurupt's journey from Pickett Middle School to a space boogie universe. *Philadelphia New Observer*, July 25, 18–19.
Spady, James G. 2002. Moving in silence: Motion, movement and music in a Hip Hop centered cultural universe. In H. Samy Alim (ed.), *Black Culture's Global Impact*. Special issue of *The Black Arts Quarterly* 6(3), Stanford, CA: Stanford University, Committee on Black Performing Arts.
Spady, James G. 2004. The Hip Hop Nation as a site of African-American cultural and historical memory. *Dumvoices Revue*, 154–166.
Spady, James G. and H. Samy Alim. 1999. Street conscious Rap: Modes of being. In *Street Conscious Rap*. Philadelphia: Black History Museum/Umum Loh Publishers.
Spady, James G. and Joseph Eure. 1991. *Nation Conscious Rap: The Hip Hop Vision*. New York/Philadelphia: PC International Press/Black History Museum.
Spady, James G., Stefan Dupres, and Charles Lee. 1995. *Twisted Tales in the Hip Hop Streets of Philly*. Philadelphia: Black History Museum/Umum Loh Publishers.
Spady, James G., H. Samy Alim, and Charles Lee (Art Director). 1999. *Street Conscious Rap*. Philadelphia: Black History Museum/Umum Loh Publishers.
Spady, James G., H. Samy Alim, and Samir Meghelli. Forthcoming. *The Global Cipha: Hip Hop culture and consciousness*. Philadelphia: Black History Museum.
Spears, Arthur K. 1982. The Black English semi-auxiliary *come*. *Language* 58: 850–872.
Spears, Arthur K. 1998. African-American language use: Ideology and so-called obscenity. In S. Mufwene, J. Rickford, G. Bailey and J. Baugh (eds), *African American English: Structure, History, and Usage*. New York: Routledge, 226–250.
Spears, Arthur K. 2000. Stressed *stay*: A new African-American English aspect marker. Paper presented at the Linguistic Society of America Convention, Washington DC, January.

Stavsky, Lois, Isaac Mozeson and Dani Reyes Mozeson. 1995. *A 2 Z: The Book of Rap and Hip-Hop Slang*. New York: Boulevard Books.

Steele, Timothy. 1999. *All the Fun's in How You Say a Thing: An Explanation of Meter and Versification*. Athens: Ohio/Swallow.

Stephens, Ronald Jamal. 1991. The three waves of contemporary rap music. The emergency of black and emergence of rap. *Black Sacred Music: A Journal of Theomusiology* 5(1): 25–40.

Stewart, William. 1972. Toward a history of American Negro Dialect. In F. Williams (ed.), *Language and Poverty: Perspectives on a Theme*. Chicago: Markham, 351–379.

Sutcliffe, David. 1992. *British Black English*. Oxford: Basil Blackwell.

Swedenburg, Ted. 2001. Islamic Hip-Hop versus Islamophobia. In Tony Mitchell (ed.), *Global Noise: Rap and Hip-Hop Outside the USA*. Middletown, CT: Wesleyan University Press.

Swedenburg, Ted. 2002. Hip Hop music in the transglobal Islamic underground. In H. Samy Alim (ed.), *Black Culture's Global Impact*. Special issue of *The Black Arts Quarterly* 6(3), Stanford, CA: Stanford University, Committee on Black Performing Arts.

Taylor, Orlando. 1985. Standard English as a second dialect? *English Today* 2, April.

Toop, David. 1984 (1994, 1999). *Rap Attack: From African Jive to New York Hip Hop*. London: Pluto Press.

Toop, David. 1991. Prince Akeem: Coming down like Babylon. *The Face* (UK), October.

Traugott, Elizabeth and Suzanne Romaine. 1983. Style in sociohistorical linguistics. Paper presented at the 6th International Conference on Historical Linguistics, Poznan, Poland. Cited in Bell, 1984.

Tsujimura, Natsuko, Kyoko Okamura, and Stuart Davis. Forthcoming. Rock rhymes in Japanese Hip-Hop rhymes. To appear in *Japanese/Korean Linguistics* 15.

Turner, Lorenzo. 1949. *Africanisms in the Gullah Dialect*. Chicago: University of Chicago Press.

Urrieta, Luis, Jr. 2004. "Performing success" and "successful performances": Chicanas and Chicanos "playing the game" or "selling out" in education. In B.K. Alexander, G. Anderson and B. Gallegos (eds), *Performance in Education: Teaching, Reform, and Identities as Social Performance*. New Jersey: Lawrence Erlbaum and Associates.

Walker, James. 2000. Rephrasing the vopula: Contraction and zero in Early African American English. In S. Poplack (ed.), *The English History of African American English*. Malden and Oxford: Blackwell.

Wa Thiongo, Ngugi. 1992. *Moving the Center: The Struggle for Cultural Freedom*. London: Heinemann.

Weiss, Anita M. 1994. Challenges for Muslim women in a postmodern world. In Akbar S. Ahmed and Hastings Donnan (eds), *Islam, Globalization and Postmodernity*. London and New York: Routledge, 127–140.

Wideman, John. 1976. Frame and dialect: The evolution of the Black voice in American literature. *American Poetry Review* 5.5 (September–October): 34–37.

Williams, Raymond. 1976. *Keywords: A Vocabulary of Culture and Society*. London: Fontana.

Williams, Robert (ed.). 1975. *Ebonics: The True Language of Black Folks*. St. Louis: Institute of Black Studies.

Winford, Donald. 1998. On the origins of African American Vernacular English—A Creolist perspective, Part 2: Linguistic features. *Diachronica* 15(1): 99–154.

Wolfram, Walter. 1969. *A Sociolinguistic Description of Detroit Negro Speech.* Washington, DC: Center for Applied Linguistics.

Wolfram, Walt. 1974. The relationship of white southern speech to Vernacular Black English. *Language* 50: 498–527.

Wolfram, Walt. 1993. A proactive role for speech-language pathologists in sociolinguistic education. *Language, Speech and Hearing Service in Schools* 24: 181–185.

Wood, Brent. 1999. Understanding Rap as rhetorical folk poetry. *Mosaic: A Journal for the Interdisciplinary Study of Literature* 32(4).

Woods, Emilee. 2005. Language socialization and cultural ideologies in underground Hip Hop. Senior honors thesis, Department of Linguistics, University of California, Santa Barbara.

Yancy, George. 1991. Rapese. Cited in James G. Spady and Joseph Eure, *Nation Conscious Rap: The Hip Hop Vision.* Philadelphia: Black History Museum Press.

Yancy, George. 2000. Feminism and the subtext of whiteness: Black women's experiences as a site of identity formation and contestation of whiteness. *Western Journal of Black Studies* 24(3): 155–165.

Yasin, Jon. 1999. Rap in the African-American music tradition: Cultural assertion and continuity. In Arthur Spears (ed.), *Race and Ideology: Language, Symbolism, and Popular Culture.* Detroit: Wayne State University Press.

Zekri, Bernard. 1992. *Rap et Islam.* Documentary film.

Zion I. 2000. Interview with H. Samy Alim, San Francisco. June.

Index

Related titles from Routledge

African American Literacies

Elaine Richardson

African-American Literacies is a personal, public and political exploration of the problems faced by student writers from the African-American Vernacular English (AAVE) culture.

Drawing on personal experience, Elaine Richardson provides a compelling account of the language and literacy practices of African-American students. The book analyses the problems encountered by the teachers of AAVE speakers, and offers African American-centred theories and pedagogical methods of addressing these problems. Richardson builds on recent research to argue that teachers need not only to recognise the value and importance of African-American culture, but also to use African-American English when teaching AAVE speakers standard English.

African-American Literacies offers a holistic and culturally relevant approach to literacy education, and is essential reading for anyone with an interest in the literacy practices of African-American students.

ISBN10: 0–415–26882–6 (hbk)
ISBN10: 0–415–26883–4 (pbk)
ISBN13: 978–0–415–26882–0 (hbk)
ISBN13: 978–0–415–26883–7 (pbk)

Available at all good bookshops
For ordering and further information please visit:
www.routledge.com

Related titles from Routledge

Black Linguistics
Language, Society and Politics in Africa and the Americas

**Sinfree Makoni, Geneva Smitherman, Arnetha Ball,
Arthur K. Spears**

Foreword by Ngugi wa Thiong'o

Enslavement, forced migration, war and colonization have led to the global dispersal of Black communities and to the fragmentation of common experiences.

The majority of Black language researchers explore the social and linguistic phenomena of individual Black communities, without looking at Black experiences outside a given community. This groundbreaking collection re-orders the elitist and colonial elements of language studies by drawing together the multiple perspectives of Black language researchers. In doing so, the book recognises and formalises the existence of a "Black Linguistic Perspective" highlights the contributions of Black language researchers in the field.

Written exclusively by Black scholars on behalf of, and in collaboration with local communities, the book looks at the commonalities and differences among Black speech communities in Africa and the Diaspora. Topics include:

* the OJ Simpson trial
* language issues in Southern Africa and Francophone West Africa
* the language of Hip Hop
* the language of the Rastafaria in Jamaica

With a foreword by Ngugi wa Thiong'o, this is essential reading for anyone with an interest in the linguistic implications of colonization.

ISBN10: 0–415–26137–6 (hbk)
ISBN10: 0–415–26138–4 (pbk)
ISBN13: 978–0–415–26137–1 (hbk)
ISBN13: 978–0–415–26138–8 (pbk)

Available at all good bookshops
For ordering and further information please visit:
www.routledge.com

Related titles from Routledge

Hiphop Literacies

Elaine Richardson

Hiphop Literacies is an exploration of the rhetorical, language and literacy practices of African Americans, with a focus on the Hiphop generation. Richardson analyses the lyrics and discourse of Hiphop, explodes myths and stereotypes about Black culture and language and shows how Hiphop language is a global ambassador of the English language and American culture.

In locating rap and Hiphop discourse within a trajectory of Black discourses, Richardson examines African American Hiphop in secondary oral contexts such as rap music, song lyrics, electronic and digital media, oral performances and cinema.

Hiphop Literacies brings together issues and concepts that are explored in the disciplines of folklore, ethnomusicology, sociolinguistics, discourse studies and New Literacies Studies.

Elaine Richardson is Associate Professor of English and Applied Linguistics at Pennsylvania State University. She is the author of *African American Literacies* (Routledge, 2003) and co-editor of *Understanding African American Rhetoric: Classical Origins to Contemporary Innovations* (Routledge, 2003).

ISBN13: 978– 0–415–32928–6 (hbk)
ISBN13: 978–0–415–32927–9 (pbk)

Available at all good bookshops
For ordering and further information please visit:
www.routledge.com

Related titles from Routledge

Word from the Mother

Geneva Smitherman

Word from the Mother presents a definitive statement on African American Language (AAL) from the internationally respected linguist, Geneva Smitherman. Her message is clear: all Americans, regardless of cultural background, must appreciate the linguistic conventions and richness of AAL if they are to participate in society as informed citizens.

Illuminated by Geneva Smitherman's evocative and inimitable writing style, the work gives an overview of past debates on the speech of African Americans and provides a vision for the future. The author explores the contributions of AAL to mainstream American English, and includes a list of idioms and expressions as a suggested linguistic core of AAL.

As global manifestations of Black Language increase, Geneva Smitherman argues that, through education, we must broaden our conception of AAL and its speakers, and examine the implications of gender, age and class on AAL. Most of all, we must appreciate the artistic and linguistic genius of AAL, presented in this book through Hip Hop song lyrics and the rhyme and rhetoric of the Black speech community.

Word from the Mother is an essential read for students of African American speech, language and culture and sociolinguistics, as well as the general reader interested in the worldwide "crossover" of Black Popular Culture.

ISBN13: 978–0–415–35875–0 (hbk)
ISBN13: 978–0–415–35876–7 (pbk)

Available at all good bookshops
For ordering and further information please visit:
www.routledge.com

F